★

NORTHERN CALIFORNIA BEST PLACES

COOKBOOK

★

~ NORTHERN CALIFORNIA BEST PLACES ~
COOKBOOK

Recipes

from the Outstanding

Restaurants and Inns of

Northern California

Cynthia C. Nims & *Carolyn Dille*

SASQUATCH BOOKS
SEATTLE

Printed in the United States of America.
Distributed in Canada by Raincoast Books Ltd.
03 02 01 00 99   5 4 3 2 1

Cover and interior design: Karen Schober
Cover photograph: Angie Norwood Browne
Interior illustrations: Debbie Hanley
Composition: Dan McComb
Copy editing: Barbara Fuller

Library of Congress Cataloging in Publication Data
Nims, Cynthia C.
The Northern California best places cookbook : recipes from the outstanding restaurants and inns of Northern California / Cynthia C. Nims, Carolyn Dille.
        p.   cm.
Includes index.
ISBN 1-57061-183-1
1. Cookery, American—California style. I. Dille, Carolyn.
II. Title.
TX715.2.C34N55 1999
641.59794—dc21   99-15349

Sasquatch Books
615 Second Avenue
Seattle, Washington 98104
(206)467-4300
books@sasquatchbooks.com
www.sasquatchbooks.com

CONTENTS

ACKNOWLEDGMENTS

I dedicate this book to the memory of my father—the first man in my life—and to Bob, the only other man in my life. *Seni seviyorum*. Many thanks to the hordes of willing taster-critics who stuck by through many months of recipe testing, as well as to those who helped with the testing: Joanne Koonce, Susan Volland, Mike Amend, and Jeff Ashley.

— C. N.

Even more than most books, this one is a collaboration. The farmers, fishers, cheesemakers, bakers, foragers, and orchardists nurture the distinctive flavors of Northern California so home cooks and chefs can create wonderful-tasting dishes. I'd like to thank each and every one of the many in these fields for their generosity and informed enthusiasm. I'm especially grateful to Peggy Smith of Tomales Bay Foods, Tom Worthington of Monterey Fish, Michael Watchorn of Hog Island Oysters, Cindy Callahan of Bellwether Farms, Sylvia Tucker of Matos Cheese Company, Mimi Luebberman of Windrush Farms, and to Paul Bertolli of Oliveto Restaurant and Gerald Hirigoyen of Fringale and Pastis Restaurants.

— C. D.

INTRODUCTION

This collection of recipes and essays tells a unique story of the cuisine of Northern California, from its bustling urban centers to its quiet countryside outposts. The recipes come from more than 60 restaurants and inns featured in the third edition of *Northern California Best Places.* Best Places® guidebooks have long been a respected resource for authoritative reviews of West Coast dining and accommodations. Now their publisher is happy to bring Northern California's cuisine home to you.

In this cookbook, we first let the chefs tell the story of the region by way of their recipes, as well as through anecdotes about favorite local ingredients and techniques for preparing the dishes. The collection blends highly sophisticated fare with comforting, homey recipes. You'll find everything from the celebrated Lobster Salad with Tomato Confit from The Dining Room at the Ritz-Carlton in San Francisco to Rabbit Braised in Herbs from Le Bilig in Gold Country and Mendocino Mud Cake from the North Coast Brewing Company.

In the early 1970s, when America was thrilling over the novelty of Hamburger Helper and a new era of culinary convenience was dawning, the trend in Northern California was starting to move in a different direction. Architects of this new culinary style, beginning with Alice Waters and her groundbreaking Chez Panisse restaurant in Berkeley, reaffirmed that foods from close to home—grown and tended thoughtfully and enjoyed in their natural peak season—were inherently better tasting (and better for the planet) than the year-round red tomato and other marvels of modern food production. Today, this is still the mantra of many chefs in the region, showing that what was once a trend can now be considered a way of life.

Northern California will surely always be one of the most celebrated food regions of the United States. The close proximity among winemakers, food producers, talented chefs, and a worldly, well-palated clientele is the equation that makes this region so gastronomically significant. Enjoy this taste of what Northern California has to offer.

 REAKFAST

ZUCCHINI LEMON MUFFINS

Abigail's, Sacramento

"Like everyone else who has a home garden and grows zucchini,
we're always looking for a delicious way to use this versatile vegetable,"
says innkeeper Susanne Ventura. The muffins are also "great for
sneaking a little vegetable to the kids," she adds.

2 cups all-purpose flour	2 eggs
½ cup sugar	1 cup milk
1 tablespoon baking powder	¼ cup vegetable oil
1 teaspoon salt	Grated zest of 1 lemon
½ teaspoon freshly grated or ground nutmeg	1½ teaspoons freshly squeezed lemon juice
½ teaspoon ground cinnamon	1 cup grated zucchini (about 1 medium
½ cup chopped pecans	zucchini)
½ cup chopped dates	

PREHEAT THE OVEN to 375°F. Grease 12 muffin cups.

IN A LARGE BOWL, combine the flour, sugar, baking powder, salt, nutmeg, and cinnamon and stir to mix. Stir in the pecans and dates. In a medium bowl, beat the eggs just to mix. Add the milk, oil, lemon zest, and lemon juice and stir until well blended. Stir in the zucchini. Add the wet ingredients to the dry and stir just until evenly mixed. Spoon the batter into the prepared muffin cups, filling each nearly to the top.

BAKE THE MUFFINS until the tops are well rounded and lightly browned, 20 to 25 minutes. Turn the muffins out onto a cake rack and let cool before serving.

Makes 12 muffins

ARTICHOKE FRITTATA

Grey Whale Inn, Fort Bragg

This is based on a recipe from Helen King, former innkeeper at the
Babbling Brook Inn in Santa Cruz. The recipe can also be halved and baked in a
9-inch square baking dish. You could substitute about 3 cups of any
coarse bread crumbs for the English muffin crumbs.

3 sourdough English muffins	*1 tablespoon Worcestershire sauce*
1 can (14 ounces) quartered artichoke hearts	*1 tablespoon powdered mustard*
in water, drained	*2 teaspoons seasoning salt or table salt*
2 jars (6½ ounces each) marinated artichoke	*3 cups grated Monterey Jack cheese*
hearts, drained	*½ cup grated Parmesan cheese*
1 cup chopped onion	*½ cup Italian seasoned bread crumbs*
12 eggs	*Chopped flat-leaf (Italian) parsley or*
2½ cups half-and-half	*paprika, for garnish*

PREHEAT THE OVEN to 350°F. Lightly grease a 9- by 13-inch baking dish.

TEAR THE ENGLISH MUFFINS into pieces, put them in a food processor, and process
to form crumbs (you should have about 3 cups). Set aside in a medium bowl. Brush
excess crumbs from the food processor bowl and add both kinds of artichoke hearts. Pulse
to coarsely chop them together, about 30 seconds. Spread the artichokes in the bottom of
the prepared baking dish and scatter the onion evenly over.

IN A LARGE BOWL, whisk together the eggs with the half-and-half, Worcestershire
sauce, mustard, and salt. Pour half of the egg mixture over the artichokes and onions.
Sprinkle the Monterey Jack cheese evenly over. Stir the English muffin crumbs and
Parmesan cheese into the remaining egg mixture and pour it over the Monterey Jack
cheese. Sprinkle the bread crumbs over, with parsley or paprika. Bake until the center is
set, about 1 hour. Let sit for a few minutes, then cut the frittata into pieces and serve.

Makes 12 to 15 servings

ARTICHOKES: GOOD AND GOOD FOR YOU

Descendants of the Italians who introduced commercial artichoke growing to California still give artichoke tips at their farm stands. These include the information that the blistered-looking artichokes have the most complex, nutty flavor, because they've been frost-kissed. Another tip regards the peeling of the stems: pare to the ivory white center for an extra delicacy; after all, the stems are part of the hearts. Some offer secrets for the best-tasting steamed artichokes: use garlic and/or lemon and/or dried chile pepper in the steaming water.

For steamed artichokes—the easiest preparation from the cook's point of view—many prefer the large sizes. Others say the medium sizes have more flavor and succulence. For sautés, stews, and combination with other ingredients, baby artichokes are good value and require less trimming; very small ones have no fuzzy chokes. For artichoke dishes, see pages 4, 41, 58, 68, and 108.

Delicious flavor and fun finger food are the usual reasons people eat artichokes, though a good case could be made for saving on vitamin and mineral supplements by eating artichokes regularly. Artichokes are very rich in minerals, especially in potassium, magnesium, chromium, and manganese, all essential for human health. They also have significant amounts of vitamin C and folate, a part of the B-complex whose positive role in reducing serum cholesterol is favorably noted by researchers. Considering the artichoke has very few calories (25 per medium size), no fat, and 12 percent dietary fiber, it is a virtual vegetable one-a-day, all-in-one.

When trimming artichokes of any size, work with a cut lemon to keep all those minerals from oxidizing and discoloring when they come in contact with the air. If you're out of lemons, a cup of water with a tablespoon or so of vinegar will work.

HOMEMADE BUTTERHORNS

The Gables Inn, Santa Rosa

This unexpected combination of ingredients for a breakfast roll, from innkeeper Judy Ogne, is tasty and surprisingly tender and flaky. It is important to chill the dough before rolling it out, which makes it easier to work with and seems to ensure that the rolls will be at their fluffiest. If you're using salted butter, you could omit the extra salt. These are just easy enough to make that you might find them becoming a weekend habit.

1 cup unsalted butter, softened at room temperature	½ teaspoon salt
	2½–3 cups flour
1 pint small-curd cottage cheese	½ cup sliced almonds, lightly toasted

ICING

2 cups powdered sugar	3–4 tablespoons whipping cream
1 teaspoon vanilla extract	or half-and-half

IN THE BOWL OF A MIXER, combine the butter, cottage cheese, and salt and work with the paddle attachment until well blended. Incorporate the flour, ½ cup at a time, and continue mixing until a stiff dough is formed. (Alternatively, mix the dough with a wooden spoon in a large bowl.) Cover the bowl and refrigerate the dough for at least 6 hours or overnight.

PREHEAT THE OVEN to 350°F. Lightly grease a baking sheet.

DIVIDE THE DOUGH in half and roll each half out into a circle about 14 inches in diameter. Cut each circle into 8 equal wedges. Roll up each piece from the large end toward the point, as for a croissant. Arrange the butterhorns on the baking sheet and bake until browned, 30 to 40 minutes.

WHILE THE BUTTERHORNS ARE BAKING, make the icing. In a small bowl, stir together the powdered sugar and vanilla with enough cream to make a smooth icing.

TAKE THE BUTTERHORNS from the oven and let cool slightly. Drizzle with the icing, sprinkle the sliced almonds over, and serve warm.

Makes 16 butterhorns

APPLES AL VINO

Indian Creek Bed & Breakfast, Plymouth

Plenty of fruit is always part of the breakfast spread at Indian Creek
Bed & Breakfast, often simply offered fresh but sometimes served in warm,
comforting recipes such as this. To cut strips of zest from a lemon, simply peel the
zest away in long pieces with a vegetable peeler as you would peel an apple. This
recipe can be made in advance and the apples served chilled if you prefer.

4 cups dry white wine	*Strips of zest from 1 lemon*
1 cup sugar	*1–2 vanilla beans, split lengthwise*
8 Golden Delicious apples, peeled, cored, and quartered	*Edible flowers and/or mint sprigs, for garnish*

IN A LARGE SAUCEPAN or a soup pot, combine the wine and sugar and bring just to
a boil over medium-high heat, stirring to help the sugar dissolve. Add the apple quarters,
lemon zest, and vanilla bean(s). Cover the pan, reduce the heat to medium-low, and gently
simmer just until the apples are tender, about 15 minutes. Take care not to boil or over-
cook the apples, or they will begin to fall apart; they should be tender but retain their
shape. Scoop out the apple pieces with a slotted spoon and put them in individual bowls
or a large serving bowl.

BRING THE COOKING LIQUIDS TO A BOIL and boil until reduced to a thick
syrup, 15 to 20 minutes. Remove and discard the lemon zest and vanilla beans, pour the
syrup over the apples, garnish with edible flowers and/or mint sprigs, and serve.

Makes 8 servings

MULTI-GRAIN PORRIDGE

Mendocino Hotel, Mendocino

At the Mendocino Hotel, this porridge is served with raw sugar, cream,
and fresh fruit. You could also embellish this satisfying hot cereal with cinnamon,
freshly grated nutmeg, raisins, or other dried fruits. Tiny amaranth seeds come
from the protein-packed leafy green plant of the same name. All of these grains are
available in health food stores or in well-stocked grocery stores.

1 cup rolled oats
1 cup barley flakes
1 cup toasted buckwheat groats (kasha)
1 cup polenta
1 cup amaranth seeds

1 cup graham cracker crumbs
3 cups water
2 cups milk
1 cup apple juice

FOR THE PORRIDGE mixture, combine the oats, barley, buckwheat groats, polenta,
amaranth seeds, and graham cracker crumbs in a large bowl and stir to mix well. Set aside
2 cups of the mixture and store the rest in an airtight container for later use. (You'll have
enough for 3 batches of porridge in all.)

COMBINE THE WATER, milk, and apple juice in a large saucepan and bring just to
a boil. Slowly add the 2 cups of porridge mixture, stirring constantly. Lower the heat and
simmer, stirring occasionally, until the grains are tender and the porridge is thickened,
about 20 minutes. Spoon the porridge into 4 to 6 individual bowls, add any desired
toppings, and serve warm.

Makes 4 to 6 servings

BAKED EGGS
with Tarragon and Leeks

Flume's End Bed & Breakfast, Nevada City

This is a simple combination of ingredients but a delicious blend of rich eggs, sweet tarragon, and aromatic leeks. If you're feeding a crowd, you can easily double this recipe and bake it in a 9- by 13-inch baking dish.

1 tablespoon unsalted butter
2 large leeks, white and pale green parts only, cleaned and sliced
¾ cup grated Gruyère cheese
¼ cup grated Parmesan cheese

4 eggs
1 cup whipping cream or half-and-half
2 tablespoons minced fresh tarragon or 1 tablespoon dried, crumbled tarragon
Salt and freshly ground black pepper

PREHEAT THE OVEN to 375°F. Lightly grease an 8-inch square baking dish.

HEAT THE BUTTER in a medium skillet over medium heat. Add the leeks and sauté until tender, about 5 minutes. Spread the leeks evenly on the bottom of the baking dish.

COMBINE THE CHEESES in a bowl and toss to mix. Spread all but ¼ cup of the cheeses evenly over the leeks. In a large bowl, whisk together the eggs, cream, and tarragon with salt and pepper to taste. Pour the egg mixture into the dish and bake until the top is golden and the center is set, about 30 minutes. Take the dish from the oven, sprinkle the reserved cheese over, and continue baking just until the cheese melts, 3 to 5 minutes longer. Let sit for a few minutes, then cut into squares to serve.

Makes 4 servings

BUCKWHEAT PANCAKES

Woodrose Café, Garberville

When was the last time you had a fluffy, nourishing, fresh-from-the-griddle buckwheat pancake? Here's your chance. Just add a pat of sweet butter, some warmed real maple syrup, and a steaming cup of coffee, and you've got a breakfast to start off any day right.

1 cup buckwheat flour	2 eggs
1 cup whole-wheat flour	2 cups buttermilk
2 tablespoons sugar	¼ cup vegetable oil, plus more
1½ teaspoons baking powder	for cooking pancakes
1½ teaspoons baking soda	¼ teaspoon vanilla extract

IN A LARGE BOWL, stir together the flours, sugar, baking powder, and baking soda. In a separate bowl, whisk the eggs to lightly mix, then whisk in the buttermilk, oil, and vanilla. Add the wet ingredients to the dry ingredients and stir just until blended. Do not overbeat or the pancakes will be tough.

HEAT A LIGHTLY OILED GRIDDLE or a large, heavy skillet over medium-high heat. When hot, pour in the batter by ¼-cupfuls and cook until the edges begin to brown and the tops are bubbly, 1 to 2 minutes. Flip the pancakes and continue cooking until browned on the bottom and just cooked through, about 1 minute longer. Continue with the remaining batter, adding more oil to the griddle or skillet as needed.

Makes 6 servings (about 18 large pancakes)

BERRY STREUSEL COFFEE CAKE

Johnson's Country Inn, Chico

A generous addition of almonds to this simple coffee cake—served both at breakfast and for afternoon tea—is no surprise; the inn is set amidst an almond farm. The blackberries, too, are from the inn's property. If you use frozen berries, you don't need to thaw them before adding them to the batter.

2 cups all-purpose flour	¼ cup unsalted butter, melted and cooled
¾ cup sugar	1 egg, beaten
2 teaspoons baking powder	1 cup fresh or frozen blackberries, blueberries,
¼ teaspoon salt	or boysenberries
¾ cup milk	1 cup chopped toasted almonds or walnuts

STREUSEL TOPPING

½ cup sugar	¼ cup cold unsalted butter
⅓ cup all-purpose flour	

PREHEAT THE OVEN to 375°F. Grease a 9-inch square baking dish or deep cake pan.

IN A LARGE BOWL, combine the flour, sugar, baking powder, and salt, and stir to mix. Stir in the milk, butter, and egg, then fold in the berries and nuts. Stir gently until well blended, about 2 minutes. Spread the batter into the prepared baking pan.

FOR THE STREUSEL TOPPING, stir together the sugar and flour in a medium bowl. Cut in the butter with a pastry blender or 2 table knives until the mixture has a crumbly texture. (Or combine the sugar, flour, and butter in a food processor and pulse until just crumbly.)

SPRINKLE THE STREUSEL over the batter and bake until a wooden toothpick inserted near the center comes out clean, about 40 minutes. Let cool slightly before cutting into pieces to serve.

Makes 8 to 10 servings

IN A FEW NUTSHELLS:
ALMONDS, PISTACHIOS, AND WALNUTS

Almond orchards are found in the northern reaches of the Central Valley, as well as scattered throughout inland microclimate zones around the San Francisco Bay. Almonds are one of the large-scale nut export crops in the state. Since the almond finds a home on many menus, from appetizers to desserts, it is naturally a favorite of many cooks and chefs. Bitter almonds, prized for their special flavor, contain a tiny amount of prussic acid. It is illegal to sell them in the United States. Most cooks substitute oil of bitter almond, actually derived from apricot or peach pits, almond relatives.

Pistachios appear in the same regions of the state as almonds, particularly clustered around the town of Corning in Tehama County, where olive orchards also flourish. The premium prices paid for imported pistachios induced some growers in the mid-1970s to set out pistachio plantations. This was serendipitous for their own fortunes and the domestic market, as before the late '70s most pistachios had been imported from Iran. Arguably, Middle Eastern nuts have a more intense flavor, but reliable availability and fairly moderate prices have brought pistachios closer to the culinary mainstream. They are now used with pasta, with fish, and in salads, as well as in dessert, but no longer in green pistachio ice cream.

Walnut groves and individual trees mark the country and suburban landscapes of Northern and Central California. These are principally the Persian or English walnut, usually grafted on native rootstock. The black walnut, preferred by many pastry chefs for its ability to stand up to cooking, is a scarce commodity. It, along with the butternut, a close relative, has very thick, hard shells. As most of the public prefer the thin-shelled nuts, so do the growers. The salad and dessert courses still see most of the harvest. Of course, almonds, pistachios, and walnuts remain very popular nuts to shell and eat out-of-hand.

COBBLESTONE HOBO BREAKFAST

Four Sisters Inns

This is one of those breakfasts that will keep you going through a long, hard day—not for the "I'll just have toast and coffee" crowd. Instead of poaching the eggs, you could fry them if you prefer. The recipe comes from one of the Four Sisters Inns, which include the White Swan and Petite Auberge in San Francisco, as well as the Maison Fleurie in Yountville.

3 large red potatoes
2 tablespoons unsalted butter
½ large onion, chopped
1 tablespoon vegetable oil
½ teaspoon paprika
Salt and freshly ground black pepper

3 tablespoons chopped flat-leaf
(Italian) parsley
¾ cup grated cheddar cheese
1 tablespoon white vinegar, for poaching
4 eggs

CREAM SAUCE

3 tablespoons butter
3 tablespoons flour
¾ cup half-and-half or milk

¼ cup crumbled cooked bacon
1 tablespoon freshly squeezed lemon juice

PUT THE POTATOES in a large pot of cold water, bring to a boil, lower the heat, and simmer until the potatoes are just tender, 20 to 25 minutes. Drain the potatoes and let cool, then cut them into cubes. Heat 1 tablespoon of the butter in a skillet over medium heat, add the onion, and cook, stirring, until tender, 3 to 5 minutes. Transfer the onion to a bowl and set aside. Heat the remaining tablespoon of butter with the oil in the same skillet over medium-high heat. Add the cubed potatoes and paprika with salt and pepper to taste. Fry the potatoes, stirring as little as possible, until brown and crisp, about 15 minutes. Stir in the onion with the parsley. Spoon the potatoes into a shallow baking dish.

PREHEAT THE OVEN to 350°F.

SCATTER THE CHEESE over the potatoes and bake until the potatoes are heated through and the cheese is melted, about 10 minutes.

WHILE THE POTATOES are baking, make the cream sauce. Melt the butter in a small saucepan. Stir in the flour and cook, stirring, over medium heat until the mixture becomes frothy, about 3 minutes. Stir in the half-and-half and cook, stirring, until the sauce is thickened, 2 to 3 minutes. Stir in the bacon and lemon juice with salt and pepper to taste. Keep the sauce warm over low heat.

FILL A DEEP SKILLET half-full with water and add the vinegar. Bring the water to a gentle boil and then carefully crack the eggs into the water. Simmer gently until the whites are set and the yolks remain runny, about 3 minutes. Scoop out the eggs with a slotted spoon, drain gently on paper towels, and set the eggs on top of the potatoes. Spoon the cream sauce over and serve, scooping out 1 egg and some potatoes for each serving.

Makes 4 servings

LEMON CHEESE FRENCH TOAST
with Berry Sauce

Quail Mountain Bed & Breakfast, Calistoga

Choose a rustic, crusty bread for this dish. If baguette is all you can find, cut the loaf on the bias to make larger pieces; you may need more than the 12 slices called for here. You can use fresh or frozen berries for the sauce, but if you use frozen, thoroughly defrost them and drain well beforehand. You can purchase lemon curd (look in the jam section) or make your own by following the recipe for Mandarin Orange Curd on page 226 and using lemon juice in place of the orange juice.

8 ounces cream cheese	12 slices country-style bread, about ¾ inch
¾ cup lemon curd	thick and 4 inches across
2 tablespoons sugar	6 eggs
2 tablespoons freshly squeezed lemon juice	1 cup milk
1 tablespoon grated lemon zest	¼ cup unsalted butter, melted

BERRY SAUCE

3 cups mixed berries (blueberries, strawberries, raspberries, and/or cranberries)	2 tablespoons cornstarch mixed with
½ cup water	1 tablespoon cold water, if needed to
2 tablespoons sugar, more to taste	thicken the sauce

IN THE BOWL of a mixer, beat the cream cheese with the paddle attachment until smooth and fluffy. Add the lemon curd, sugar, lemon juice, and lemon zest and continue beating until thoroughly blended and smooth. (Alternatively, beat the cream cheese mixture in a large bowl with a wooden spoon or handheld beaters.)

GREASE A 9- BY 13-INCH BAKING DISH. Arrange half of the bread slices in the dish, spread the cream cheese mixture over the bread, and top with the remaining bread slices. In a medium bowl, whisk together the eggs, then whisk in the milk until well blended. Pour the egg mixture over the bread, cover the dish, and refrigerate at least 2 hours or overnight. The bread should absorb the egg mixture before it is baked.

PREHEAT THE OVEN to 350°F.

DRIZZLE THE MELTED BUTTER over the egg-soaked bread and bake until the bread is firm and browned, 30 to 40 minutes.

WHILE THE TOAST IS BAKING, prepare the sauce. In a medium saucepan, combine the berries, water, and sugar and bring to a boil over high heat, stirring occasionally. Reduce the heat and simmer until the berries are very tender and the sauce has thickened slightly, 15 to 20 minutes. If the sauce needs further thickening, add the cornstarch and cook a few minutes longer, stirring. Add more sugar to taste if the berries are tart.

ARRANGE ONE LAYERED PIECE of French toast on each plate and spoon a bit of the warm berry sauce over. Serve right away, and pass the rest of the sauce separately.

Makes 6 servings

TREATING BERRIES WITH CARE

Ripe berries have distinct aromas (except for blueberries, which are more subtle). Getting to know each berry's aroma and color will help you decide which to buy. Berries will not ripen after being picked. If the berries are staining their containers, at least some are overripe and may be moldy, which can affect the flavor of the whole container. All berries are quite fragile and susceptible to molds. Ideally, you should buy berries the day you will use them. If you need to store berries overnight or longer, layer unwashed berries between paper toweling in an airtight plastic container and store in the refrigerator.

If you're sure of the condition of your garden-grown berries, they need not be washed, as this rinses away flavor, aroma, and sheen. Washing purchased produce is a good practice for health's sake, however, so plan to rinse those berries carefully under a soft spray just before using them. Wash strawberries before hulling so they do not fill with water. Drain all berries very well after washing.

CELERY ROOT, POTATO, AND LEEK HOME FRIES

Dunbar House, 1880, Murphys

Fresh herbs make all the difference in a dish as simple as this.
At Dunbar House, herbs are snipped from the garden or, during the winter,
from herb pots growing in the kitchen so the fresh flavor is always
available—even when there's snow on the ground.

The home fries can be prepared through browning the vegetables the night before.
Refrigerate and then finish in the oven the next morning just before serving.

3 medium leeks, white and pale green parts only, cut in ¼-inch slices
2 tablespoons olive oil
2 medium russet potatoes (about 1 pound), peeled and cut in ¼-inch julienne strips

1 small or ½ large celery root (about 1 pound), peeled and cut in ¼-inch julienne strips
2 teaspoons minced rosemary
1 teaspoon thyme leaves
Salt and freshly ground black pepper

PUT THE LEEKS in a large bowl of cold water and let sit for 5 to 10 minutes to rid
them of dirt and sand. Lift the leeks out of the water and drain well, then pat dry.

PREHEAT THE OVEN to 350°F.

HEAT THE OIL in a large ovenproof skillet over medium-high heat. Add the potatoes,
celery root, leeks, rosemary, and thyme, with salt and pepper to taste. Cook, stirring frequently, until the vegetables begin to brown, about 10 minutes. Transfer the skillet to the
oven and bake until tender, about 20 minutes.

Makes 4 servings

WALNUT GOLDEN RAISIN SCONES

Schat's Courthouse Bakery and Café, Ukiah

Schat's pastry chef Donald Pittman, a graduate of the California Culinary Academy in San Francisco, created this recipe, which won honorable mention in the 1997 California Walnut Association Baking Contest.

2 cups all-purpose flour	*½ cup chopped walnuts*
⅓ cup plus 1 tablespoon sugar	*½ cup golden raisins*
1 tablespoon baking powder	*½ cup milk*
1 teaspoon ground cinnamon	*1 egg, beaten*
¼ teaspoon salt	*1 teaspoon vanilla extract*
½ cup unsalted butter, cut in pieces and chilled	*1 tablespoon whipping cream*

PREHEAT THE OVEN to 400°F. Lightly grease a baking sheet.

IN A LARGE BOWL, combine the flour, ⅓ cup of the sugar, the baking powder, cinnamon, and salt. Stir to evenly blend. Add the butter and, using a pastry blender or 2 table knives, cut it into the flour mixture until it has a crumbly consistency. Stir in the walnuts and raisins. In a small bowl, stir together the milk, egg, and vanilla and add this to the dry ingredients. Stir gently just until evenly mixed.

TRANSFER THE DOUGH to a lightly floured work surface. With floured hands, shape the dough into an 8-inch round. Cut the dough into 8 wedges, brush them lightly with the cream, and sprinkle with the remaining tablespoon of sugar. Arrange the wedges on the baking sheet and bake until puffed and lightly browned, 15 to 18 minutes.

Makes 8 servings

HEARTH BREADS WITH HEART: ARTISANAL BAKERIES

The bakery's role as supplier of the community's staff of life is alive and well in Northern California. Some notable bakeries were started with the intention of nourishing the soul along with the body: Brother Juniper's of Santa Rosa, begun by a group of lay Christians, and The Tassajara Bakery of San Francisco, originally a Zen Center activity. When a bakery sets roots in a community, when it offers honest bread and good pastries, it becomes more than a retail outlet. It becomes a place where friends and strangers meet and exchange news and views. It becomes the village bakery, as Joe Ortiz, nationally acclaimed baker of Gayle's Bakery, puts it.

Lingering over coffee and pastry or a sandwich lunch is encouraged by the cozy setting and welcoming staff of many Northern California bakeries. Capitola's Gayle's Bakery, Healdsburg's Downtown Bakery and Creamery, Point Reyes Station's Bay Village Bakery, St. Helena's Model Bakery, and Ukiah's Schat's Courthouse Bakery and The Garden Bakery all keep a cozy, small-town friendliness, along with their award-winning baked goods.

The bakers take the dictum "not by bread alone" to heart in more than one sense. They are willing and able to search for and perfect the best recipes for almond and coconut macaroons, frangipane tarts, galettes, tiramisu, chocolate cheesecake, and scores of other sweet toothsomes. Many cultivate a network of suppliers for local fruit and nuts to put their nectarine tarts, cherry pies, or walnut sticky buns over the flavor top.

Not that they've neglected the basics. Many of the artisanal bakers have been bitten by the bread bug while traveling in France, Germany, or Italy. They have felt art and science in the crackle of crust between their teeth. They heard the stories of *pain de campagne, pane Toscano,* and *volkornbrot*—traditional country breads of France, Tuscany, and Germany—and saw the dramas of old and new hearth ovens. Some went to Europe especially to learn baking techniques. They watched and worked, listened and talked until they had the knowledge and confidence to come home and begin baking.

Some bakers fell under the wood-fired oven spell. Some of these—Bay Village Bakery of Point Reyes Station, the Della Fattoria Bakery of Petaluma, and The Wood-Fire Bakery of Mountain View—provide their communities and some of the finest restaurants with baked goods. Among other reasons, the region is a good place for them to work because of the availability of hardwoods. In addition to a plentiful supply of California oak, many fruit and nut orchards grow there, with old trees continually being replaced. Bakers establish contacts with orchard owners for a supply of seasoned wood. The varieties of wood add subtle nuances of flavor to the baked goods. Almond, cherry, or plum may scent a bakery's signature loaves, flat breads, or pastries.

Two East Bay bakeries, The Acme Bread Company and Semifreddi, started small and have managed to establish branches and produce truly artisanal breads on a commercial scale. They are among a handful of bakeries that furnish many of the San Francisco Bay Area's best restaurants. Artisan Bakery of Sonoma is another whose breads have become the standard by which others are measured.

More than a century of traditional breadmaking stands behind the latest breadmaking efforts. The first sourdoughs, produced by the gold miners, were crude rather than refined. But quite soon, Basque, French, and Italian bakers turned their hands to sourdough, which quickly became identified as a San Francisco specialty. These immigrants developed other breads, such as sheepherders', and re-created breads from their homelands.

The bakeries they established made the region synonymous with fine bread and baked goods for many decades. Appreciation for artisanal breads declined markedly after the Second World War, though some sourdough specialists, such as Larrabu, baked very fine commercial breads in wood-burning ovens.

The bread-baking renaissance of the 1980s and '90s seems to be a deepening of the region's traditions. The work of contemporary artisanal bakers is valued enough for them to support their families and employees. They have already begun training the next generation of bakers, those who see alchemy in the infinite forms flour, water, and yeast take in presence of heat.

VEGETABLE FRITTATA

Johnson's Country Inn, Chico

Herbs freshly snipped from the inn's garden embellish the enticing aroma of this dish, serving as an organic wake-up call for guests as it wends through the halls. Feel free to alter the vegetables and herbs a bit, depending on what's freshest at the market (or from your own garden).

4 tablespoons olive oil	*1 teaspoon thyme leaves*
1 small onion, chopped	*8 eggs*
1 red or yellow bell pepper, cored, seeded, and chopped	*Salt and freshly ground black pepper*
3 plum (roma) tomatoes, chopped	*3 medium red rose potatoes, precooked and cut in ½-inch wedges*
1 cup chopped Swiss chard or spinach	*1 cup grated sharp cheddar cheese*
2 cloves garlic, minced	*¾ cup grated provolone or swiss cheese*
½ cup loosely packed basil leaves, coarsely chopped	*¼ cup grated Parmesan cheese*
1 tablespoon minced oregano	*1 tablespoon minced cilantro*

PREHEAT THE OVEN to 375°F.

HEAT HALF OF THE OLIVE OIL in a medium skillet over medium heat. Add the onion, bell pepper, tomatoes, Swiss chard, and garlic. Sauté, stirring, until tender, about 5 minutes. Take the skillet from the heat. Stir in the basil, oregano, and thyme and set aside.

HEAT THE REMAINING OIL in a medium paella pan or another large, sloping-sided skillet over medium-high heat. Whisk together the eggs, season to taste with salt and pepper, and add the eggs to the hot pan. Scatter the sautéed vegetable mixture, potatoes, and cheddar and provolone cheeses evenly over the eggs. Transfer the pan to the oven and bake the frittata until the eggs are set, about 25 minutes. Use a spatula to loosen the frittata and slide it onto a serving platter. Sprinkle with the Parmesan cheese and cilantro, cut into wedges, and serve.

Makes 6 to 8 servings

BLUE CORNMEAL PANCAKES

Hidden City Café, Point Richmond

Cornmeal pancakes are among the favorite breakfast options of the many regulars who flock to this popular café. You'll want to serve them only the best sweet butter, real maple syrup, and possibly a scattering of fresh fruit to go with the pancakes.

1 cup blue cornmeal	*2 tablespoons unsalted butter,*
1–2 tablespoons honey	*melted and cooled*
½ teaspoon salt	*½ cup all-purpose flour*
1 cup boiling water	*2 teaspoons baking powder*
1 egg	*Butter or oil, for frying pancakes*
½ cup milk	

IN A MEDIUM BOWL, stir together the cornmeal, honey, and salt. Slowly stir in the boiling water until the mixture is evenly blended and smooth. Set aside until cool, about 20 minutes.

IN ANOTHER BOWL, lightly whisk the egg, then whisk in the milk and butter. Stir this into the cooled cornmeal mixture until smooth. Sift the flour and baking powder over and stir just until incorporated.

HEAT A LIGHTLY BUTTERED or oiled griddle or a large, heavy skillet over medium-high heat. When hot, add the pancake batter in generous tablespoons and cook until the bubbles that form on top burst, about 1 minute. Turn the pancakes and continue cooking until browned on the bottom. Continue with the remaining batter, adding butter or oil to the skillet as needed.

Makes 4 to 6 servings (about 36 small pancakes)

OATBRAN MUFFINS

Half Day Café, Kentfield

These wholesome muffins have great texture and flavor from the addition of applesauce and a touch of molasses. They're lowfat, too! Feel free to add other embellishments, such as nuts, raisins, chopped dried fruits, and other spices.

2 cups all-purpose flour	2 eggs
1½ cups oatbran	1½ cups applesauce
½ cup packed brown sugar	½ cup vegetable oil
2 teaspoons baking powder	¼ cup lowfat milk
2 teaspoons ground cinnamon	¼ cup molasses
½ teaspoon salt	½ teaspoon vanilla extract

MUFFIN TOPPING

¼ cup all-purpose flour	2 tablespoons finely chopped walnuts
¼ cup rolled oats	½ teaspoon ground cinnamon
¼ cup packed brown sugar	½ teaspoon powdered ginger
2 tablespoons granulated sugar	Pinch salt
3 tablespoons unsalted butter, cut in pieces and chilled	

FOR THE MUFFIN TOPPING, combine the flour, oats, sugars, butter, walnuts, cinnamon, ginger, and salt in the bowl of a mixer and mix with the paddle attachment until well blended and the topping has a crumbly texture. Don't overmix; the butter should remain in little visible bits. Set aside.

PREHEAT THE OVEN to 350°F. Line 18 muffin cups with paper liners, or grease the muffin cups.

IN A LARGE BOWL, combine the flour, oatbran, brown sugar, baking powder, cinnamon, and salt. Stir to mix well. In a medium bowl, lightly beat the eggs, then stir in the applesauce, oil, milk, molasses, and vanilla. Add the wet ingredients to the dry ingredients and gently stir until just evenly mixed. Scoop the batter into the prepared muffin cups, nearly filling them (about ⅓ cup). Scatter the muffin topping evenly over and bake until puffed and lightly browned, 30 to 40 minutes.

Makes 18 muffins

PEACH SQUARES
with Sour Cream Topping

Lost Whale Bed & Breakfast, Trinidad

Though this warm and filling breakfast dish is at its best when peaches
are fresh and ripe, the recipe can also be made with frozen peaches. It could even
double as dessert or as a snack with afternoon tea.

6 peaches, pitted and sliced | *4 egg yolks*
1 cup packed brown sugar | *3 tablespoons granulated sugar*
2 teaspoons ground cinnamon | *1 teaspoon almond extract*
2 cups sour cream |

CRUMB CRUST

1 cup unsalted butter, softened at room | *4 cups all-purpose flour*
temperature | *1 teaspoon baking powder*
¼ cup granulated sugar | *½ teaspoon salt*

PREHEAT THE OVEN to 400°F. Grease and flour a 9- by 13-inch baking dish.

FOR THE CRUMB CRUST, cream together the butter and sugar in a mixer. In a separate bowl, stir together the flour, baking powder, and salt. Gradually add the flour mixture
to the butter until evenly blended. Press the crust evenly along the bottom and partially
up the sides of the prepared baking dish.

LAYER THE PEACH SLICES over the crust. Sprinkle the brown sugar and cinnamon
evenly over the peaches and bake for 15 minutes.

WHILE THE PEACHES ARE BAKING, stir together the sour cream, egg yolks, granulated sugar, and almond extract.

TAKE THE BAKING DISH from the oven and reduce the oven temperature to 350°F. Spread the sour cream topping over the peaches and continue baking until the topping is well set and the crust begins to pull away slightly from the sides of the pan, 35 to 40 minutes longer. Take the dish from the oven and let sit for a few minutes before cutting the baked peaches into squares. Serve warm.

Makes 12 servings

OF CURDS AND WHEY

Dutch, Greek, Italian, and Scotch dairy farmers came to the pastoral landscapes of Mendocino, Sonoma, and Santa Cruz Counties about a century ago. For most of the intervening years, decent, sometimes excellent, factory cheeses have been made, following traditions the immigrants had developed. Monterey Jack cheese is perhaps Northern California's most famous, sold in supermarkets everywhere in the nation and made in Wisconsin, too. Jack was developed by an immigrant Scots dairyman, David Jacks, who settled near the city of Monterey. Jack is no longer made in Monterey, but the Sonoma Cheese Factory produces excellent Sonoma Jack, Dry Jack, and Teleme. Members of the Viviani family, who operate the Sonoma Cheese Factory, still follow small-batch, attentive methods, though they make many thousands of pounds of cheese.

Other small dairies and factories make credible versions of popular European cheeses. Bulk Farms owners in Oakdale have kept true to their Dutch heritage, specializing in plain, cumin-flavored, or garlic-flavored Gouda and an excellent aged Gouda. Rouge et Noir of Marin County produces only small rounds of Camembert-style cheeses, which are local favorites for simple wine-and-cheese picnic lunches. Mozzarella Fresca, also of Marin, makes Italian-style fresh mozzarella and ricotta.

Artisanal cheeses have been made for many years. The Vella Cheese Company's Bear Flag brand is synonymous with the finest of craftsman-made cheeses. In the hands of cheesemaker Ignazio Vella, eight-pound wheels of cow's milk Jack cheese are rubbed with cocoa, pepper, and olive oil to form a rich deep chocolate rind. After two years of aging, this becomes Dry Jack: complex, nutty, and buttery, inviting comparisons with Italian grana cheeses. Bear Flag's Asiago Italian Table Cheese is equally delicious. The Vellas began cheesemaking in the 1930s in Sonoma, in partnership with the Vivianis (of the Sonoma Cheese Factory). They continue to refine their craft and build regional traditions.

Peluso Cheese of Los Banos makes a rice-flour-rind Teleme that stands as an exemplar of this soft cows'-milk cheese. It is excellent on its own and with bread and fruit; when the chewy, nutty-flavored rind is removed, Teleme is a fine melting cheese for cooking. The name is thought to have come from the Touloumi cheese made in Crete, as Cretan settlers near Tomales Bay were the first to make it.

In the last few decades, there has been a resurgence of artisanal cheesemaking, with many newcomers trying their hands and succeeding. (For a look at goat cheeses in the region, see Goat Cheeses Gather the Gold, page 213.) The best cheesemakers depend on quality of milk just as fine winemakers depend on the quality of grapes. Pasturage is important, as everything dairy animals eat shows in the milk. Breed of animal is also important to an artisanal cheesemaker, as are a dairy's husbandry habits.

The Straus Family Organic Dairy has an excellent reputation with the cheesemakers it supplies. The Cowgirl Creamery of Point Reyes Station uses Straus Family milk for cottage cheese, fromage blanc, and award-winning crème fraîche, all made daily in small batches. The Creamery also makes some slightly aged rounds, which develop character while retaining a fresh appeal.

The Matos Cheese Company of Santa Rosa produces a distinctive cows'-milk cheese from its own dairy herd. Its cheese, St. George, makes fans of those lucky enough to taste it. The cheese may be described as semisoft, buttery, something between cheddar and Jack in flavor, but this gives little idea of the clean, rich, yet light flavor. Members of the Matos family, originally from St. George Island in the Azores, are continuing a tradition of five generations.

Bellwether Farms of Petaluma has pioneered the area's sheep's-milk cheeses, beginning in 1990. Bellwether follows many Italian methods and uses Italian forms to produce the award-winning Toscano, an aged pecorino-style cheese. It also makes Italian-style ricotta with whey and several young pecorinos: St. Andreas, Pecorino Pepato, and Caccioto. It has begun to make artisanal cows'-milk cheeses as well, including ricotta, fromage blanc, and Crescenza—a soft, young tart cheese modeled after the Italian cheese.

The variety and quality of regional cheeses has spurred an interest in the cheese course at restaurants. Imported cheeses are also offered, but the selection at many places includes a Northern California cheese or two. Cheesemakers have begun to work with restaurateurs as produce suppliers do, conducting tastings and exchanging information about cooking with and serving cheese.

SALSA JACK SOUFFLÉ

Glenelly Inn, Glen Ellen

From the veranda of this 1916 inn, you look out over the
Sonoma Valley, known nearly as well for its cheese production as for the local
winemaking traditions. So it's Sonoma Jack cheese that is preferred for this easy
breakfast soufflé. The addition of salsa also seems natural in this region of
distinctive Mexican heritage.

This isn't like the traditional fold-in-beaten-egg-whites-and-hold-your-
breath-while-it-bakes soufflés, though the puffy, golden presentation belies its simple
technique. Baked and served in individual ramekins, the results are even more
dramatic. The optional pieces of corn tortilla added to this dish make it a bit more
filling. You can leave them out for a slightly lighter dish or simply
serve warmed corn tortillas alongside.

1 pound Jack cheese, cut in small cubes
1 cup cottage cheese
1 cup salsa, red or green, mild to hot
depending on your taste

1–2 corn tortillas, torn into bite-size
pieces (optional)
9 eggs
1 cup buttermilk or regular milk

PREHEAT THE OVEN to 425°F. Lightly grease a 9- by 13-inch baking dish.

SCATTER THE JACK CHEESE evenly in the bottom of the prepared dish, spread the
cottage cheese evenly over, and spoon the salsa on top. Sprinkle the corn tortilla bits over,
if using.

IN A LARGE BOWL, whisk the eggs to lightly blend, then whisk in the buttermilk.
Pour the egg mixture into the dish and bake until the eggs are set in the center and
golden brown on top, 30 to 40 minutes.

Makes 8 to 10 servings

CROATIAN CORN BREAD

Grey Whale Inn, Fort Bragg

This slightly sweetened and super-moist variation
on corn bread makes a nice change on the breakfast plate, possibly served
with a drizzle of maple syrup and a side of bacon or sausage. Or you could turn it
into a sort of breakfast "shortcake," served with fresh berries and a dollop of lightly
sweetened whipped cream. Any leftovers will make a great snack later in the day.
The recipe is from the family files of the inn's breakfast cook, Debbie Dooley.

2 cups cottage cheese	½ cup polenta
2 eggs	½ cup all-purpose flour
¼ cup raw sugar or regular granulated sugar	¼ cup unsalted butter, melted and cooled
½ teaspoon salt	¼ teaspoon baking soda
1 cup sour cream	Freshly grated or ground nutmeg

PREHEAT THE OVEN to 425°F. Grease a 9-inch square baking dish or a 10-inch quiche pan.

IN A LARGE BOWL, stir together the cottage cheese, eggs, sugar, and salt until well mixed. Stir in the sour cream, polenta, flour, butter, and baking soda. Pour the mixture into the prepared dish and sprinkle the top lightly with nutmeg. Bake until golden brown, about 30 minutes. Let cool slightly before cutting into pieces to serve.

Makes 8 servings

GRAND MARNIER FRENCH TOAST

Seal Cove Inn, Moss Beach

In addition to the orange butter, maple syrup can
be served with this toast. For a teetotaling "just plain orange"
version of the recipe, omit the Grand Marnier.

6 eggs	*¼ cup freshly squeezed orange juice*
2 cups milk, preferably whole milk	*Vegetable oil or spray, for frying*
¼ cup Grand Marnier	*12 thick slices French bread*

ORANGE BUTTER

½ cup unsalted butter	*Grated zest of 1 orange*
¼ cup Grand Marnier	*1¼ cups powdered sugar, plus*
¼ cup freshly squeezed orange juice	*more for serving*

FOR THE ORANGE BUTTER to serve with the French toast, melt the butter over
medium heat in a small saucepan. Take the pan from the heat and stir in the Grand
Marnier, orange juice, and orange zest. Gradually stir in the powdered sugar until well
blended. Let cool. Refrigerate until ready to serve, stirring occasionally.

IN A LARGE BOWL, whisk the eggs until well blended, then whisk in the milk with
the Grand Marnier and orange juice. Heat a large skillet over medium heat and lightly
coat the skillet with vegetable oil. Dip 3 or 4 pieces of the bread in the egg mixture until
well soaked, and then fry in the hot skillet until nicely browned, about 2 minutes on each
side. Repeat with the remaining bread, adding more oil to the skillet as needed.

ARRANGE THE FRENCH TOAST on individual plates and top each piece with a
spoonful of the orange butter. Dust the toast lightly with powdered sugar and serve while
hot, passing extra orange butter separately.

Makes 4 to 6 servings

OATMEAL FENNEL SEED SCONES

Sutter Creek Inn, Sutter Creek

A nice twist on the traditional scone, this not-too-sweet recipe benefits from the added texture of oatmeal and the subtle anise flavor of fennel seeds. Tasty with coffee in the morning, these scones are delicious with that afternoon cup of tea.

2 cups all-purpose flour	*½ teaspoon celery salt*
1 cup rolled oats	*½ cup unsalted butter, cut in pieces*
¼ cup packed brown sugar	*and chilled*
1 tablespoon baking powder	*½ cup milk*
2 teaspoons fennel seeds	*2 eggs, lightly beaten*

PREHEAT THE OVEN to 400°F. Lightly grease a large baking sheet.

IN A LARGE BOWL, combine the flour, oats, brown sugar, baking powder, fennel seeds, and celery salt and stir to evenly mix. Add the butter and, using a pastry blender or 2 table knives, cut it into the flour mixture until it has a crumbly consistency. Add the milk and eggs and stir gently just until blended; do not overmix or the scones will be tough. Turn the dough onto a lightly floured work surface and knead just a few turns until smooth.

DIVIDE THE DOUGH in half and pat each half into a round about ½ inch thick and 6 inches across. Score the top of each round to mark 6 wedges for easy serving. Arrange the rounds a couple of inches apart on the baking sheet and bake until lightly browned, about 18 minutes. Transfer the rounds to a cake rack to cool, then cut into wedges for serving.

Makes 12 scones

APPETIZERS

TZATZIKI

Wine Spectator Restaurant at Greystone, St. Helena

This tangy sauce is a part of every Greek meze table. To achieve a texture
similar to Greek yogurt, which is made with sheep's milk and thicker than what
we get here, the yogurt is drained in the refrigerator for at least
4 hours to remove excess water.

Serve the tzatziki as a dip with slices of pita bread and fresh vegetables,
spoon it over fried eggplant and zucchini, or serve as a sauce accompaniment for
grilled lamb. It will have a more developed flavor if made at least a couple
of hours before serving and stored, covered, in the refrigerator.

32 ounces plain yogurt	*3 large cloves garlic, very finely minced*
1 large English cucumber, seeded and coarsely	*3 tablespoons olive oil*
grated (or 2 small regular cucumbers,	*1 tablespoon red wine vinegar or lemon juice*
peeled, seeded, and grated)	*¼ cup chopped mint or part mint, part*
Salt and freshly ground black pepper	*flat-leaf (Italian) parsley*

LINE A STRAINER with cheesecloth and set it inside a large bowl. Spoon the yogurt
into the strainer, cover with plastic, and refrigerate for 4 to 6 hours. Discard the liquid that
collects in the bowl.

PUT THE GRATED CUCUMBER in a colander or strainer and sprinkle generously
with salt. Let sit in the sink to drain for about 30 minutes, then squeeze the cucumber to
remove excess water.

IN A LARGE BOWL, stir together the drained yogurt, garlic, olive oil, and vinegar or
lemon juice. Add the cucumber and stir it evenly into the yogurt mixture. Stir in the mint
with salt and pepper to taste.

Makes about 2½ cups

STEAMED DUNGENESS CRAB DUMPLINGS

with Lemongrass Dressing and Chile-Garlic-Lime Dipping Sauce

Albion River Inn, Albion

Chef Stephen Smith served these dumplings when invited to cook
at the celebrated James Beard House in New York City. The occasion was a delicious
showcase for the Dungeness crab caught locally on the Mendocino coast.

*4 ounces rock shrimp or regular shrimp,
peeled and deveined*

1 egg white

2 tablespoons minced ginger

2 tablespoons whipping cream

2 tablespoons chopped cilantro

1 tablespoon sugar

1 teaspoon salt

½ teaspoon freshly ground black pepper

8 ounces Dungeness crabmeat

½ cup finely diced napa cabbage heart

1 package (14 ounces) wonton wrappers

1 egg, lightly beaten

LEMONGRASS DRESSING

½ cup chicken stock

¼ cup soy sauce

2 stalks lemongrass, trimmed and minced

1 tablespoon minced garlic

½ cup vegetable oil

1 tablespoon minced cilantro

2 cups finely shredded napa cabbage

*½ large cucumber, peeled, seeded, and
thinly sliced*

CHILE-GARLIC-LIME DIPPING SAUCE

2 tablespoons vegetable oil

2 tablespoons minced ginger

2 tablespoons minced garlic

2 tablespoons minced shallot

1 tablespoon minced Thai or jalapeño chile

1 cup chicken stock

2 tablespoons sugar

2 tablespoons tomato paste

Juice of 2 limes

2 tablespoons minced cilantro

*1 tablespoon cornstarch dissolved in
2 tablespoons cold water*

Salt and freshly ground pepper

PUT THE SHRIMP, egg white, ginger, cream, cilantro, sugar, salt, and pepper in a food processor and purée until very smooth. Transfer the mixture to a bowl. Pick over the crabmeat to remove any bits of shell or cartilage. Add the crabmeat and cabbage to the shrimp purée and stir until evenly blended. Refrigerate until well chilled, about 2 hours.

WHILE THE FILLING CHILLS, make the lemongrass dressing. Combine the chicken stock, soy sauce, lemongrass, and garlic in a small saucepan. Bring to a boil and boil until reduced by about half, 8 to 10 minutes. Pour the broth mixture into a small bowl and let cool. When cool, whisk in the oil and cilantro. Refrigerate until needed.

FOR THE DIPPING SAUCE, heat the oil in a medium saucepan over medium heat. Add the ginger, garlic, shallot, and chile. Cook, stirring, until tender and aromatic, 3 to 5 minutes. Stir in the chicken stock, sugar, and tomato paste. Bring just to a boil, then lower the heat and simmer for 15 minutes. Stir in the lime juice, cilantro, and cornstarch and simmer until the sauce is thickened, stirring often, about 5 minutes longer. Take from the heat and season the sauce to taste with salt and pepper. Set aside.

TO FORM THE DUMPLINGS, brush one wonton wrapper lightly with beaten egg. Put 1 tablespoon of the chilled filling in the center and lift the corners up to meet above the filling, pressing the folded edges together to form an "X." Continue with the remaining filling and wonton wrappers.

PREPARE A STEAMER with a few inches of water in the bottom. Arrange the dumplings on the perforated steamer racks without touching. Bring the water to a boil, add the racks, cover the pan, and steam the dumplings until the wrappers are translucent and the filling is cooked through, about 10 minutes.

WHILE THE DUMPLINGS are steaming, gently reheat the dipping sauce. Rewhisk the lemongrass dressing to mix and pour it over the shredded cabbage and thinly sliced cucumber in a large bowl. Toss to evenly coat, then arrange the salad to one side of each of 4 individual plates. Arrange the steamed dumplings on the plates, passing the dipping sauce separately.

Makes 4 servings (about 24 dumplings)

SOUTHEAST ASIAN INGREDIENTS

The staple flavors of most Southeast Asian dishes are fairly easy to find in the San Francisco Bay Area and in towns in Northern California with immigrant populations. For Thai and Cambodian curries and soups, fresh galangal, lemongrass, and purple Asian basil wait in the produce departments of independent supermarkets, as well as in Asian specialty stores. Several plants are sold as Vietnamese coriander, including *Polygonum odoratum*. Cooks have their favorites for garnishing *pho*, the very popular Vietnamese beef soup with a hundred variations. Lemongrass, anise-scented basils, Southeast Asian varieties of scallions and winter onions, and common leaf coriander with the roots are also sold at farmers' markets. Kaffir lime *(Citrus hystrix)* leaves require a little more searching but are available fresh or frozen. Banana leaves for wrapping vegetables, meat, or fish or steaming rice are also available fresh or frozen.

Such ingredients are essential to authentic re-creation of the cuisine's dishes. When an imported ingredient is out-of-season, the frozen form can substitute; Southeast Asian cooks seldom use dried forms of aromatic herbs and plants. For example, fresh galanga, related to ginger, has a more complex flowery perfume and a flavor that is more citruslike and less biting. Dried galangal is virtually tasteless. Fresh kaffir lime leaves and the fruit's rind add another note of citrus complexity to soups and curries. Dried lime leaves, like dried lemongrass, don't come close.

Dried and manufactured ingredients do play an important role in much Southeast Asian cooking, from Thai to Vietnamese, Indonesian to Burmese. One can find dried shrimp (in whole, powder, and paste form) and fish sauces from almost every Southeast Asian country. Indonesian shops carry ketchups—sweet and salt soy sauces—candlenuts, canned coconut milk and shredded coconut, palm sugar, and many *sambals* (chile paste condiments with different flavorings). With these, cooks make the typical peanut sauces and curries. Filipino shops are stocked with annatto seeds, palm vinegar, tamarind pulp, and saffron for the adobos, sour soups, and Spanish-influenced dishes that characterize Philippine cuisine.

Since all Southeast Asian countries are represented in Northern California, the pan-Asian food emporiums that increasingly dot the urban and suburban landscape frequently offer sections dedicated to specific countries. Restaurant and home cooks find them convenient for experimenting with other cuisines and enlivening their own.

ARTICHOKES BARIGOULE

L'Amie Donia, Palo Alto

Barigoule is a traditional preparation of braised artichokes
from Provence in southern France. Sometimes the artichokes are stuffed with
vegetables and/or meat, but here they are not, making for a light first-course serving.
Meyer lemons are common in Northern California, especially in the more temperate
coastal regions. The Meyer is larger and slightly sweeter than the common
lemon, but generally the two are interchangeable.

4 large artichokes	*6 cloves garlic, crushed*
1 Meyer lemon or large common	*Bouquet garni of 1 bay leaf and 3 sprigs*
lemon, halved	*thyme tied together with kitchen string*
½ cup olive oil	*1 teaspoon saffron threads (optional)*
1 onion, thinly sliced	*1 teaspoon crushed coriander seeds*
2 carrots, thinly sliced	*Salt and freshly ground black pepper*
2 stalks celery, thinly sliced	*Chopped flat-leaf (Italian) parsley, for serving*
2 cups dry white wine	

TRIM AND RINSE the artichokes. Rub the cut surfaces with half of the lemon; squeeze
the remaining juice from the lemon halves and set aside.

HEAT THE OLIVE OIL over medium heat in a deep pan large enough to hold the artichokes upright. Add the onion, carrots, and celery and cook, stirring, until tender, 3 to 5
minutes. Add the reserved lemon juice and 1 cup of the wine with the garlic, bouquet garni,
saffron, coriander seeds, and salt and pepper to taste. Arrange the artichokes upright over the
vegetables and pour over the remaining wine with enough water to reach the bottom edge
of the leaves, 1 to 2 cups. Bring the liquids to a gentle boil, then reduce the heat, cover the
pan, and simmer until the artichokes are cooked through, about 45 minutes. To check if the
artichokes are fully cooked, tug at one of the leaves—it should pull away easily.

ARRANGE THE ARTICHOKES on a large serving platter or in 4 individual shallow
soup bowls. Spoon some of the cooking liquids over, sprinkle with the chopped parsley, and
serve warm. You'll want to have an extra bowl on the table for discarded artichoke leaves.

Makes 4 servings

TUNA TARTARE
with a Ginger Emulsion

Highlands Inn, Carmel

Seaweed salad, a Japanese delicacy, is available in better seafood
markets and Asian food stores. Its distinctive colors and crisp texture are a perfect
accompaniment to the tender, rich tuna tartare.

Be sure to use regular olive oil for the ginger emulsion. Extra virgin would be too
strongly flavored for this delicate sauce. This recipe makes more emulsion than is
needed here; extra will be delicious on sandwiches, drizzled over seafood,
or used in salad dressing.

1 medium tomato	*2 tablespoons minced chives*
1 pound sashimi-grade tuna, finely diced	*Juice of 1 small lemon*
(about 2 cups)	*1 cup seaweed salad*
2 tablespoons minced shallot	

GINGER EMULSION

1 egg yolk	*1½ cups olive oil*
Juice of 3 limes	*Salt and freshly ground white or black pepper*
1 tablespoon minced ginger	

FOR THE GINGER EMULSION, combine the egg yolk, lime juice, and ginger in a
blender or food processor and pulse to blend. With the blades running, very slowly add
the olive oil, beginning with a few drops at a time until the mixture begins to emulsify,
then continuing with a slow, steady stream. Season to taste with salt and pepper, transfer to
a bowl, and refrigerate until needed.

BRING A MEDIUM PAN of water to a boil and prepare a large bowl of ice water. With
the tip of a sharp knife, score a small "X" on the bottom of the tomato. Add the tomato
to the boiling water and blanch until the skin begins to split, 20 to 30 seconds. Scoop the
tomato out with a slotted spoon and put it in the ice water for a quick cooling. When
cool, drain the tomato, then peel away and discard the skin. Quarter the tomato lengthwise, scoop out and discard the seeds, then finely chop the flesh and put it in a large bowl.

ADD THE TUNA, shallot, chives, and ¼ cup of the ginger emulsion to the bowl with the tomato. Stir gently until well mixed. Stir in the lemon juice, with salt and pepper to taste. Form the tartare into 4 molds (such as ½-cup ramekins) and refrigerate until ready to serve, at least 30 minutes or up to 2 hours.

TO SERVE, spoon about 2 tablespoons of the ginger emulsion in the center of each of 4 chilled plates. Form a small circle of the sauce; then draw the sauce outward with the back of the spoon to form a star pattern. Spoon the seaweed salad into the center of the star and unmold the tuna tartare on top of the seaweed. Serve right away.

Makes 4 servings

STEAMED MUSSELS WITH CELERY, APPLES, AND HAZELNUTS

Wente Vineyards, Livermore

This simple, aromatic steamed-mussel recipe is full of warming fall flavors. Use a nice, dry white wine that you'll want to drink alongside. The chef suggests a sauvignon blanc.

Be sure to serve some good, crusty bread alongside for dipping in the tasty cooking juices left in the bowl. This recipe will serve two for a main course, and it can easily be doubled to serve more.

1 tablespoon olive oil

6 green onions, white and pale green parts only

1 cup chicken stock

¼ cup dry white wine

2 tablespoons Calvados

2 pounds mussels, scrubbed and debearded

1 stalk celery, finely diced

½ Fuji or other crisp apple, finely diced

Juice of ½ lemon

1 tablespoon finely chopped toasted hazelnuts

HEAT THE OIL in a large saucepan over medium heat. Add the whole green onion pieces and cook, stirring occasionally, until they are light golden, about 5 minutes. Add the chicken stock, reduce the heat to low, cover the pan, and cook until the onions are very tender, about 10 minutes. Using a slotted spoon, scoop the onions onto a cutting board and coarsely chop them when cool enough to handle.

RETURN THE GREEN ONIONS to the pan with the wine. Increase the heat to high and bring just to a boil. Stir in the Calvados, then add the mussels to the pan. Cover the pan and cook, shaking the pan occasionally, until the mussels have opened, 3 to 5 minutes. Discard any mussels that do not open.

TAKE THE PAN from the heat and stir in the celery, apple, lemon juice, and hazelnuts. Scoop the mussels into 4 individual bowls, spooning the cooking liquids over. Serve right away.

Makes 4 servings

AQUACULTURE: BRINGING UP CLAMS, MUSSELS, AND OYSTERS

Most clams, mussels, and oysters are now farmed rather than harvested from the wild for many good reasons: declining wild stocks, more reliable production, improved ability to counteract pollution and natural bacteria, customer confidence in aquaculture.

Tomales Bay, Marin County, is an excellent aquaculture site, with cold, clean waters protected by a peninsula. Michael Watchorn of Hog Island Oyster Company decided to work here more than 20 years ago and has supplied fine restaurants and retail sources in the San Francisco Bay Area with bivalves ever since. He uses the French rack-and-bag system to raise them. He places the quarter-inch oyster, clam, and mussel spat separately in horizontal layers in plastic fine-mesh bags and attaches the bags to rebar rods in the bay. Mussels generally take a year to develop to market size, oysters two years, and clams about two and a half years.

Hog Island raises the Sweetwater Hog Island oyster and the Kumamoto (a Pacific variety), Atlantic Bluepoints, and French Belons, as well as Mediterranean mussels and Manila clams. When the bivalves are mature, Watchorn and his colleagues harvest them, test them for bacteria, sort and pack them, and then transport them to Hog Island's clients. That is, if all goes well. Technology has aided the art of bivalve aquaculture, but it is ultimately an agricultural pursuit, subject to nature's quirks and surprises. Predators, such as green crabs or rays, may take some of the harvest, even with attentive monitoring. Bags will wash away in big storms, no matter how well they are lashed to their supports.

The flavor of bivalves, particularly of oysters, depends highly on their environments. In that they are like wines. As grape varietals show their heritage but also pick up savor from the earth, amount of sunshine, rain, and ambient temperature, so do bivalves. The salinity of the waters where they grow and the flora and fauna that influence microlevels of nutrients and minerals all play a part in the flavor of a given mussel, oyster, or clam.

TOMATO AND ROQUEFORT TART PROVENÇAL

Fandango, Pacific Grove

A delicious way to start a meal, this tart could also be served in larger pieces as a light main course, with a crisp salad and bread alongside.

2 tablespoons olive oil	*4 ounces ham, finely diced*
1 shallot, sliced	*2 tablespoons minced flat-leaf (Italian) parsley*
1 clove garlic, sliced	*2 tablespoons minced basil*
3 eggs	*Paprika*
2½ cups whipping cream or half-and-half	*Salt and freshly ground black pepper*
4–5 ounces Roquefort cheese or other blue cheese, crumbled	*4 medium tomatoes, thinly sliced and drained on paper towels*

PIE CRUST

1½ cups all-purpose flour	*½ teaspoon salt*
½ cup unsalted butter, cut in pieces and chilled	*5–6 tablespoons cold water*
	1 tablespoon olive oil

FOR THE PIE CRUST, combine the flour, butter, and salt in a food processor and pulse just until the mixture has a crumbly texture. Add the water 1 tablespoon at a time, pulsing a few times between each addition, just until the dough begins to have a smooth texture. (Be careful not to overwork the dough or it will become tough.) Turn the dough onto a lightly floured work surface and form it into a ball. (Alternatively, make the dough by cutting the butter into the flour with a pastry blender or 2 table knives; then stir in the water until well blended.) Wrap the dough in plastic and refrigerate for at least 30 minutes.

HEAT 2 TABLESPOONS OLIVE OIL in a small skillet over medium heat and sauté the shallot and garlic until just tender but not browned, 2 to 3 minutes. Set aside to cool completely.

ROLL THE CHILLED PASTRY dough out to line a deep 9-inch pie pan, trimming excess from the edges and crimping to form a decorative rim. Refrigerate for at least 30 minutes.

PREHEAT THE OVEN to 375°F.

LINE THE PASTRY CRUST with foil and partially fill it with pie weights or dry beans. Bake the crust until just set but not too browned, 12 to 15 minutes. Take the crust from the oven, remove the foil and weights, and brush the pastry with 1 tablespoon olive oil. Set aside to cool. Leave the oven set at 375°F.

IN A LARGE BOWL, lightly beat the eggs, then whisk in the cream and beat until well mixed. Stir in the cooled shallot-and-garlic mixture, the cheese, ham, 1 tablespoon of the parsley, and 1 tablespoon of the basil with paprika, salt, and pepper to taste.

ARRANGE HALF OF THE TOMATO SLICES on the bottom of the pastry crust. Pour the egg mixture over and bake for 20 minutes. Take the tart from the oven, arrange the remaining tomato slices on top, sprinkle with the remaining parsley and basil, and season lightly with salt and pepper. Return the tart to the oven and continue baking until the center is set, about 5 minutes longer. Turn on the broiler and lightly brown the top of the tart to finish, about 3 minutes. Let cool slightly before serving.

Makes 8 servings

PAN-FRIED OYSTERS WITH PANCETTA AND WILTED SPINACH

Restaurant 301, Carter House Victorians, Eureka

The Carter House chefs are able to use super-fresh Humboldt Bay oysters, collected from this bay that skirts the western edge of Eureka. Any recipe calling for oysters is best when the oysters are just-shucked, with fall and winter the best seasons for buying fresh oysters in the shell. If fresh in-shell oysters aren't available, you can use jarred oysters, drained and rinsed. One 10-ounce jar of medium oysters will have about 10 oysters in it.

2 tablespoons olive oil, more if needed
4 ounces pancetta or top-quality bacon, diced
½ cup fine yellow cornmeal, more if needed
Pinch freshly ground or grated nutmeg
Salt and freshly ground black pepper
½ cup buttermilk or regular milk

10 oysters, shucked
1 tablespoon unsalted butter
1 clove garlic, minced
1 bunch spinach, washed and dried,
*   tough stem ends trimmed*

HEAT 2 TABLESPOONS OLIVE OIL in a medium nonstick skillet over medium-high heat. When very hot, add the pancetta and cook, stirring, until it is crisp. Scoop the pancetta out with a slotted spoon and drain on paper towels. Reserve the drippings in the skillet and set aside.

ON A PLATE or in a small bowl, stir together the cornmeal and nutmeg with salt and pepper to taste. Put the buttermilk in another small bowl. Dip each oyster in the buttermilk, and then coat evenly in the cornmeal, patting to remove excess.

REHEAT THE PANCETTA DRIPPINGS in the skillet over medium-high heat. Add the oysters and cook until nicely browned and just firm to the touch, about 3 minutes on each side. You might need to add a drizzle of olive oil if there aren't enough pancetta drippings. Transfer the oysters to a warmed platter lined with paper towels, cover with foil to keep warm, and set aside.

WIPE OUT THE SKILLET with paper towels and heat the butter over medium-high heat until just foaming. Add the garlic and sauté until aromatic, about 1 minute. Add the spinach leaves and cook, stirring, until wilted, 1 to 2 minutes.

TO SERVE, spoon the spinach onto 2 individual plates, arrange the oysters on top, and sprinkle the crisped pancetta over.

Makes 2 servings

BYWORDS FOR BIVALVES

A time-honored rule of thumb applies equally to oysters, mussels, clams, and any other bivalves in the shell. The shells should be closed when you buy them, open when you eat them; this is a quick visual test to tell whether bivalves are wholesome to eat. Sometimes bivalves open just a bit to breath while they are under refrigeration. Mussels are particularly prone to opening. To be sure they are still alive, tap them gently; they should close. Oysters and clams may be still alive but too cold to react quickly and discernibly to tapping.

If you're not certain whether bivalves are alive, smell them before serving them on the half shell or cooking them. Ones with an unpleasant or "off" odor should not be eaten. They are rarely encountered in this age of aquaculture and careful refrigeration of seafood, but practice letting your nose be your guide. Bivalves should have a slightly salty, appetizing aroma.

To open clams, mussels, and oysters, either shuck them or heat them. If you're serving them on the half shell, follow your nose before placing them on ice, and then refrigerate immediately for up to an hour. Most people who appreciate the flavor of bivalves on the half shell shuck them just before serving. When you are cooking, discard any bivalves that do not open after their pan mates have.

Though it is perfectly possible to eat bivalves in summer, most agree that the flavor is not as tasty then as during the rest of the year. Mussels are usually leaner and less meaty in summer. Oysters spawn when the water warms, which leaves them softer and rather fatty tasting. Once out of the water, clams are quite sensitive to warm temperatures, so it is best to eat them close to their source.

Some people are allergic to raw bivalves, though not necessarily to cooked ones. It's wise to ask before planning a menu whether your guests have such allergies. Those with immune-system and liver deficiencies or other serious health problems are advised not to eat raw shellfish, especially bivalves.

SALSA ROMESCO

Wine Spectator Restaurant at Greystone, St. Helena

This Spanish sauce takes its name from a variety of dried pepper that
is not very hot. If you like your romesco a bit on the zippy side, add a little mince
of fresh jalapeño chile or extra cayenne pepper. At the Wine Spectator Restaurant,
the romesco is served with grilled shellfish, grilled asparagus, and grilled green
onions. "It is also an addictive dipping sauce for fried potatoes," adds Joyce
Goldstein, a San Francisco restaurant consultant who has been visiting
executive chef at this Culinary Institute of America campus.

The recipe calls for almonds and hazelnuts, but you could also use
1 cup of either rather than a mixture. The sweet smoked Spanish paprika adds a
subtle smoky element to this sauce, though other top-quality sweet paprika can be
used in its place. It might be a good time to replace that dusty can of paprika in
your cupboard if it has been around for some unknown period of time.

2 medium dried ancho chiles	*½ cup toasted hazelnuts, skins removed*
1 large tomato	*3 tablespoons red wine or sherry vinegar,*
1 large red bell pepper	*more to taste*
¾ cup olive oil	*3–4 large cloves garlic, minced*
1 slice white bread, ½ inch thick, crust	*1 tablespoon sweet smoked Spanish paprika*
removed (about 1 ounce)	*¼ teaspoon cayenne pepper, more to taste*
½ cup toasted blanched almonds	*Salt and freshly ground black pepper*

PUT THE ANCHO CHILES in a small bowl and cover with hot water. Let sit until
tender, about 1 hour. Drain the chiles, remove the stems and seeds, and chop. Set aside.

BRING A MEDIUM PAN OF WATER to a boil and prepare a large bowl of ice water.
With the tip of a sharp knife, score a small "X" on the bottom of the tomato. Add the
tomato to the boiling water and blanch until the skin begins to split, 20 to 30 seconds.
Scoop the tomato out with a slotted spoon and put it in the ice water for quick cooling.
When cool, drain the tomato and then peel away and discard the skin. Quarter the
tomato lengthwise, scoop out and discard the seeds. Chop the tomato and drain on paper
towels. Set aside.

ROAST THE BELL PEPPER over a gas flame or under the broiler until the skin blackens, turning occasionally to roast evenly, 5 to 10 minutes total. Put the pepper in a plastic bag, securely seal it, and set aside to cool. When cool enough to handle, peel away and discard the skin. Remove the core and seeds and chop the pepper. Set aside.

HEAT 2 TABLESPOONS OF THE OLIVE OIL in a small skillet and fry the bread over medium-high heat until golden, 1 to 2 minutes on each side. When cool enough to handle, break up the bread and put it in the bowl of a food processor or blender with the ancho chiles, tomato, bell pepper, nuts, vinegar, garlic, paprika, and cayenne. Process until very finely chopped. With the motor running, gradually add the remaining olive oil. Season the sauce to taste with salt and pepper and let sit for 15 minutes before tasting again for heat.

Makes about 2 ½ cups

SESAME CRUSTED SHRIMP

Covey Restaurant, Quail Lodge Resort, Carmel Valley

This recipe is quite quick and easy to put together, but these crunchy
sesame seed–crusted shrimp make an impressive appetizer, especially if you combine
both white and black sesame seeds. The chef suggests serving the shrimp with
rice or polenta for something more substantial.

½ cup sesame seeds (preferably half white
and half black)
¼ cup all-purpose flour
2 egg whites, beaten with 1 tablespoon water

16 large shrimp (about 1 pound),
peeled and deveined
2–3 tablespoons olive oil or clarified butter

CASHEW SAUCE

1 cup dry white wine
1 tablespoon soy sauce, more to taste
1 clove garlic, minced
½ teaspoon Thai fish sauce
(nam pla—optional)

½ teaspoon sugar
3 tablespoons cashew butter or
creamy peanut butter
Cayenne pepper
Freshly ground black pepper

FOR THE SAUCE, combine the wine, soy sauce, garlic, fish sauce, and sugar in a small
saucepan; whisk in the cashew butter. Bring to a boil and boil until slightly thickened,
2 to 3 minutes. Season to taste with cayenne, black pepper, and more soy sauce. Keep
warm over very low heat.

IF USING both black and white sesame seeds, stir to mix. Put the seeds on a small plate.
Put the flour and egg whites in 2 separate dishes. Working with a few shrimp at a time,
dredge the shrimp in flour, patting well to remove excess; then dip in the egg white mixture and finally coat the shrimp in sesame seeds, again patting to remove excess.

HEAT THE OIL in a large, heavy skillet over medium-high heat. Add the shrimp and
cook until they start to curl and are almost completely opaque, about 2 minutes per side.
Arrange the shrimp on 4 individual plates and drizzle the cashew sauce around.

Makes 4 servings

CHINESE INGREDIENTS

If you like the fun and challenge of making your own dim sum, you'll find fresh bamboo shoots, water chestnuts, live shrimp, and wheat starch wrappers for *siu mai* in San Francisco's Chinatown. You can also find red rice vinegar for dipping sauce. If you don't want to bother, there are plenty of choices in ready-to-eat dim sum: *ha gau, cha siu bau, chai dim sum, cheung fun,* or *jien dui,* to name a few. More adventures in ingredients are found in two streets—Stockton between Clay and Vallejo and Grant between Pacific and Broadway—than anywhere else in the nation, except for New York City's Chinatown.

Sights and smells are intriguing enough to stimulate the appetite of the most I-can-take-or-leave-Chinese-food type. The hearts of Chinese food lovers throb for the overwhelming selection of common soy, oyster, hoisin, plum, chili, barbecue, and black bean sauces, as well as for many more exotic ingredients. Chicken or duck feet for dim sum, cooked Peking duck, and pork in myriad forms from sausage to spareribs fill the meaty menu. Fresh lotus leaf, litchi nuts, and jujubes in season gratify the authentic-taste cook. Live water creatures—crayfish from the Sacramento Delta, imported eel, spiny and Maine lobster, bass and carp—are offered for the discriminating. Dried abalone, oysters, scallops, and squid are available for snacks, soups, and congees.

Noodle emporiums make wonton and spring roll wrappers, as well as egg noodles, and usually sell cooked noodle dishes. Dried rice noodles *(ho fun)* and cellophane noodles *(fun see)* are found in shops with other dried, packaged, and preserved ingredients. Many of these are *sine qua non* for soups: cloud and wood fungus, tiger lily buds, Szechuan preserved greens, thousand-year eggs. Some, such as rock sugar and black rice vinegar, are used primarily in braised dishes. Fresh vegetables in bins and baskets spill onto the sidewalks. Greens from *gai lan* to *pak choi,* cabbages, snow peas, bunching onions, and bitter and winter melons promise Chinese flavor in stir-fries, braises, and soups.

The silicon boom and increasing Chinese immigrant population of the past two decades have led to small Chinese markets scattered throughout most counties touching San Francisco Bay. Ranch Markets, a recent arrival, combine supermarket size, ease, and well-lighted shelves with the specialties from many Asian cuisines.

BRANDADE-STUFFED GIANT MOREL MUSHROOM

Farallon, San Francisco

This recipe is absolutely luxurious, with cream, butter, and olive oil.
But it's oh, so delicious and shows why Farallon has been such a hugely popular
restaurant since it opened in San Francisco in 1997. Salt cod, long appreciated
in other countries, especially Spain and Portugal, is regaining favor in this country.
Disconcertingly leathery and crusted with salt when purchased, the fish emerges
with wonderful flavor and texture after soaking and poaching. Brandade
is a classic Mediterranean appetizer, often served as is with bread or toast for
spreading, with good olives and other snacks alongside.

Unless it's a bumper-crop year for morels (often the case the year following forest
fires, which create a fertile growing condition that morels thrive on), you're likely to
have trouble finding the giant morels chef Mark Franz uses for this recipe.
You can use the brandade stuffing in other mushrooms, such as large white or
crimini mushroom caps, shiitakes, or small portobello mushroom caps.

At Farallon, the chef embellishes the sauce by first simmering the fish stock
and wine with crushed lobster shells. We've streamlined the sauce preparation here,
but if you have some lobster shells on hand (they can be rinsed and frozen to save
after shelling a whole steamed lobster), sauté them with the shallots and herbs
at the beginning of the sauce preparation.

3 tablespoons olive oil	½ cup dry white wine
6 giant morel mushrooms	1¾ cups fish stock
(about 4 inches long)	1 cup plus 1 tablespoon unsalted butter
Salt and freshly ground black pepper	1 cup fava beans, shelled and blanched
1 cup sliced shallots	¾ cup fresh corn kernels, blanched
2–3 sprigs thyme plus 1 tablespoon	(about 1 small ear)
thyme leaves	¼ cup finely chopped tomato
1 bay leaf	

BRANDADE

4 ounces salt cod, soaked for 24 hours in
multiple changes of cold water
2 cups whipping cream

¼ cup olive oil (preferably half regular
and half extra virgin)
2 cloves garlic, crushed whole

FOR THE BRANDADE, drain the soaked salt cod and remove and discard any bones
and skin. Put the cod in a medium saucepan with the cream and cook over medium heat
until the fish becomes tender, about 10 minutes. Strain the cod, reserving the cream. In a
small saucepan, combine the olive oil(s) and garlic cloves. Cook over medium heat until
the garlic is aromatic, about 3 to 4 minutes, then take the pan from the heat. Scoop out
and discard the garlic (or save it for another use). Flake the salt cod into the bowl of a
mixer fitted with the wire whisk. Blend the fish at medium speed until flaked, then slowly
drizzle in 2 tablespoons of the poaching cream. With the motor running, carefully drizzle
the olive oil(s) toward the edge of the bowl. (Alternatively, you could mix the brandade by
hand, blending the ingredients vigorously with a wooden spoon.) The texture of the brandade should be firm but smooth; add another drizzle of the cream if needed. Check for
seasoning, adding salt and pepper to taste, then set aside.

HEAT 1 TABLESPOON OLIVE OIL in a medium skillet over medium heat. Add the
mushrooms, season lightly with salt and pepper, and sauté until they are just tender, 5 to
10 minutes, depending on the type and size of mushroom used. Take from the heat and let
cool. When the mushrooms are cool enough to handle, use a pastry bag to stuff the brandade into them. (Alternatively, use a small spoon to fill the mushrooms.) Set aside.

PREHEAT THE OVEN to 350°F.

FOR THE SAUCE, heat 1 tablespoon of olive oil in a medium saucepan over medium-
high heat. Add the shallots, thyme sprigs, and bay leaf and sauté until aromatic, about 3
minutes. Add the wine, bring to a boil, and boil until the liquid is reduced by about half.
Add 1½ cups fish stock, bring to a boil, and boil until about ¼ cup of liquid remains.
Reduce the heat to medium-low and whisk in 1 cup butter, a little at a time, until fully
incorporated. Strain the sauce into another pan, season to taste with salt and pepper, and
keep warm over very low heat. (Don't overheat the sauce or the butter will turn from
creamy to oily.)

ARRANGE THE STUFFED MUSHROOMS on a baking sheet and bake until just
heated through, 5 to 10 minutes.

WHILE THE MUSHROOMS ARE HEATING, prepare the vegetable ragout. In a medium skillet, heat 1 tablespoon olive oil over medium heat. Add the thyme leaves, followed by the fava beans and corn, stirring for about 1 minute. Add the tomato with ¼ cup fish stock and season to taste with salt and pepper. Cook, stirring, until just evenly heated, 2 to 3 minutes. Then stir in the remaining 1 tablespoon butter.

SPOON THE RAGOUT into the centers of 6 individual plates and drizzle some of the sauce around the vegetables. Set the warm stuffed mushrooms on the ragout and serve right away.

Makes 6 servings

FORAGERS' FUNGI

The secrets of mushroom hunting can be well learned only by going on field trips with those who know from long experience which mushrooms are safe to eat, which are delicious, and where to find them. Virtually all mycological societies agree that identifying mushrooms from photographs is very difficult. Misidentification can be dangerous, even deadly. It is worth noting that most wild mushrooms should be cooked before they're eaten. Some people don't react to the allergens in raw boletes and chanterelles; be careful in consumption if you aren't sure whether you will or not.

Most of the wild mushrooms that turn up at markets and in restaurants are gathered by knowledgeable hunters. Retailers and chefs are also careful about the kinds of mushrooms they offer to the public. There haven't been any incidents of mushroom poisoning in public venues for many years, in fact, though there have been several, including deaths, among people who have gathered mushrooms for home consumption.

The coastal season extends from October to March; in the Sierra, mushrooms also appear after summer rainstorms and after the snowmelt in May and June. Early season begins with the boletes, including the prized *Boletus edulis*: porcino in Italian, cèpe in French. According to a longtime fungophile, *B. edulis* never places worst than first in every blind tasting. Boletes are called the king of mushrooms in Italy, fitting their meaty flavor, al dente texture, and complex wood-and-smoke aroma. The mild meadow agaricus (*Agaricus campestris*), close cousin to the cultivated mushroom, also appears early.

Midseason, the chanterelles (*Cantharellus cibarius*), both golden and white, spring up. Their nutty flavor and clean woodsy fragrance make them popular even with people who usually don't eat mushrooms. Their close cousins, black trumpets (*Craterellus fallax*) and horns of plenty (*C. cornucopioides*) follow closely. Earthy-tasting, humus-scented morels, black and yellow *Morchella* spp., close the season. They are rarer here than in the Pacific Northwest, where more moisture and wooded habitat favor them.

The varieties mentioned here are the ones most often seen in restaurants, but other fungi are tasty and usually abundant. Candy cap (*Lacterius fragilis*) has a maple-syrup-like flavor and is used to flavor cookies and cakes. Honey (*Armillaria mellea*) and oyster (*Pleurotes ostreatus*) are not complex in flavor but are delicious in omelets, on toast, and in other simple dishes.

ARTICHOKE TART

Belle de Jour Inn, Healdsburg

When fresh baby artichokes are available, it's worth the bit of extra work
to use them in this tart. Simply trim the stems and tips from the artichokes and pull
away a few layers of the tough outer leaves. Steam or boil the artichokes until tender,
slip them directly into cool water with the juice of half a lemon, drain the
artichokes, and quarter them.

This tart also makes a wonderful lunch or light supper with a salad of baby greens
and a glass of sauvignon blanc. At Belle de Jour, though, it is often served
at breakfast, accompanied by fresh fruit and scones.

5 eggs	*2 tablespoons chopped sun-dried tomatoes*
¾ cup ricotta cheese	*(oil-packed or plumped dried)*
1 can (14 ounces) quartered artichoke hearts	*1 teaspoon herbes de Provence*
in water, drained	*Salt and freshly ground black pepper*
1 cup grated Swiss cheese	*2 tablespoons grated Parmesan cheese*

PASTRY

1¼ cups all-purpose flour	*⅓ cup shortening*
¼ teaspoon salt	*¼ cup cold water*

PREHEAT THE OVEN to 400°F.

FOR THE PASTRY, stir together the flour and salt in a large bowl. Cut in the short-
ening using a pastry blender or 2 table knives until the mixture has a crumbly consistency.
Sprinkle the water over and toss the dough with a fork until thoroughly combined. Form
the dough into a ball and roll out on a lightly floured work surface to a 12-inch circle.
(If the kitchen's warm, the dough may be too soft to roll out right away; wrap the dough
in plastic and refrigerate for about 30 minutes before continuing.)

LINE A 10-INCH removable-base tart pan or a deep 9-inch pie pan with the dough and
prick the bottom a few times with a fork. Line the pastry crust with foil and partially fill
it with pie weights or dry beans. Bake the pastry for 8 minutes. Take the pan from the

oven, remove the foil and weights, and continue baking until the pastry is set but not browned, about 10 minutes longer. Set the pastry aside to cool. Reduce the oven temperature to 350°F.

FOR THE FILLING, whisk the eggs in a large bowl until smooth, then whisk in the ricotta cheese until well blended. Add the artichoke hearts, Swiss cheese, sun-dried tomatoes, and *herbes de Provence* with salt and pepper to taste and stir until well blended.

SPRINKLE THE PARMESAN CHEESE in the bottom of the pastry crust. Pour the filling over and bake until the filling is set and beginning to turn brown, 25 to 30 minutes in a tart pan, 30 to 35 minutes in a pie pan. Serve the tart hot, warm, or cold.

Makes 6 to 8 servings

LIQUID GOLD IN THE HILLS: OLIVE OIL

So much of what we take for granted was not always thus. The ubiquity of little plates or cruets of olive oil in Northern California restaurants is a recent example. In Mediterranean countries, olives are frequently served with bread; oil is not. In those countries, oil marinates everything from cheese to fish to vegetables, is poured into soup, drizzled over salad and grilled meat, brushed onto hearth-toasted bread, and baked into sweets and savories. Here, a tradition-in-the-making—bread with oil to dip it in—began in the late 1980s, though no restaurant or oil producer has yet claimed this bid for immortality. "Mediterranean-style" had buzzed over to being de rigueur menu talk of the time, studies on monounsaturated fats and country-by-country comparisons of heart disease were in the daily papers, and butter was banished from many tables. In the kitchens, too, the tide of olive oil was rising and the shores of solid fats receding.

The fortunes of olive groves have waxed and waned throughout the region's history, subject to food fashions and housing developments, but olives have been cultivated continuously in the southern reaches since the Spanish established missions at Monterey and Santa Clara in the late 18th century. Italians brought their own cuttings when they arrived later. Spanish and Italian varieties—Mission, Sevillano, Manzanillo, Ascolano—still make up the bulk of the crop.

Throughout this time, most oil was pressed for home, mission, or very local consumption. At the end of the 19th century, a few canned black-ripe olives began to make an impression on the gourmet restaurant, hotel, and first-class railway trade. These were from the large groves in the upper Sacramento Valley. A few years later, with the invention of an effective mechanical olive-pitter and a tin-canning process, both green and black olives began to be canned. Many Californians found these olives tasty when eaten as part of the cocktail course or in mild mission versions of Mexican food. But the rest of the nation was slow to relish olives.

It took almost a century before Americans would be convinced of what some doctors were sure of in 1891: olive oil was good for human health. Northern California, with groves already in place and a climate virtually perfect for olives, was positioned for a significant press, as happened during the last two decades.

Local oils began to dribble out and to find many consumers willing to switch from expensive imported oils.

People with a passion for the olive discovered abandoned but still abundantly producing groves. Others with devotion and cash brought cuttings from Tuscany and Provence to start new groves, as well as the latest and/or the oldest in European pressing equipment. Some experimented with American pressing technology. A number of growers and producers formed the California Olive Oil Council to set and maintain standards for regional extra virgin oil. They work with similar international groups on educational and promotional programs.

Much local oil is from the Mission variety of olive. It has a high percentage of oil in its thin flesh, but to many palates it does not have the nuanced flavor of the best European oils. The popularity of herb- and spice-flavored oils has enabled producers to sell most of their harvests at a good price. Owners of old groves with other oil-producing varieties, such as Columella, Picholine, and Rubra, are confident that these will find favor and distinction.

Several salient parallels exist between the region's olive oil and wine. Both are relatively expensive agricultural products, subject to many vagaries of weather and market pricing. The olive and the vine have very old traditions; they need some time to become deeply established as part of the cuisine. Whether producers work with newly planted or long-established groves, Italian, French, or Spanish varieties, they are of a mind that it's only a matter of time before California olive oil ranks with the world's finest. And, like the winemakers who took California wines from the region to the world, the olive oil producers are people with passion and commitment.

TAGLIATELLE
with Nettles and New Olive Oil

Oliveto Restaurant, Oakland

Paul Bertolli, chef/owner of this renowned Oakland restaurant, makes
this recipe only in the late fall and early spring, when nettles are abundant and
recently pressed olive oil is available. Nettles, the bane of many hikers and gardeners,
become a magical ingredient when they're invited into the kitchen. Here, they turn
fresh egg pasta brilliant green, adding their subtle earthy perfume and flavor to
this simple dish. If you can't get your hands on freshly pressed olive oil,
just use the best you can find.

Be sure to handle the nettles with gloves until they're cooked, to avoid their
harmless but irritating sting.

6 ounces tender fresh nettles	*6 tablespoons new extra virgin olive oil*
1 egg	*6 tablespoons freshly grated Parmigiano-*
2 cups all-purpose flour	*Reggiano cheese*
1 teaspoon salt	

BRING A LARGE SAUCEPAN OF WATER to a boil and prepare a large bowl of ice
water. Add half of the nettles to the boiling water, blanch for 30 seconds, then drain and
add them immediately to the ice water. When cooled, drain well, squeeze excess water
from the nettles, and purée in a food processor or blender with the egg to make a smooth
paste. Combine the flour, salt, and the nettle paste in a medium bowl and stir until evenly
blended. Knead the dough on a lightly floured work surface until it is evenly blended and
satiny to the touch, 8 to 10 minutes. Wrap the pasta dough in plastic and set aside for 30
minutes.

AFTER THE DOUGH HAS RESTED, use a hand-cranked pasta machine to roll it
out to a thickness of about 1/16 inch (to setting 5 or 6), using a bit of flour as needed to
prevent sticking. Cut the pasta sheets into roughly 12-inch lengths and stack the pieces,
with a dusting of flour between them. Roll the sheets up into a cylinder, leaving about
1 inch unrolled at the end. Cut across the roll to make tagliatelle about ⅜ inch thick and

12 inches long. Pick up the pasta strands by the unrolled end and scatter them loosely on a floured baking sheet.

JUST BEFORE SERVING, bring a large pot of generously salted water to a boil. Add the tagliatelle and cook until al dente, about 3 minutes. Add the remaining nettles to the pasta water about 30 seconds before draining the pasta. Drain the pasta and nettles thoroughly and then transfer to a warmed large bowl. Add the olive oil and quickly toss. Arrange the pasta in 6 individual shallow bowls or plates, sprinkle the cheese over, and serve right away.

Makes 6 servings

TO CLEAN AND CRACK CRAB

Hold the crab from underneath and remove the top bright red shell by lifting it from the body. Spoon out any crab butter (the soft yellowish fat) and reserve it. Rinse and reserve the shell if you want to use it for presentation. Remove the gills, mouthparts, and firm, white, centered intestine from the body cavity. Turn the crab over and remove the triangular piece. Rinse the body cavity and set aside.

Twist the legs from the body as close as possible to the body. Crack the leg and claw sections with a heavy tool, such as a mallet or the back of a cleaver. Hold the legs or claws so that a ridged or angled side will be struck by the mallet or cleaver. This, along with the weight of the tool, decreases the possibility that the meat will be mashed or imbedded with pieces of shell. Now you're ready for the delicious crab dishes on pages 38, 64, and 96. You don't even have to find a place to park or listen to the serenades of barking sea lions on Fisherman's Wharf!

CRAB FRITTERS

Lisa Hemenway's, Santa Rosa

Chef/owner Lisa Hemenway recently spent more than a year
on a taste exploration through Vietnam and Singapore, an experience that manifests
itself in her menu, which includes dishes such as this. She serves these fritters, similar
to egg rolls, both as an appetizer (1 to 2 per serving) and a main course
(3 per serving). For a smaller, bite-size variation, you could instead
enclose the filling in wonton wrappers.

The fritters are tied with strips of banana leaf (or green onion tops), which is an
addition more aesthetic than essential for holding together the fritters. If you do use
the green onions, don't try to tie them too firmly or they'll break.

2 tablespoons unsalted butter	*Pinch powdered mustard*
½ cup minced onion	*Salt and freshly ground black pepper*
½ cup minced celery	*12 egg roll wrappers (about half of a*
½ cup dried bread crumbs	*1-pound package)*
1 cup crabmeat (about 8 ounces)	*½ banana leaf or 3–4 green onion tops, cut in*
1 egg, lightly beaten	*strips ¼ inch wide and about 4 inches*
2 tablespoons whipping cream	*long, for tying the fritters*
1 tablespoon minced flat-leaf (Italian) parsley	*Vegetable oil, for deep-frying*

HOT LIME MAYONNAISE

1 egg yolk	*1 teaspoon sambal oelek or other hot chile*
Juice of 1 lime	*sauce, or to taste*
¾ cup vegetable oil	*½ teaspoon finely grated lime zest*

IN A MEDIUM SKILLET, heat the butter over medium heat. Add the onion and celery
and sauté, stirring occasionally, until the vegetables are just tender but not browned,
about 3 minutes. Stir in the bread crumbs and continue cooking, stirring often, until
evenly blended and the bread crumbs have absorbed moisture from the vegetables, 1 to 2
minutes. Set aside to cool.

PICK OVER THE CRABMEAT to remove any bits of shell or cartilage. Stir the crab-meat, egg, cream, parsley, and mustard into the cooled bread crumb mixture, with salt and pepper to taste. Transfer the mixture to a bowl and refrigerate until fully chilled.

WHILE THE FILLING IS CHILLING, prepare the mayonnaise. Put the egg yolk and lime juice in a blender or food processor and whirl to mix. With the blades running, begin adding the vegetable oil a few drops at a time until the emulsion has begun to form. (The egg yolk will turn pale and the mixture will become very thick.) Add the rest of the vegetable oil in a very fine stream. Add the *sambal oelek* or other chile sauce and lime zest with salt and pepper to taste. Transfer to a bowl and refrigerate the mayonnaise until ready to serve.

TO FORM THE FRITTERS, lay one egg roll wrapper on the work surface and put 2 level tablespoons of the crab mixture into the center of the wrapper. Form the filling in a horizontal strip about 1 inch wide, leaving a 1-inch edge on either end. Brush the edges of the wrapper lightly with water, then wrap up the filling in a cylinder, twisting the ends gently to fully enclose the filling. Using strips of banana leaf or green onion top, tie each end of the fritter. Repeat with the remaining filling and wrappers.

HEAT ABOUT 2 INCHES OF OIL in a deep sauté pan or a large saucepan to about 350°F. Fry the crab fritters in batches until golden brown, 3 to 5 minutes, then drain on paper towels. Arrange the fritters on a large platter or individual plates, passing the hot lime mayonnaise separately.

Makes 6 to 12 servings

ROCKFISH SEVICHE

Farallon, San Francisco

At Farallon, chef Mark Franz uses a variety of fish for this citrus-cured recipe, from Hawaii's onaga to Floridian snapper. Closer to the San Francisco Bay Area, options include rockfish, lingcod, scallops, and halibut. Though the acid reaction with the fish changes the color and texture of the flesh, the fish is never technically "cooked," so whichever you choose, be certain that it is the highest quality you can get.

The chef often makes a dramatic presentation of the seviche, serving it in a cleaned sea urchin, abalone, or scallop shell perched on a bed of rock salt on a glass plate. At home, you can serve it in small dishes or on a bed of greens. For a party, spoon the colorful seviche into endive leaves for tasty finger fare.

1½ pounds very fresh rockfish, skin and pin bones removed
1 cup freshly squeezed grapefruit juice
½ cup freshly squeezed lime juice
½ cup freshly squeezed lemon juice

½ small red onion, sliced paper thin
4 small grapefruit, peeled and sectioned (see below)
Salt and freshly ground black pepper

DRESSING

2–3 tablespoons brined green peppercorns, rinsed and lightly chopped
1 red Fresno or jalapeño chile, cored, seeded, and finely diced

1 tablespoon chopped cilantro
½ cup olive oil

CUT THE FISH FILLETS into ½-inch dice. In a large bowl, combine the citrus juices; set aside ¼ cup of the juice mixture for the dressing. Stir the fish and red onion into the remaining juice. Cover and refrigerate until the fish is "cooked" to your taste, about 15 to 30 minutes.

FOR THE DRESSING, whisk together in a small bowl the reserved citrus juice with the green peppercorns, chile, and cilantro, then whisk in the olive oil.

WHEN THE FISH IS MARINATED to taste, drain off all the juices. (Leaving the fish in contact with the acidic juices for too long with make the fish tough.) Add the grapefruit sections and dressing to the fish and onions and toss to mix well. Season to taste with salt and pepper and serve right away.

Makes 6 servings

SECTIONING CITRUS

Here's an easy technique for peeling and sectioning grapefruit and other citrus fruits so that the sections have no pith or membrane, making them tidier and easier to eat.

Cut both ends from the grapefruit just to the flesh. Set the grapefruit upright on a cutting board and use the knife to cut away the peel and pith, following the curve of the fruit. It takes a bit of practice, but try not to cut away too much of the flesh with the peel.

Working over a large bowl to catch the sections and juice, hold the peeled grapefruit in your hand and slide the knife blade down one side of a section, cutting it from the membrane. Cut down the other side of the same section and let it fall into the bowl. Continue for the remaining sections, turning back the flaps of membrane like the pages of a book.

FEUILLETÉE OF MOREL MUSHROOMS, ARTICHOKES, ROASTED FENNEL, AND FAVA BEANS

with Asparagus Beurre Blanc

Lalime's, Berkeley

This recipe was created with spring and vegetarians in mind. "I try to include a vegetarian menu every other month on our flyer for regular vegetarians so that they don't feel left out!" explains chef Frances Wilson. "[This recipe] is a celebration of spring using such vegetables as fava beans, asparagus, artichokes, and morel mushrooms. For a lighter version of the sauce, thin the asparagus purée with some vegetable stock instead of using beurre blanc." When fava beans aren't available, use fresh peas or other beans. And other mushrooms can be used in place of the morels. Be sure to pick the smallest of the baby artichokes available, so they'll be plenty tender for this preparation.

*6 pieces puff pastry, each 5 by 3 inches
(1 commercial frozen sheet)*

1 egg, beaten

FILLING

*12 baby artichokes
2 fennel bulbs, trimmed, cored, and sliced
3 tablespoons olive oil
2 teaspoons minced garlic
Salt and freshly ground black pepper*

*1 pound morel mushrooms, halved, very
lightly rinsed, and well dried
2 cups fava beans, peeled and blanched
1 tablespoon minced tarragon*

ASPARAGUS BEURRE BLANC

*1 pound asparagus
2 cups whipping cream*

*½ cup dry white wine
1 cup unsalted butter, cut in pieces and chilled*

PREHEAT THE OVEN to 375°F.

FOR THE FILLING, cut about ½ inch off the top of the baby artichokes and trim the base. Pull away a few layers of the outer leaves until you reach the tender, paler green inner leaves, then halve the artichokes. Bring a medium pan of lightly salted water to a boil, add the artichokes, and simmer until just tender, 7 to 10 minutes. Drain, refresh under cold running water, drain well, and set aside.

PUT THE SLICED FENNEL in a baking dish. Drizzle 1 tablespoon of the olive oil and 1 teaspoon of the garlic over. Season to taste with salt and pepper and toss to mix. Roast the fennel until just tender, 10 to 12 minutes. Transfer the fennel to a large bowl and set aside.

SCATTER THE MUSHROOMS in the same baking dish. Drizzle with another tablespoon of olive oil and the remaining garlic, with salt and pepper to taste. Toss to mix and roast until tender, 5 to 7 minutes for morels, 10 to 12 minutes for regular mushrooms. Add the mushrooms to the bowl with the fennel, along with the baby artichokes, fava beans, and tarragon. Toss gently to evenly mix and taste for seasoning, adjusting if needed. Set aside. Keep the oven set at 375°F.

ARRANGE THE PASTRY RECTANGLES on a baking sheet with at least 1 inch between them. Lightly brush the tops with the beaten egg. Bake the pastry until browned and puffed, 12 to 15 minutes. Set aside to cool on a cake rack.

FOR THE ASPARAGUS BEURRE BLANC, cut the tender tips from the asparagus stalks and trim away any tough white from the ends. Bring a small pan of lightly salted water to a boil, add the asparagus tips, and blanch for 2 minutes. Scoop out the asparagus tips with a slotted spoon, drain well, and set aside for garnish. Return the water to a boil, add the asparagus stalks, and boil until very tender, about 7 minutes. Drain well, then purée the stalks in a food processor until smooth. Rub the purée through a sieve to remove the fibrous parts.

PUT THE CREAM in a heavy medium saucepan, bring to a boil, reduce the heat, and simmer until reduced by half. In another small saucepan, boil the wine until reduced by half. Add the wine to the cream and put the pan over low heat. Whisk in the butter, bit by bit, careful that the butter melts creamily without becoming oily. Move the pan off the heat as needed to avoid overheating. Whisk in the asparagus purée with salt and pepper to taste. Keep warm over low heat.

HEAT THE REMAINING TABLESPOON OF OLIVE OIL in a large skillet and reheat the vegetable filling over medium-high heat. Split each of the pastry rectangles in half horizontally and set the bottom halves on 6 individual plates. Spoon the filling over and top with the remaining pastry halves. Pour the sauce around, garnish the plates with the asparagus tips, and serve right away.

Makes 6 servings

GRAVLAX AND HERB TERRINE

City Hotel, Columbia

This is a silky, luxurious way to start a meal, with the fresh herbs nicely complementing the richness of the cured salmon (gravlax) and cream cheese. For a cocktail party, you could spread the terrine onto small crackers ahead of time and lay them out on a tray for easy one-handed nibbling.

14 ounces cream cheese, at room temperature
2 eggs
1 cup whipping cream
4–5 ounces gravlax, diced
¾ cup grated Gruyère cheese

2–3 tablespoons minced herbs (chervil, parsley, chives, tarragon, and/or basil)
¼ teaspoon freshly ground white pepper
Pinch freshly ground or grated nutmeg

PREHEAT THE OVEN to 325°F. Lightly grease six ½-cup ramekins.

BEAT THE CREAM CHEESE in a mixer with the paddle attachment or in a bowl with a wooden spoon until soft and smooth. Beat in the eggs, then stir in the cream until evenly blended. Stir in the gravlax, Gruyère cheese, herbs, pepper, and nutmeg. Spoon the mixture into the prepared ramekins and set them in a baking dish large enough to hold them all generously. Add boiling water to the baking dish to come about halfway up the sides of the ramekins. Carefully transfer the baking dish to the oven and bake until the terrines are firm and a knife inserted in the center comes out clean, 25 to 30 minutes. Take the ramekins from the baking dish and let cool, then refrigerate until ready to serve. Serve chilled or at room temperature, with crackers, toast, or crusty bread alongside for spreading.

Makes 6 servings

HEDGEHOG OF THE SEA

The question of how to extract anything edible from a sea urchin hinges on a prior question: how to handle the urchin at all. Fortunately for those fans of the urchin's delicately flavored coral, some anonymous adventurer of the edible discovered that one side of the urchin yielded to pressure rather than inflicted it. This must rank with the opening of the oyster as human advancement in understanding which creatures of the sea were not only edible, but delicious.

Tidepools along the Northern California coast harbor large colonies of purple sea urchins, relatives of sand dollars and starfish. Urchins bristle with more than a hundred spines. These help defend their fragile, roughly hemispherical shells against predators: sea otters, people, and starfish cousins. Along the North Coast from Mendocino to the Oregon border, collectors harvest urchins while wearing gloves to protect themselves from wounds. Much of the commercial trade has turned to the green-shelled urchin, a more flavorful East Coast variety. These are shucked and shipped to the sushi trade, ready to be rice- and nori-wrapped.

The edible parts of an urchin are the five pale rose orange–colored corals. The nonspiny face of the urchin, where its mouth is located, is softer than the rest of the shell. This is where to cut around with scissors to extract the coral. The corals are very fragile and are best loosened with a spoon, slipped into the hand, and rinsed carefully of any extraneous matter.

Sea urchins are now considered a gourmet treat and priced accordingly. Few are still sold live. Some cooks serve these corals in the trimmed shells like oysters, accented with a touch of lemon juice and perhaps a sprinkle of chives. Others find ways to highlight the urchin's delicate texture and briny flavor in urchin omelets or by coating them in a light tempura batter (see page 72).

SEA URCHIN TEMPURA

Mendocino Hotel, Mendocino

For devotees of *uni*, or raw sea urchin roe, this recipe might seem
like gilding for the lily. But the light, crisp batter helps temper the distinctive flavor
and texture of sea urchin roe that others find a bit overwhelming. The fresh salad of
mango, cucumber, and green onion served alongside is the perfect foil
for this rich tempura.

Chef Colleen Murphy heads to the Mendocino docks, where she picks out
fresh sea urchin in the shell. "Choose small purple ones if possible; they're the
sweetest," she explains. "Each urchin has five lobes of roe. Carefully crack around the
bottom edge and open the shell, then tenderly scoop out the roe and rinse them off.
Keep the roe between layers of paper towel and chill until ready to use. We use the
shells to serve the sea urchin tempura, rinsing out the shell very well and dividing it
in two." You can also look for cleaned sea urchin roe in some top-quality seafood
or Asian markets, a less dramatic but much easier approach to obtaining
the unusual sea creatures.

The tempura batter should be used right after mixing, and the quick-cooking
tempura should be served right away. Be sure all the other elements are ready—not
to mention your dining companions—before you begin the final process.

20 sea urchin roe	*1 cup mixed edible seaweeds, for serving*
2 tablespoons vegetable oil, plus more	*(optional)*
for deep-frying	*1 cup cake flour*
1 tablespoon finely shredded ginger	*1 cup cold water*
1 cucumber, peeled, seeded, and thinly sliced	*1 egg, lightly beaten*
1 mango, peeled, seeded, and thinly sliced	*2 tablespoons wasabi paste*
4 green onions, sliced	

TERIYAKI SAUCE

½ cup freshly squeezed orange juice

¼ cup soy sauce

2 tablespoons dry sherry

1 tablespoon sesame oil

1½ teaspoons sesame seeds

½ teaspoon powdered mustard

½ teaspoon honey, preferably orange blossom

½ teaspoon minced shallot

¼ teaspoon minced ginger

Pinch Szechuan pepper

IF YOU ARE STARTING with whole sea urchins or otherwise have access to the shells, you can rinse them well and let drain to use them as serving dishes if you like. Very gently rinse the sea urchin roe under cold water, arrange the roe on paper towels, and refrigerate until ready to use.

FOR THE TERIYAKI SAUCE, combine all the ingredients in a medium bowl and stir to mix well. Set aside.

HEAT 2 TABLESPOONS OIL in a small saucepan over medium heat and fry the shredded ginger just until lightly browned and aromatic, about 1 minute. Drain on paper towels and set aside. In a medium bowl, combine the cucumber, mango, and green onions and toss gently to mix. Set aside.

ARRANGE THE SEAWEEDS attractively on 4 individual plates. If using sea urchin shells, set one on each plate and distribute the cucumber, mango, and green onion evenly among the shells. Otherwise, simply make a bed of those ingredients on top of the seaweed. Pour the teriyaki sauce into 4 individual bowls and set them on the plates for dipping.

HEAT ABOUT 3 INCHES OF OIL in a deep fryer or a heavy, deep saucepan over medium-high heat. In a medium bowl, combine the flour, water, and egg and briefly stir with a fork just until blended.

WHEN THE OIL IS HEATED (test with a small piece of bread; it should sizzle vigorously within a few seconds), carefully drop a few of the sea urchin roe into the batter and scoop out with a fork. Carefully transfer the roe to the hot oil and fry just until the outside is lightly browned and crisp, about 1 minute. Drain the fried roe on paper towels and keep warm in a low oven. Continue with the remaining roe.

ARRANGE THE SEA URCHIN TEMPURA on the cucumber-mango-onion beds on each plate, top with some of the frizzled ginger, and garnish with a dab of wasabi. Serve right away.

Makes 4 servings

PEEL-AND-EAT SHRIMP IN BEER

North Coast Brewing Company, Fort Bragg

The house brew used for this recipe at North Coast
is the company's Acme Pale Ale, but any pale ale will do. Of course, you'll want
to have plenty more of the same chilled to serve with the shrimp. Though delicious
in the buff, these shrimp would also be tasty with a zesty cocktail sauce or
rémoulade sauce alongside for dipping. This is an easy recipe to double,
triple—whatever—if you've got a crowd coming over.

1 pound medium or large shell-on shrimp	*2 dried red peppers (such as pasilla)*
1 bottle (12 ounces) pale ale	*4 sprigs fresh dill or ½ teaspoon dried dill*
1 cup water	*¼ teaspoon thyme leaves*
Juice of 1 lemon	*Lettuce leaves, for serving*
2 bay leaves	*Lemon wedges, for serving*
¼ cup loosely packed celery leaves	

IN A LARGE POT, combine the shrimp, beer, water, lemon juice, and bay leaves and
bring just to a boil. Stir in the celery leaves, dried red peppers, dill, and thyme. Cover the
pot and simmer over medium heat for 5 minutes. Take from the heat and let cool, then
chill for about 1 hour. (Letting the shrimp cool in the cooking liquids allows them to
absorb a maximum of flavor from the seasonings.)

DRAIN THE SHRIMP and arrange them on a large lettuce-covered platter, scattering
the lemon wedges around. Pass sauce separately, if you like, and be sure to have a big bowl
for shrimp shells and lots of napkins for your guests.

Makes 4 servings

LITTLE FISH WITH BIG FLAVOR:
SARDINES AND ANCHOVIES

Cannery Row in Monterey, now a tourist destination housing gift shops and restaurants and a world-class aquarium and cannery museum, was once the interim resting place for uncounted millions of sardines and anchovies. The fish were pulled from the offshore waters of Monterey Bay in such quantities that the fishing fleet and canneries prospered for about 50 years before they shrank to a fraction of their former size in the 1950s. Silvery sardine and anchovy schools are not only some of the aquarium's most mesmerizing exhibits. Increasingly, larger shoals of each variety are seen in the bay, and some are brought to market as specialty fish, largely for restaurants.

Anchovies and sardines are related, though from different families. They share a rather rich flesh, with a 20 to 22 percent fat content and delicate flavor and texture. They are also quite perishable, a major reason for canning or salting them and the reason they are not often seen in retail markets. Anchovies are kept live in salt water until sold. As more people taste fresh anchovies and sardines, perhaps the distribution of the catch will shift toward human consumption from the current most popular use as salmon bait.

Simple Mediterranean-style preparations bring out the particular fine flavor of these small fish. Preparation of a classic dish involves marinating sardines in olive oil with bay leaves and then wrapping them in grape or fig leaves and finishing by grilling the fish over vine or fig branch trimmings. A slightly more elaborate dish is Sicilian stuffed sardines, with bread crumbs, pine nuts, and raisins. A fresh anchovy classic is an appetizer, often served with olives. The anchovies are lightly cured in a saltwater bath and then marinated in olive oil, with the addition of lemon zest or herbs according to the chef's fancy. Pasta dishes, especially those from the islands of Sardinia and Sicily, show off both kinds of fish with a bit of fennel or oregano, garlic, and lemon or orange juice and rind.

MOROCCAN-INSPIRED FLATBREAD

with Eggplant, Peppers, Garlic, Preserved Lemons, and Olives

Wine Spectator Restaurant at Greystone, St. Helena

It's tempting to call this a Moroccan pizza, but
visiting executive chef Joyce Goldstein describes it as a flatbread topped
with a Moroccan salad. "Usually the eggplant is cooked down to a purée but that
would look pretty homely on a flatbread," she explains. "So the aesthetic choice is
yours. You can leave it in slices or chop it coarsely. In the summer, you could
add a dice of fresh tomatoes to the mixture before baking," she adds.

You may have some of the charmoula left, which will hold well for a few
days in the refrigerator. It would be delicious brushed on toasted bread rounds for a
cocktail snack or tossed with pasta for a zesty side dish to grilled meats.

Preserved lemons are quite easy to make, but you need to plan
a few weeks in advance of using them. You may be able to find preserved lemons in
fine-food shops, though often they are sold more as a decorative kitchen accent in a
pretty jar than as a food product. In a pinch, you could use fine strips
of zest from half a fresh small lemon, simmered in two cups of water
with one tablespoon of salt for about 15 minutes.

1 eggplant (about 1 pound)	*8 Moroccan olives, pitted and coarsely chopped*
1 small red bell pepper	*1 tablespoon chopped flat-leaf (Italian) parsley*
Peel of ½ preserved lemon (see page 78)	*1 tablespoon chopped cilantro*

CHARMOULA

½ cup olive oil	2 teaspoons ground cumin
¼ cup freshly squeezed lemon juice	2 teaspoons paprika
¼ cup chopped flat-leaf (Italian) parsley	½ teaspoon cayenne pepper, or to taste
¼ cup chopped cilantro	Salt and freshly ground black pepper
2 tablespoons minced garlic	

CRUST

1½ cups all-purpose flour	1 tablespoon olive oil
½ cup warm water (105° to 110°F)	½ teaspoon salt
2 teaspoons active dry yeast	

FOR THE CHARMOULA, combine the olive oil, lemon juice, parsley, cilantro, garlic, cumin, paprika, and cayenne with salt and pepper to taste. Stir to mix well and set aside.

FOR THE CRUST, put the flour in a large bowl and make a well in the center. Add the warm water in the center of the well and sprinkle the yeast over. Let sit until the yeast is bubbly, about 5 minutes. Stir the flour and water together, adding the olive oil and salt as you mix. When the dough forms a ball, turn it onto a lightly floured work surface and knead the dough until satiny and smooth, 5 to 10 minutes. (Alternatively, you could make the dough in a mixer, using the paddle attachment until the dough forms a ball, then changing to the dough hook for kneading.) Lightly oil the bowl, add the dough, and turn so it is lightly but evenly coated in oil. Cover the bowl with a dish cloth and set aside until doubled in bulk, about 1 hour.

PREHEAT A GRILL or preheat the oven to 375°F.

PEEL AND TRIM THE EGGPLANT and cut it into ½-inch-thick slices (¾-inch-thick if grilling). Brush the slices with a little of the charmoula and season lightly with salt. Grill or bake the slices until tender and cooked through, about 15 minutes per side in the oven, 7 to 10 minutes per side on the grill. You can leave the slices whole or halve or chop them, depending on your preference for the look of the finished presentation.

ROAST THE BELL PEPPER over a gas flame or under the broiler until the skin blackens, turning occasionally to roast evenly, 5 to 10 minutes total. Put the pepper in a plastic bag, securely seal it, and set aside to cool. When cool enough to handle, peel away and discard the skin. Remove the core and seeds and cut the pepper into thin strips. Cut the preserved lemon peel into very thin slivers and set aside 4 to 5; cut the remaining slivers into a fine mince.

REHEAT THE OVEN TO 375°F. Lightly oil a pizza pan or baking sheet, or sprinkle it lightly with fine cornmeal. (If you have a pizza stone, this is a good time to use it. The stone doesn't need oil or cornmeal.)

PUNCH DOWN THE DOUGH and press it out into a circle about 9 inches across. Transfer the dough to the prepared pizza pan, spread it with a thin layer of the charmoula, and sprinkle with the minced preserved lemon. Arrange the grilled eggplant and bell pepper strips on top and scatter with the reserved preserved lemon slivers and the olives. Bake until golden and the toppings are bubbly, 15 to 20 minutes. Sprinkle the top with parsley and cilantro just before cutting into wedges to serve.

Makes 6 servings

PRESERVED LEMONS

Preserved lemons are used in many Mediterranean and Middle Eastern dishes, including stews and tagines (braised meats).

8 lemons (about 2 pounds total) | *Freshly squeezed lemon juice, as needed*
About 10 tablespoons coarse salt |

With a small, sharp knife and holding the lemon upright on the chopping board, cut each lemon in quarters downward through the lemon to within an inch of the bottom. Put 1 tablespoon of salt in the bottom of each of 1 or 2 mason jars just large enough to hold the lemons snugly. Spoon 1 tablespoon of salt down into the cut sections of each lemon and put the lemons in the jar, pressing down firmly to release some of their juices. Add enough fresh lemon juice to thoroughly cover the lemons. Cover the jar tightly and set aside in a cool, dark place to preserve for 3 to 4 weeks before using.

GAMBERI E FUNGHI

(Shrimp and Oyster Mushrooms)

Café Maddalena, Dunsmuir

Chef/owner Maddalena Sera leaves the shells on the
shrimp in this recipe for added presentation and extra flavor. For easier eating,
you could shell the shrimp before cooking.

24 medium shrimp, shells on
(about ¾ pound)
3 tablespoons extra virgin olive oil
3 tablespoons chopped flat-leaf (Italian)
parsley, plus more for serving
1 tablespoon minced garlic
1 tablespoon coarsely chopped, toasted
almonds (skin on)

¼ teaspoon cinnamon
Salt and freshly ground black pepper
1 pound oyster mushrooms, wiped clean
and torn into strips
6 ounces baby greens

PREHEAT THE OVEN to 375°F.

PUT THE SHRIMP in an even layer in an ovenproof nonstick skillet and sprinkle with
the olive oil, half of the parsley, the garlic, almonds, and cinnamon, with salt and pepper to
taste. Put the skillet in the oven and bake until the shrimp begin to turn pink, about 5
minutes. Take the skillet from the oven, scatter the mushrooms and remaining parsley over,
and stir to mix. Continue baking until the mushrooms are tender and the shrimp are just
cooked through, 8 to 10 minutes longer.

ARRANGE THE GREENS on 4 individual plates and top with the roasted shrimp and
mushrooms. Sprinkle with a bit of chopped parsley and serve right away.

Makes 4 servings

TROUT CAKES
with Sesame Soy Vinaigrette

The Groveland Hotel, Groveland

These cakes are deep-fried at The Groveland Hotel restaurant,
but we've adapted the recipe for pan-frying. You can certainly deep-fry if you
wish, cooking them in 375°F oil until golden brown.

For the 1 pound of cooked trout, you'll need to start with 2 large
(1 pound each) or 3 medium (¾ pound each) trout. Lay them on a foil-lined
baking sheet and bake at 375°F for 20 to 25 minutes, or poach or steam the
fish for about 10 to 15 minutes. You could also use other cooked fish,
such as salmon or halibut.

1 pound cooked, boned, skinned trout meat, crumbled	*3 cloves garlic, minced*
	Salt and freshly ground black pepper
3 eggs	*2 cups dried bread crumbs, preferably*
1 cup finely diced jicama	*Japanese-style panko crumbs*
1 stalk celery, finely diced	*3–4 tablespoons vegetable oil*
2 tablespoons minced ginger	*4 cups mixed tender greens*
2 tablespoons minced shallot	

SESAME SOY VINAIGRETTE

½ cup soy sauce	*1½ teaspoons toasted sesame seeds*
¼ cup rice wine vinegar	*½ teaspoon sesame oil*
1 tablespoon packed brown sugar or honey	*½ cup vegetable oil*

FOR THE VINAIGRETTE, combine the soy sauce, vinegar, brown sugar, sesame seeds,
and sesame oil in a blender or food processor and blend for about 1 minute. With the
blades running, slowly add the oil in a thin stream so the vinaigrette emulsifies. Transfer
the dressing to a bowl and set aside.

IN A LARGE BOWL, combine the trout, eggs, jicama, celery, ginger, shallot, and garlic
with salt and pepper to taste. Stir to mix well, then stir in the bread crumbs. Form the
mixture into 8 cakes about 1 inch thick.

HEAT THE OIL in a large, heavy skillet over medium heat. Add the trout cakes and cook until nicely browned and heated through, 5 to 7 minutes on each side. (You may need to cook the cakes in batches.)

JUST BEFORE SERVING, toss the mixed greens with about ¼ cup of the sesame soy vinaigrette. Arrange the greens on 4 individual plates and set the trout cakes on top. Drizzle a bit more of the vinaigrette over the cakes and serve right away.

Makes 4 servings

FARINATA

with Sage, Olives, and Caramelized Onions

Rose Pistola, San Francisco

At Rose Pistola, this signature appetizer is baked in a very hot wood-fired oven on a steel plate. For this home version, the best choice is a cast-iron skillet or another heavy, ovenproof skillet. The restaurant offers variations on this chickpea cake theme, with other toppings that might include broccoli raab and Meyer lemon. Try experimenting with other toppings if you're so inspired. Many well-stocked grocery stores carry a variety of flours, including chickpea. You can also find it in Middle Eastern food stores and health food shops.

4 tablespoons olive oil, plus more for serving
1 medium onion, thinly sliced
¼ cup niçoise or other small olives

8–10 small, tender sage leaves
Freshly ground black pepper

FARINATA BATTER

½ cup chickpea flour
1 tablespoon olive oil

½ teaspoon salt
1 cup water

HEAT 2 TABLESPOONS of the olive oil in a medium skillet over medium heat. Add the sliced onion, stir to coat lightly in the oil, and lay a piece of foil loosely over the onion. Cook the onion, stirring occasionally, until very tender and caramelized to a light brown color, about 30 minutes.

WHILE THE ONION IS COOKING, prepare the farinata batter. Combine the chickpea flour, 1 tablespoon olive oil, and salt in a medium bowl, then whisk in the water to form a smooth batter. Let sit for 30 minutes to allow the flour to absorb the water, stirring occasionally.

PREHEAT THE OVEN to 500°F.

PUT THE REMAINING 2 tablespoons of the olive oil in a large, heavy skillet, preferably cast iron, and swirl so the oil evenly coats the bottom and lower sides of the pan. Strain the farinata batter into the skillet, discarding the solids (or add them to a batch of hummus or falafel). Evenly scatter the caramelized onions, olives, and sage leaves over the batter and bake until nicely browned on the bottom and crisp, about 20 minutes.

TO SERVE, carefully slide the farinata from the skillet onto a cutting board and cut it into wedges. Season with pepper to taste, drizzle with a bit of olive oil, and serve.

Makes 4 servings

CLEANING AND COOKING SQUID

To clean squid in the quickest way, as the professionals do, cut the tentacles from the body just above the eyes. Hold the tentacles just where they begin and squeeze out the beak, a small, hard ball with a tiny black center. Discard the beak and reserve the tentacles.

Place the squid on a cutting board. Use the blunt side of a chef's knife to press the body firmly from tail to head. Most of the innards, the head, and the thin purple-spotted skin will be removed. Turn the body to the other side and repeat. The transparent quill should be protruding from the body. Hold it with the point of the knife and pull the body away from it. If you wish, carefully use the blade of the knife to scrape any remaining skin, though it is edible and its color desirable for some dishes. Rinse the squid body and tentacles and cut into desired shapes.

Drain the squid well and pat dry before cooking. The rule of thumb is to cook squid quickly at high heat or slowly at low heat. If you are sautéing or deep-frying fresh squid, they will take only a minute or two to cook over high heat. If you stuff and braise them, cook them at a bare simmer for about 30 minutes.

CRISPY PANKO CALAMARI WITH
SPICY SAMBAL AÏOLI

Brix, Yountville

Everyone's favorite fried calamari takes a tasty Asian twist here,
with the tender rings served on top of a sesame- and ginger-scented slaw. Japanese
seven-spice seasoning—a blend of black and white sesame seeds, dried seaweed,
orange peel, sansho and chile peppers, and poppy seeds, also known as
shichimi togarashi—adds distinctive flavor to the calamari breading and can be
found in Asian markets or on well-stocked grocery shelves.

¼ cup vegetable oil, plus more for frying calamari	*½ cup finely julienned napa cabbage*
¼ cup sesame oil	*½ cup finely julienned romaine lettuce*
Juice of ½ orange	*¼ cup kaiware (radish) sprouts*
2 tablespoons rice wine vinegar	*1 cup panko bread crumbs*
2 tablespoons soy sauce	*½ cup all-purpose flour*
1 teaspoon minced ginger	*1 teaspoon salt*
Pinch sugar	*1 teaspoon Japanese 7-spice seasoning*
½ cup finely julienned cucumber	*6 ounces calamari tubes and tentacles, cleaned,*
½ cup finely julienned carrot	*tubes cut in 1-inch rings*
½ cup finely julienned jicama	*8 wonton wrappers, cut in ¼-inch strips*

SAMBAL AÏOLI

½ cup mayonnaise, preferably homemade	*1 teaspoon sambal oelek or other hot chile*
Juice of 1 lime	*sauce, or to taste*
	½ teaspoon minced garlic

FOR THE AÏOLI, in a small bowl, stir together the mayonnaise, lime juice, chile sauce,
and garlic until well mixed. Refrigerate until ready to serve.

IN A LARGE BOWL, combine ¼ cup vegetable oil, sesame oil, orange juice, rice wine
vinegar, soy sauce, ginger, and sugar. Whisk to emulsify the dressing. Add the cucumber,
carrot, jicama, cabbage, lettuce, and sprouts, and toss to mix well. Set aside to marinate
while preparing the calamari.

IN A DEEP FRYER or large heavy pot, heat about 3 inches of vegetable oil to 375°F over medium-high heat.

WHILE THE OIL IS HEATING, stir together the panko crumbs, flour, salt, and 7-spice seasoning in a large bowl. Add the calamari and toss well to evenly coat the pieces in the crumb mixture. Shake excess coating from the calamari and set aside in a single layer on a plate.

TO TEST IF THE OIL IS HOT enough, add one wonton strip; it should bubble vigorously right away and turn golden within a minute. Working in batches, fry the remaining wonton strips, stirring a bit to keep the pieces from sticking together, until golden and crisp, about 1 minute. Transfer to paper towels to drain and set aside.

GIVE THE OIL 30 SECONDS to 1 minute to reheat, then gently add a handful of calamari to the hot oil and fry until golden, 1 to 2 minutes. Scoop out the calamari with a slotted spoon and drain on paper towels. Continue cooking the remaining calamari in batches, allowing the oil to reheat between batches.

ADD THE FRIED WONTON STRIPS to the marinated vegetables and toss to mix. Arrange the vegetable slaw in the center of individual plates and scoop the fried calamari on top. Spoon a bit of the spicy sambal aïoli over and serve right away, passing extra aïoli separately.

Makes 2 serving

Soups & Salads

CALDO VERDE

Wine Spectator Restaurant at Greystone, St. Helena

Caldo verde, a classic Portuguese recipe translated as "green soup," couldn't be easier to make but is surprisingly full of flavor. In place of the Portuguese dark green cabbage traditionally used, kale and collard greens make fine substitutes. "This soup is usually accompanied by a crusty corn bread called *broa,*" notes Joyce Goldstein, a visiting executive chef of this Mediterranean-inspired restaurant.

¼ cup olive oil, plus more for serving (optional)
1 large onion, chopped
1 pound russet potatoes (about 2 medium), peeled and cut in ¼-inch slices
2 cloves garlic, minced
6 cups water
2 teaspoons salt, plus more to taste
¼ pound chorizo or linguiça sausages
¾ pound kale or collard greens (about 1 big bunch), washed, tough stems removed, and dried
Freshly ground black pepper

HEAT ¼ CUP OLIVE OIL in a large saucepan over medium heat. Add the onion and sauté until tender, 8 to 10 minutes. Add the potatoes and garlic, increase the heat to medium-high, and sauté for 2 to 3 minutes, stirring often. Add the water and 2 teaspoons salt, cover the pan, and simmer until the potatoes are tender, about 20 minutes.

WHILE THE POTATOES are simmering, cook the sausages in a pot of boiling water until firm and cooked through, about 5 minutes. Drain and let cool slightly. When cool enough to handle, slice the sausages. Set aside. Stack the kale leaves in batches, roll them up like a cigar, and cut across the leaves into very thin strips.

WHEN THE POTATOES ARE TENDER, coarsely mash them against the side of the pot with a wooden spoon or a potato masher. Add the sliced sausages and cook 5 minutes longer. Add the greens, stir well, and simmer uncovered for 3 to 5 minutes. Do not over-cook the greens; they should remain bright green and slightly crunchy. Taste the soup for seasoning, adding pepper and more salt to taste. Ladle the soup into 4 individual bowls, drizzle each with a bit of extra olive oil if you like, and serve at once.

Makes 4 servings

PORTOBELLO MUSHROOM SOUP
with Goat Cheese and White Truffle Oil

Highlands Inn, Carmel

To make this soup even richer and more flavorful, chef Cal Stamenov often cooks the vegetables in fat from duck foie gras. The results are plenty delicious if you just cook them in butter, though, as we suggest here.

White truffle oil is available in gourmet shops and well-stocked grocery stores. The small bottles seem expensive, but a few drops go a long way. Once you have it around, you'll love to add a bit to mashed potatoes or toss the flavorful oil into fresh pasta for a stunning first course.

¼ cup plus 1 tablespoon unsalted butter	Salt and freshly ground black pepper
¼ cup thinly sliced shallots	1 bottle (750 ml) cabernet sauvignon
¼ cup thinly sliced leeks	4 cups chicken stock, preferably homemade
1 tablespoon thinly sliced garlic	½ cup whipping cream
6 large portobello mushrooms,	1–2 teaspoons white truffle oil
trimmed and diced	½ cup crumbled fresh goat cheese

IN A LARGE SAUCEPAN, heat 1 tablespoon butter over medium heat. Add the shallots, leeks, and garlic and cook until tender and aromatic, 3 to 5 minutes, stirring often. Add the diced mushrooms and 1 teaspoon salt and continue cooking until the mushrooms have given off their juices and the liquids have cooked off, 7 to 10 minutes. Add the wine, bring to a boil, and boil until reduced by about three-quarters, about 20 minutes. Add the chicken stock, reduce the heat, and gently simmer for about 45 minutes. Stir in the cream and bring just to a boil, then take the pan from the heat. Cut the remaining ¼ cup butter into chunks and add them to the pan, stirring until the butter has gently melted.

PURÉE THE SOUP with an immersion blender, or purée it in batches in a food processor or blender and return the soup to the pan. If the soup is very thick, add a bit more chicken stock or water. Taste the soup for seasoning, adding more salt or pepper if needed. Ladle the hot soup into 8 large, shallow soup bowls. Drizzle ⅛ to ¼ teaspoon of the truffle oil over each bowl and scatter with the crumbled goat cheese. Serve right away.

Makes 8 servings

CHILLED YELLOW TOMATO SOUP
with Lobster

City Hotel, Columbia

Lobster makes a luxurious addition to this simple but flavorful chilled soup. The pink-and-white lobster pieces make an attractive contrast to the bright yellow tomatoes, but red tomatoes can be used if yellow aren't available. Because this is such a simple recipe, it's crucial that the tomatoes be ripe and flavorful. Other cooked seafoods, such as crabmeat or cooked shrimp, could be used in place of the lobster. At City Hotel, this soup is often served with a small mound of couscous salad mixed with lemon and mint in the center.

If you shell your own lobster for the meat needed here, you can use the shells to make a quick lobster stock for the soup. Rinse the shells well and clean the carapace, discarding the feathery gills along either side. Simmer the shells in water to cover for about 20 minutes, then drain. Add a few herb sprigs and chopped carrot or onion if you like, but it's not necessary.

5 large, vine-ripe yellow tomatoes	*1½ cups lobster stock or vegetable stock,*
¼ cup olive oil	*preferably homemade*
1 onion, finely diced	*½ teaspoon cumin powder*
2 tomatillos, husks removed,	*Salt and freshly ground black pepper*
cleaned, and sliced	*1 cup chopped, cooked lobster meat*
1 small serrano chile, cored,	
seeded, and minced	

BRING A MEDIUM PAN OF WATER to a boil and prepare a large bowl of ice water. With the tip of a sharp knife, score a small "X" on the bottom of each tomato. Add the tomatoes to the boiling water, 2 or 3 at a time, and blanch until the skin begins to split, 20 to 30 seconds. Scoop the tomatoes out with a slotted spoon and put them in the ice water for quick cooling. When cool, drain the tomatoes, then peel away and discard the skin. Quarter the tomatoes lengthwise, scoop out and discard the seeds, and coarsely chop the tomatoes.

HEAT THE OLIVE OIL in a large saucepan over medium heat, add the onion, and cook until the onion gives off its liquids and becomes tender, about 5 minutes. Add the tomatillos and serrano chile and cook until they are tender, stirring occasionally, about 3 minutes. Add the tomatoes and stock, bring to a boil, lower the heat, and simmer until the tomatoes are tender, about 10 minutes. Stir in the cumin, with salt and pepper to taste. Purée the soup with an immersion blender, or purée it in batches in a food processor or blender, and transfer to a large bowl. Taste the soup for seasoning, then refrigerate until thoroughly chilled before serving.

LADLE THE CHILLED SOUP into 4 large, shallow soup bowls, garnish each with the lobster meat, and serve.

Makes 4 servings

CARROT AND CORIANDER SOUP

with Cilantro–Pine Nut Pesto

Applewood Inn Restaurant, Pocket Canyon

This soup gets points for beauty as well as for flavor, with a striking drizzle
of vivid green pesto and white sour cream added to the rust-colored soup just before
serving. The pesto echoes the coriander seeds used in the soup, based on cilantro
(also known as coriander leaves) in place of the traditional basil. You'll have more
pesto than is needed to garnish the soup, but you can save the rest to toss with pasta
or vegetables, or toss it with cooked shrimp for a salad.

1 tablespoon olive oil	*4 cups chicken stock, preferably homemade,*
4 cups diced carrots (about 2 pounds)	*or water*
1½ cups diced onion	*⅓ cup whipping cream*
1 tablespoon minced garlic	*2 tablespoons sour cream*
2 teaspoons coriander seeds, toasted and	*1 tablespoon freshly squeezed lemon*
ground, or 2 teaspoons ground coriander	*or lime juice*

CILANTRO-PINE NUT PESTO

½ cup lightly packed cilantro leaves	*1 teaspoon minced garlic*
½ cup extra virgin olive oil	*Salt and freshly ground black pepper*
¼ cup pine nuts (or other nuts such as	
almonds or hazelnuts)	

HEAT THE OLIVE OIL in a large saucepan over medium heat. Add the carrots, onion,
and garlic and cook, stirring, until the onions are translucent, 8 to 10 minutes. Add the
ground coriander and stir to evenly coat the vegetables. Add the stock, bring the liquid
just to a boil, reduce the heat, and simmer until the carrots are tender, 10 to 15 minutes.

WHILE THE SOUP IS SIMMERING, prepare the pesto. Combine the cilantro
leaves, olive oil, pine nuts, and garlic in a blender or food processor and purée until
thoroughly blended. Transfer the pesto to a small bowl, season to taste with salt and
pepper, and set aside.

TAKE THE CARROTS from the heat and let cool for a few minutes, then purée the mixture with an immersion blender. (Alternatively, purée the soup in batches in a food processor or blender and return the soup to the pan.) Stir in the whipping cream and return the soup just to a boil. Take from the heat and season to taste with salt and pepper.

LADLE THE CARROT SOUP into 4 individual bowls. In a small bowl, stir together the sour cream and lemon juice. Randomly drizzle about 2 tablespoons of the pesto and the sour cream mixture over the bowls of soup and serve right away.

Makes 4 servings

BUZ'S FAMOUS CRAB CIOPPINO

Buz's Seafood Market and Restaurant, Redding

Don't let this inland locale fool you. Buz's takes seafood very seriously.
After all, the trip over the mountains from the coast isn't all that far, and plenty of
coastal seafood makes the journey almost every day. Legend has it that Italian
immigrants in San Francisco invented this robust shellfish stew. It is traditional to sop
up the thick, red sauce with lots of extra-sour sourdough bread, another San
Francisco food tradition. Have a big bowl on the table for discarded shells, not to
mention plenty of napkins or a big roll of paper towels.

⅓ cup olive oil	2–3 teaspoons salt
1 large onion, sliced	1 bay leaf
1 bunch green onions, trimmed and sliced	¼ teaspoon dried rosemary, crushed
1 green bell pepper, cored, seeded, and coarsely chopped	¼ teaspoon dried thyme, crushed
3 large cloves garlic, chopped	¼ teaspoon freshly ground black pepper
2 cups water	3 whole cleaned Dungeness crabs, portioned, shells lightly cracked
2 cups canned tomato purée	12 live clams, scrubbed
1 cup canned tomato sauce	1 pound large shrimp, peeled and deveined
1 cup dry white or red wine	1 loaf sourdough bread
⅓ cup lightly packed flat-leaf (Italian) parsley leaves	

HEAT THE OLIVE OIL over medium-high heat in a large, deep sauté pan or soup pot
that has a tight-fitting lid. Add the onions, bell pepper, and garlic and sauté, stirring often,
until tender, about 5 minutes. Add the water, tomato purée, tomato sauce, wine, parsley,
salt, bay leaf, rosemary, thyme, and pepper. Bring the mixture just to a boil, lower the heat
to medium-low, cover the pan, and simmer for 1 hour, stirring occasionally. (The cioppino
can be prepared to this point up to a day in advance and refrigerated; reheat before finishing the dish.)

RETURN THE SAUCE to a simmer, then add the cleaned crab portions, scatter the
clams over the crab, and distribute the shrimp evenly over the top, gently pressing the
seafood into the sauce. Cover the pot and cook the shellfish over medium heat until the
clams have opened and the shrimp are cooked, 20 to 30 minutes.

SCOOP THE SHELLFISH from the pot and distribute evenly among 6 large, wide soup bowls. Ladle the tomato sauce over and serve right away, passing the sourdough bread alongside.

Makes 6 servings

AT HOME WITH DUNGENESS CRAB

The Dungeness has served as the quintessential gustatory sea creature of Fisherman's Wharf in San Francisco for almost a century, though it is at home in the cold Pacific coastal waters from Alaska to Big Sur and takes its name from New Dungeness Bay in Washington State. San Francisco can, however, lay claim to spreading the crab's fame. The Wharf can still boast sweet, juicy crab just hours from the ocean and the steamer. And cioppino, that delicious seafood invention of the Wharf's original Italian fishermen, could hardly exist without the Dungeness.

The next best thing to eating crab at the Wharf is cooking and eating your own crab. Buy a lively live crab—ask the fishmonger to prod the crab to be sure it moves well. Some like smaller crabs, saying the meat is finer and fills the shell completely, making a better bargain. Others are happy with the usual size, about 1½ pounds. A crab this size yields a generous cup of dressed meat or serves two as an appetizer.

Keep the crab cold until you plan to cook it, which should be the same day you buy it. Bring to boil a gallon of water with a generous tablespoon of salt in a pot large enough to hold the crab. Plunge the crab into the pot and cook it for 12 minutes from the time the water returns to the boil. (For each additional crab, add a quart of water and a generous teaspoon of salt.) Remove the crab from the pot and let cool.

As soon as the crab is at room temperature, dress it to remove the meat, or refrigerate it on a plate. The crab may be cooked several hours ahead. For cracked-crab appetizer, clean and crack the crab within an hour or two of serving

ROASTED PUMPKIN PECAN SOUP

The Village Pub, Woodside

You could save the seeds from the pumpkin, clean them well, and then toast them in the oven to serve as a garnish for this soup or simply as a snack. You could also garnish the soup with chopped, toasted pecans.

1 cooking pumpkin (about 7 or 8 pounds), such as sugar pumpkin
1 cup pecan pieces, lightly toasted
2 tablespoons vegetable oil
1 onion, diced
¼ cup walnut or pecan oil

2 tablespoons tamari or soy sauce
1 tablespoon cider vinegar
Pinch freshly grated or ground nutmeg
Pinch cayenne pepper
Salt and freshly ground white pepper

PREHEAT THE OVEN to 350°F.

CORE AND QUARTER the pumpkin, removing the seeds. Lay the pumpkin pieces in a roasting pan and bake until tender, about 1 hour.

WHILE THE PUMPKIN IS ROASTING, put the pecans in a food processor and process until they reach the consistency of cream, about 2 minutes. Be patient: the pecans will resemble finely chopped nuts, then something that looks like peanut butter, and finally a liquidy purée. Set aside.

WHEN THE PUMPKIN IS TENDER, take it from the oven and cool until easy to handle. Scrape the flesh from the skin; there should be about 5 to 6 cups of flesh.

HEAT THE VEGETABLE OIL in a soup pot over medium heat. Add the onion and cook, stirring, until tender, 3 to 5 minutes. Add the pumpkin with enough cold water to cover by 1 to 2 inches (about 8 to 10 cups of water). Bring the water to a boil, then lower the heat and simmer for 5 minutes. Stir in the puréed pecans, return to a boil, and simmer 5 minutes longer, stirring often. Stir in the walnut oil, tamari, vinegar, nutmeg, and cayenne, with salt and pepper to taste.

PURÉE THE SOUP with an immersion blender or in batches in a food processor or blender. If the soup is very thick, stir in a bit more water. Taste the soup for seasoning and reheat if necessary. Ladle the soup into 8 individual bowls and serve, garnished with toasted pumpkin seeds or pecans if you like.

Makes 8 servings

VELOUTÉ BONGO BONGO

Fandango, Pacific Grove

This recipe originated with famed San Francisco–based restaurateur, Trader Vic, whose eponymous restaurants have brought foods of the Pacific Islands to diners up and down the West Coast since the 1930s. Basil (Bill) Coleman—an executive with Trader Vic's for 25 years before he became a general manager at The Lodge at Pebble Beach—passed the recipe on to Fandango owner Pierre Bain. The recipe was a great favorite at Club XIX, the restaurant Bain had owned for 20 years before opening Fandango in 1986.

At Fandango, the cream is drizzled over the top of each serving of soup and the surface quickly glazed under a very hot broiler just before serving. It's hard to re-create this in a home oven, so we instead simply drizzle the cream over the hot soup.

Clam juice can be quite salty. If you prefer to control the saltiness of the soup, use fish broth or part broth, part clam juice.

1 tablespoon olive oil	Pinch dried basil
1 small onion, chopped	½ bay leaf
2 cloves garlic, chopped	6 cups clam juice or fish broth,
1 jar (about 10 ounces) medium	preferably homemade
Pacific oysters	3 bunches spinach, rinsed, dried,
1 cup dry white wine	and coarsely chopped
2 tablespoons brandy	½ cup oyster sauce
Pinch dried tarragon	Salt and freshly ground black pepper
Pinch dried thyme	½ cup whipping cream

HEAT THE OLIVE OIL in a medium saucepan over medium heat. Add the onion and garlic and sauté until tender, 3 to 5 minutes. Add the oysters, wine, brandy, tarragon, thyme, basil, and bay leaf. Cook over medium heat until the oysters are plump, about 10 minutes.

IN A SOUP POT, bring the clam juice and/or fish broth just to a boil. Add the spinach, stirring until it is evenly cooked, about 1 minute. Discard the bay leaf from the oyster mixture, then add the oyster mixture and oyster sauce to the soup. Return just to a boil and take the pot from the heat. Working in batches, purée the soup in a food processor or blender until smooth. Check the soup for seasoning, adding salt and pepper to taste. (If you used only clam juice, salt will probably not be needed.)

LADLE THE SOUP into 6 individual bowls and drizzle the cream over each serving. Serve the soup right away.

Makes 6 servings

SOUTHWESTERN-STYLE CORN SOUP

Huckleberry Springs Country Inn, Monte Rio

The subtle heat from fresh chiles is a delicious complement to the sweet corn in this soup. If you like your chiles a bit less subtle, feel free to use more, or maybe sprinkle a little extra over each bowl just before serving. For a richer soup, use half-and-half or whipping cream in place of the evaporated milk.

7 large ears sweet corn	*4 cloves garlic, coarsely chopped*
1 tablespoon olive or corn oil	*2 cups evaporated milk*
4 leeks, trimmed, halved, and rinsed, white	*3–4 tablespoons freshly squeezed lime juice*
and light green parts chopped	*Salt and freshly ground white pepper*
4 cups chicken stock, preferably homemade	*1 medium onion, diced*
2 poblano chiles, cored, seeded, and chopped	*½ cup chopped prosciutto (about 2 ounces)*
2 jalapeño chiles, cored, seeded, and chopped	*Minced cilantro (optional)*

CUT THE KERNELS from each ear of corn and set aside 1 cup to use for garnish. Heat the olive oil in a large saucepan or a soup pot over medium heat. Add the corn and leeks and sauté until the leeks are tender and the juices have cooked down, about 10 minutes. Stir in the chicken stock, chiles, and garlic. Bring to a boil, then reduce the heat to medium-low, cover, and simmer for 30 minutes.

STIR IN THE EVAPORATED MILK and continue cooking until the soup is slightly thickened, 5 to 10 minutes longer. Purée the soup with an immersion blender, or purée it in batches in a food processor or blender and return the soup to the pot. Season to taste with lime juice, salt, and pepper. Keep the soup warm over medium heat.

COMBINE THE ONION and prosciutto in a skillet and sauté over medium heat until the onion is tender, about 10 minutes.

TO SERVE, scatter the reserved corn kernels among 8 individual soup bowls and ladle the soup over. Spoon the onion-and-prosciutto mixture into the center and sprinkle the cilantro over, if using. Serve right away.

Makes 8 servings

MUSSEL SOUP
with Leeks and Saffron

Bistro Vida, Menlo Park

This is a wonderfully rich, creamy soup with plenty of flavor, ideal for starting off a dinner party.

2½ pounds mussels, scrubbed and debearded
¾ cup dry white wine
2 tablespoons unsalted butter
2 large or 3 small leeks, white part only, well cleaned and thinly sliced

1 large pinch saffron threads
1½ cups whipping cream or half-and-half
Salt and freshly ground black pepper
1 tablespoon minced chives

PUT THE MUSSELS in a large pot with the wine, cover, and cook over high heat, shaking the pan occasionally, until the mussels are opened, 5 to 7 minutes. Scoop out the mussels and let cool in a large bowl, reserving the cooking liquids. Discard any mussels that do not open. When cool enough to handle, take the mussel meats from the shells and discard the shells. Pour any accumulated cooking liquids from the bowl into the pot.

HEAT THE BUTTER in a medium saucepan over medium heat. Add the leeks and cook, stirring, until they turn translucent, 3 to 5 minutes. Stir in the saffron and cook for 1 minute longer. Add the reserved mussel cooking liquids (leaving any grit behind in the bottom of the pan), cream, and shelled mussels, with salt and pepper to taste. Simmer gently just to heat through, about 10 minutes. Ladle the soup into 4 to 6 individual bowls, sprinkle with the chives, and serve.

Makes 4 to 6 servings

CREAMY BUTTERNUT SQUASH AND GINGER SOUP

Albion River Inn, Albion

This creamy, golden soup is just the thing to warm you up on a cold evening. It is filling enough to be called dinner, with good bread alongside. Grilled cheese sandwiches would also be a tasty accompaniment.

5 tablespoons olive oil	*1 cup dry sherry*
1 fennel bulb, trimmed, cored, and diced	*1 butternut squash, peeled, seeded, and*
5 cloves garlic, peeled whole	*coarsely chopped*
½ cup unsalted butter	*8 cups chicken stock, preferably homemade,*
¾ cup all-purpose flour	*or water*
1 medium onion, diced	*½ cup half-and-half*
1 large carrot, coarsely chopped	*2 tablespoons Pernod or other anise liqueur*
2 stalks celery, coarsely chopped	*(optional)*
¼ cup minced ginger	*Salt and freshly ground black pepper*

PREHEAT THE OVEN to 400°F.

HEAT 1 TABLESPOON OF THE OLIVE OIL in an ovenproof skillet over medium heat. Add the fennel and garlic, stirring to evenly coat in oil. Transfer the skillet to the oven and roast until tender and lightly browned, about 20 minutes. Set aside.

MAKE A ROUX by melting the butter in a small, heavy saucepan, then stirring in the flour until well blended. Cook the roux over medium–low heat until it is golden and has a light, toasty aroma, stirring often, about 10 minutes. Set aside.

IN A LARGE, HEAVY SOUP POT, heat the remaining olive oil over medium-high heat until almost smoking. Add the onion, carrot, celery, and ginger. Reduce the heat to medium-low, cover the pot, and cook the vegetables until very tender, about 20 minutes, stirring occasionally. Add the sherry, increase the heat to medium-high, and simmer until most of the liquid has evaporated, about 5 minutes. Add the squash with the roasted fennel and garlic, followed by the stock. Stir to mix, bring just to a boil, then lower the heat to medium, and simmer uncovered until the squash is very tender, about 45 minutes. Stir in the roux and half-and-half. Continue cooking, stirring often, until the soup is thickened, about 10 minutes. Purée the soup with an immersion blender until very smooth. (Alternatively, purée the soup in batches in a food processor or blender and return the soup to the pot.) Stir in the Pernod, with salt and pepper to taste, and gently reheat the soup before serving.

Makes 6 to 8 servings

ITALIAN SAUSAGE SOUP

Dorrington Hotel & Restaurant, Dorrington

This rustic soup, something like minestrone with more substance,
could easily pass for a meal in itself. The amount of pasta needed depends on the
type you use. Macaroni expands quite a lot more than orzo does, for instance,
so you'd want to use the smaller amount of macaroni.

1 pound Italian sausage, cut in ½-inch pieces
4 cups beef stock, preferably homemade
4 cups water
1½ cups dry red wine
1 onion, chopped
1 red or green bell pepper, cored,
seeded, and sliced
¼ cup chopped parsley

2 cloves garlic, chopped
Salt and freshly ground black pepper
1–2 cups dry pasta (such as small macaroni,
orzo, or small shells)
1 pound zucchini (about 3 medium),
trimmed and sliced
Freshly grated Parmesan cheese, for garnish

COOK THE SAUSAGE pieces in a large skillet over medium heat until they've given off
their fat (if they have much) and are just cooked through, stirring often, about 10 minutes.
Scoop the sausage onto paper towels to drain.

IN A LARGE SOUP POT, combine the beef stock, water, wine, onion, bell pepper,
parsley, and garlic, with salt and pepper to taste. Add the sausage pieces, bring just to a boil,
lower the heat, and simmer, covered, for 30 minutes. Add the pasta and continue simmering until al dente, stirring occasionally, 10 to 15 minutes longer. Stir in the zucchini
during the last few minutes of cooking. Taste the soup for seasoning, adjusting if necessary.

LADLE THE SOUP into 8 individual bowls, sprinkle each with Parmesan cheese, and
serve right away.

Makes 8 servings

CAESAR SALAD

Cottonwood Restaurant, Truckee

The garlic in this dressing isn't subtle, so modify accordingly if you wish.
But for garlicphiles, this is about the best Caesar salad you could hope for. At the
restaurant, this salad is intended as finger food: diners pick up the whole leaves
and munch away. Permission granted for you to do the same at home!

If you think about it, stir together the olive oil and herbs used for the crostini an hour
or two ahead of time, so the oil has a chance to absorb more of the herbal flavors.

2–3 tablespoons finely minced garlic	*1 cup grated Pecorino Romano cheese*
3 anchovy fillets	*Freshly ground black pepper*
1 egg yolk	*1 large head romaine lettuce, leaves separated,*
Juice of ½ lemon	*rinsed, and dried*
⅓ cup olive oil	

CROSTINI

¼ cup olive oil	*12 bias-cut slices of baguette, ½ inch thick*
1 tablespoon minced herbs	*(about ½ loaf)*
(parsley, chives, oregano)	*2 tablespoons grated Pecorino Romano cheese*

PREHEAT THE OVEN to 400°F.

FOR THE CROSTINI, stir together the olive oil and herbs. Lightly brush the herbed oil
on one side of the bread slices and arrange them, oiled side up, on a baking sheet. Sprinkle
the tops lightly with the cheese and bake until lightly browned, 6 to 8 minutes. Set aside.

IN A LARGE BOWL, mash together the garlic and anchovies with a fork to form a
rough paste. Stir in the egg yolk, followed by the lemon juice; then blend in the oil. Add
half of the cheese, with pepper to taste. Add the whole romaine leaves and toss to evenly
coat in dressing. Arrange the leaves on individual plates, sprinkle the remaining cheese
over, and add a few crostini to each plate. Serve right away.

Makes 4 to 6 servings

ARTICHOKE, ARUGULA, AND PROSCIUTTO SALAD

with Parmesan Vinaigrette

Wente Vineyards Restaurant, Livermore

"Artichokes are notoriously difficult to pair with wine because the cynarin in the artichoke makes everything taste sweeter," points out chef Kimball Jones. He suggests a white wine with lively acidity such as pinot grigio or trebbiano.

The salty tang of Parmesan cheese is a delicious addition to the vinaigrette. You might want to whip it up sometimes just to dress a humble green salad.

4 large artichokes	*½ pound arugula, rinsed and dried, tough*
12 very thin slices prosciutto	*stem ends trimmed*
	½ small head radicchio, finely shredded

PARMESAN VINAIGRETTE

½ cup finely grated Parmesan cheese	*1 tablespoon freshly squeezed lemon juice*
2 tablespoons minced shallot	*½ cup olive oil*
2 tablespoons champagne vinegar	*Salt and freshly ground black pepper*

BRING A LARGE PAN OF SALTED WATER to a boil. While the water heats, trim the artichoke stems just to the base of the artichoke. Pull away a few outer layers of the lower leaves, until the artichoke bottom is more visible. Cut away the remaining leaves just above the artichoke bottom. For a neater presentation, trim away any remaining dark green from the leaf bases, using a small, sharp knife. Cook the artichoke bottoms in the boiling water until tender, 15 to 20 minutes. Drain and let cool, then scoop out and discard the choke from the artichokes. Cut the bottoms into quarters and set aside.

FOR THE VINAIGRETTE, combine the cheese, shallot, vinegar, and lemon juice in a medium bowl and whisk to evenly blend, then whisk in the olive oil. Taste the dressing for seasoning, adding salt and pepper to taste. (Keep in mind that the cheese is salty, so extra salt may not be needed.)

LAY THE PROSCIUTTO SLICES on 4 individual plates. In a medium bowl, combine the artichoke bottoms and arugula. Drizzle the dressing over and toss gently to mix. Arrange the arugula and artichokes over the prosciutto. Scatter the radicchio over and serve.

Makes 4 servings

ARTICHOKE CENTRAL

Most of the U.S. crop of artichokes is grown in fields near Castroville, Monterey County. In a sign of the times, Castroville is now the Artichoke Center of the World, where it used to be the Artichoke Capital of the World. It has long held the record for annual artichoke tonnage, about 75 percent of the nation's crop; the remaining 25 percent is also grown in California. Castroville holds a spring festival with all the requisite food, fun, music, and artichoke doodads. Locals like to boast that Marilyn Monroe, when she was Norma Jean Baker, was the first Artichoke Queen.

Artichoke plants (*Cynara scolymus*) produce year-round for five to ten years in this mild, marine climate with little variation in seasonal temperatures. The main crop is in March, April, and May, however, with a strong secondary crop in October. Artichokes are most plentiful and least expensive during these months.

The edible globes of the artichoke are immature flower buds and need rather pampered care to be brought to market. They are a labor-intensive and expensive crop, harvested, sorted, and packed by hand. When handled properly, artichokes keep well. To store for up to a week, spritz them with a little water and keep in an airtight bag in the vegetable section of the refrigerator.

SALAD OF CHINESE FIVE-SPICE MARINATED DUCK

with Roasted Shiitake Mushrooms, Heirloom Tomatoes, Fennel, Baby Mizuna, and Ginger-Blackberry Vinaigrette

Bridges, Danville

This is, without a doubt, a salad that makes a meal. Chef Kevin Gin uses muscovy duck breasts, preferred by many chefs because they are large, meaty, and very lean. For lighter appetites, you could use just two breasts and share each between two servings.

Mizuna, a Japanese mustard green, has distinctive jagged green leaves and is a great addition to any salad. You could use a mix of tender salad greens (which often includes mizuna) instead, if you can't find mizuna on its own.

4 muscovy duck breasts (about 8 ounces each)
16 small shiitake mushrooms, stems trimmed, caps halved (about 8 ounces)
2 tablespoons dry sherry
2 tablespoons olive oil
2 teaspoons minced garlic

1 fennel bulb, trimmed, cored, and cut lengthwise in thin strips
6 cups baby mizuna or other tender greens
1½ pounds heirloom or other vine-ripened tomatoes, cored and cut in wedges

5-SPICE MARINADE

1 cup soy sauce
½ cup dry sherry
¼ cup sesame oil
2 tablespoons minced or grated ginger

2 teaspoons minced garlic
½ teaspoon Chinese 5-spice powder
½ teaspoon sugar

GINGER-BLACKBERRY VINAIGRETTE

1 cup blackberries, fresh or thawed frozen	1 tablespoon minced shallot
½ cup olive oil	2 teaspoons minced or grated ginger
2 tablespoons champagne vinegar	1 teaspoon sugar
1 tablespoon red wine vinegar	Salt and freshly ground black pepper

TRIM EXCESS FAT from the edges of the duck breasts.

FOR THE MARINADE, combine the ingredients in a shallow dish and stir to mix. Add the duck breasts, turn to evenly coat (ending with the breasts skin side up), and set aside to marinate for 30 minutes.

WHILE THE DUCK IS MARINATING, make the vinaigrette. Combine the ingredients in a food processor or blender and pulse just to evenly mix. (Alternatively, whisk the ingredients together in a large bowl.) Season to taste with salt and pepper and set aside.

PREHEAT THE OVEN to 400°F.

IN A SMALL BAKING DISH, combine the mushrooms with the sherry, 1 tablespoon of the olive oil, and 1 teaspoon of the garlic, with salt and pepper to taste. Toss to evenly mix, then roast the mushrooms until tender and aromatic, 8 to 10 minutes, stirring the mushrooms once halfway through. Transfer the mushrooms to a plate and, in the same baking dish, toss the fennel with the remaining olive oil, garlic, and salt and pepper to taste. Roast until tender, 10 to 12 minutes, stirring once halfway through. Set aside.

REDUCE the oven temperature to 350°F.

TAKE THE DUCK BREASTS from the marinade and arrange them skin side up on a baking sheet. Roast the duck about 10 minutes for medium-rare, 12 minutes for medium. Take the duck breasts from the oven, cover with foil, and let sit for 10 minutes before cutting the breasts in ½-inch slices on the bias, keeping the slices together in a fan pattern.

IN A LARGE BOWL, combine the mizuna, tomatoes, roasted mushrooms, and roasted fennel. Drizzle the vinaigrette over and toss to mix. Arrange the salad on 4 individual plates, top with the duck breast slices, and serve.

Makes 4 servings

LIGURIAN SEAFOOD SALAD

Rose Pistola, San Francisco

This is a seafood salad that's *all* seafood, freshly cooked and simply drizzled with lemon juice, good olive oil, and a touch of garlic. Just delicious. The salad will have more distinctive flavor if it is not served chilled. If you make this salad in advance and refrigerate it, allow about 30 minutes for it to come to room temperature before serving.

At Rose Pistola, the octopus is cooked fresh in a court bouillon—a simple combination of water with aromatic vegetables and herbs—with the same flavorful liquid used to cook the other seafoods. For a shortcut, you could purchase cooked octopus and simmer the remaining court bouillon ingredients for 15 minutes to use for cooking the other seafoods. If you cook fresh octopus, you could freeze the leftover for later use.

1 cup rock shrimp (about 8 ounces)
1 cup cleaned calamari rings (about 8 ounces)
16 live mussels, scrubbed and debearded
16 live clams, scrubbed
½ cup extra virgin olive oil

Juice of 1 lemon
2 teaspoons minced flat-leaf (Italian) parsley
½ teaspoon minced garlic, preferably spring garlic
Salt and freshly ground black pepper

OCTOPUS COURT BOUILLON

1 tablespoon olive or vegetable oil
1 onion, chopped
1 carrot, chopped
1 stalk celery, chopped
1 clove garlic, chopped
1 cup chopped tomato

½ cup dry white wine
1 sprig rosemary
1 sprig thyme
1 sprig marjoram
1 whole raw octopus (3 to 4 pounds)

FOR THE OCTOPUS COURT BOUILLON, heat the oil in a large, heavy soup pot over medium heat. Add the onion, carrot, celery, and garlic, and cook until the vegetables are tender and aromatic and their liquid is released, 4 to 6 minutes. Add the tomato, wine, and herbs and cook to reduce slightly and concentrate the flavors, about 5 minutes longer.

ADD THE OCTOPUS with enough cold water to cover. Bring the water just barely to a boil and then immediately reduce the heat to a low simmer. Cook until the octopus is cooked through and tender, about 1 hour. Do not let the water boil, or the octopus will become tough. Remove the octopus and let cool. Strain the court bouillon and set aside. When the octopus is cool enough to handle, cut off one of the arms and dice the meat to give about 1 cup. (Freeze the remaining octopus for another use.)

PUT ABOUT 4 CUPS of the strained court bouillon in a medium saucepan and bring just to a boil. Add the rock shrimp, lower the heat to a simmer, and cook just until the shrimp are cooked through, 2 to 3 minutes. Scoop out the shrimp with a slotted spoon and put them in a large bowl. Return the court bouillon to a boil, add the calamari, reduce the heat to a simmer, and cook until just evenly whitened and cooked through but still tender, about 1 minute. Scoop out the calamari and add it to the bowl with the shrimp. Return the liquids to a boil, add the mussels, and cook over high heat until the mussels have opened, 3 to 4 minutes. Scoop out the mussels and add them to the bowl with the other seafoods. Return the court bouillon to a boil, add the clams, and cook over high heat until the clams have opened, 4 to 5 minutes. Discard any clams or mussels that do not open. Set the cooked seafoods aside to cool slightly. Add the diced octopus to the bowl.

DRIZZLE THE OLIVE OIL and lemon juice over the seafoods, then add the parsley and garlic, with salt and pepper to taste. Toss to evenly mix and serve slightly warm or at room temperature.

Makes 4 servings

PEAR AND ENDIVE SALAD
with Goat Cheese and Walnut Verjus
Vinaigrette

Domaine Chandon, Yountville

This salad has a lot to like about it, from the tangy goat cheese through
the fresh, crisp endive, to the caramelized crunch of the walnuts. Added inspiration
comes in the vinaigrette, which uses verjus in place of vinegar. The tart-sweet
juice made from underripe grapes gives the dressing a lower tang level and makes
the dish a bit easier to pair with wine.

1 cup walnut halves	4 ripe Bosc pears
⅓ cup powdered sugar	5–6 ounces fresh goat cheese
2–3 tablespoons vegetable oil	3 tablespoons minced chives
6 heads Belgian endive	

VERJUS VINAIGRETTE

⅓ cup verjus	¼ cup walnut oil
1 tablespoon Dijon mustard	1 teaspoon granulated sugar
½ cup olive oil	Salt and freshly ground black pepper

FOR THE VINAIGRETTE, whisk together the verjus and mustard in a medium bowl,
then slowly whisk in the olive and walnut oils. Add the sugar, with salt and pepper to
taste, whisking to thoroughly blend. Set aside.

BRING A SMALL PAN OF WATER to a boil, add the walnut halves, and cook for
2 minutes. Drain the walnuts and put them in a small bowl. Add the powdered sugar and
stir to evenly coat the nuts. (The moisture on the walnuts will dissolve the sugar.) Heat
the oil in a medium skillet over medium heat. Add the walnuts and cook, stirring, until
golden brown and caramelized, about 5 minutes. Transfer the nuts to a piece of parchment
or waxed paper, sprinkle lightly with salt, and set aside.

DISCARD ANY TATTERED OUTER LEAVES from the endive heads. Remove
3 nice large leaves from each head and set those aside for garnishing the plates. Thinly

slice the remaining endive, beginning at the tapered tip and working toward the base, discarding the last inch or so. Put the sliced endive in a large bowl; set aside.

PEEL, HALVE, AND CORE THE PEARS. Thinly slice 3 of the pear halves and set those slices aside for garnishing the salad. Dice the remaining pear and add it to the bowl with the endive. Coarsely chop the walnuts and add them to the bowl. Rewhisk the vinaigrette to mix, then drizzle the dressing over the salad ingredients. Toss gently to evenly mix.

LAY 3 OF THE WHOLE ENDIVE LEAVES on each serving plate, with the broader ends toward the center and tips pointing out. Arrange the pear slices between the endive leaves. Mound the salad in the center of each of 6 plates and crumble the goat cheese over the salad. Sprinkle the chives over all and serve.

Makes 6 servings

LOBSTER SALAD
with Tomato Confit

The Dining Room at the Ritz-Carlton, San Francisco

Praises of this lobster salad have been sung throughout the San Francisco
Bay Area. Chef Sylvain Portay accentuates the rich lobster and avocado combination
with a verjus dressing. Verjus is a tart juice pressed from underripe grapes
(generally chardonnay), used much like vinegar but without its sharp tang. It's natural
that verjus, a common ingredient in medieval cooking, should resurface in fine
restaurants near the winemaking regions of Northern California. Navarro Vineyards
in Mendocino County, one local producer of verjus, began bottling verjus for
retail distribution in 1992. Restaurants, including Chez Panisse in Berkeley,
had gotten verjus from Navarro prior to that time.

At the Ritz, the lobster salad is formed into a perfect circle using a
4-inch cylindrical mold. At home, a free-form circle will taste just as good. This is an
elaborate salad, but note that a few things can be done a day in advance, including
cooking the lobster and roasting the tomatoes. Your efforts will pay off when you see
the ecstasy on your guests' faces after they take the first bite.

2–3 tablespoons olive oil	*½ teaspoon freshly squeezed lemon juice*
4 medium tomatoes	*½–1 avocado*
Salt and freshly ground black pepper	*1½ tablespoons minced chives*
2 live lobsters (1 to 1½ pounds each)	*1½ teaspoons minced shallot*
4 ounces fine green beans (haricots verts)	*1 ounce osetra caviar*
½ cup crème fraîche	*4 ounces baby greens*

VERJUS DRESSING

¼ cup olive oil	*1 garlic clove, lightly crushed*
1½ tablespoons verjus	*½ teaspoon chopped thyme*
1 teaspoon minced shallot	

FOR THE TOMATO CONFIT, preheat the oven to 225°F.

LINE A BAKING SHEET with foil and lightly coat it with 1 to 1½ tablespoons olive
oil. Bring a medium pan of water to a boil and prepare a large bowl of ice water. With the

tip of a sharp knife, score a small "X" on the bottom of each tomato. Add the tomatoes to the boiling water, 1 or 2 at a time, and blanch until the skin begins to split, 20 to 30 seconds. Scoop the tomatoes out with a slotted spoon and put them in the ice water for a quick cooling. When cool, drain the tomatoes, then peel and discard the skin. Quarter the tomatoes lengthwise and scoop out and discard the seeds and the interior flesh compartments, leaving only the outer shell portions. Arrange the tomato pieces on the baking sheet and brush the tops with the remaining olive oil. Season lightly with salt and pepper. Bake the tomatoes until they begin to wrinkle a bit and the surface looks dry, about 3 hours. Set aside to cool.

AFTER PUTTING THE TOMATOES in the oven, make the verjus dressing. Combine olive oil, verjus, shallot, garlic, and thyme with salt and pepper to taste in a medium bowl. Set aside for at least 2 hours (or up to 24 hours).

HEAT A FEW INCHES OF WATER in the bottom of a steamer large enough to hold the lobsters. (You may have to cook them individually if you don't have a pot large enough.) Add the lobsters, cover the steamer, and cook over high heat about 7 minutes for 1-pound lobsters, 10 minutes for 1½-pound lobsters. Set aside to cool.

WHEN COOL ENOUGH to handle, separate the tails from the carapaces by twisting firmly on either side of the connection. (You'll want to work over the sink, because shelling lobster can be messy.) Remove the large clawed legs from the body and twist off the claws. With heavy crackers or a small hammer, gently crack and shell the claws, being careful not to smash the shell into the meat. Using either crackers or shears, split the remaining leg portions and remove their meat. Using kitchen shears, cut up the underside of the tails, then peel back and remove the shell. Cut each tail into 6 even slices (medallions) and dice the remaining lobster meat. Refrigerate the lobster until well chilled.

SHORTLY BEFORE READY TO SERVE the salad, bring a small pan of lightly salted water to a boil and prepare a medium bowl of ice water. Add the green beans to the boiling water and blanch until bright green and just barely tender but still with a crunch, about 1 minute. Drain the beans and add them to the ice water to cool. When cool, drain well and set aside on paper towels. Strain the verjus dressing, discarding the shallot, garlic, and thyme. In a small bowl, combine the crème fraîche and lemon juice with salt and pepper to taste; set aside.

PEEL, PIT, AND DICE the avocado and put it in a large bowl. Dice the tomato confit and add it to the bowl along with the diced lobster meat, chives, and 1½ teaspoons shallot. Add 2 teaspoons of the verjus dressing with salt and pepper to taste. Gently toss the salad and arrange it in the centers of 4 individual plates, pressing it gently into a 4-inch circle. Arrange 3 lobster medallions around the salad and put the green beans on top of the lobster salad. Spoon 4 small circles of crème fraîche around the plate and put a tiny dollop of caviar in the center of each circle. Put the baby greens in a bowl, add 2 tablespoons of the verjus dressing, and toss to mix. Set a pile of the greens on top of the beans. Serve right away.

Makes 4 servings

FRUIT OF THE VINES: WINE AND WINE COUNTRY

The grapy genius in the valleys of the area—the Anderson, Alexander, Napa, Russian River, and Sonoma—is well recognized by the world. These valleys, each with its particular charms and varietals, form a loose center of wine country. Here are scores of restaurants, country bed & breakfasts and luxury inns, and the most popular varietals: cabernet, chardonnay, merlot, pinot noir, riesling, sauvignon blanc.

Central wine country may be recognized by a relatively bucolic look; more land is covered by vines than by housing tracts. Old fruit and nut orchards dot the landscape. Rosemary, roses, and lavender make formal hedges or hug hillsides. Field flowers such as wild mustard and roadside stands of wild fennel flourish in their seasons. Marine moisture softens wine country air, morning and evening. The climate and topography are Mediterranean in feeling, which clearly appealed to the Italian and French immigrants who planted fruit and vines here during the 19th century. Some landscapes of Tuscany and Sonoma County are still remarkably similar, though the architecture of homes and wineries is decidedly American eclectic in wine country.

Less well known outside Northern California are other viticultural areas that also produce world-class wines. These include Arroyo Seco, Livermore Valley, and the Santa Cruz Mountains, whose wines and settings are as interesting and spectacular as the household-name valleys; some say more so. Excellent vintages of the popular varietals are just one aspect that interests vintners here.

Experimental winemakers are working with viognier, pinot meunier, garnacha, malvisia bianca, and other relatively recherché varietals to produce bottlings that are delicious now and harbingers of the twenty-first century. Hillside vineyards look over the green-and-gold southern Salinas Valley to the fabulously contorted mountains of Pinnacles National Monument, or nestle among the ancient, imposing redwoods in the Santa Cruz Mountains. These areas also provide plenty in the way of the creature comforts of fine inns and restaurants, without the tourist highway sense of central wine country.

Two centuries of wine in the region have seen a gradual return to European roots; wine and food are partners here as they were for the Spanish missionaries who planted the region's first vineyard at Mission Sonoma in 1805. Winemakers and chefs of today are contributing to one of civilization's most enduring traditions: the creation of a cuisine. This evolves, year by year, century by century, and requires a fortunate combination of climate, culture, and many individuals to express a genius of place.

Of course, it takes more than vintners and restaurant cooks to make cuisine. Wine country is well supported by people who grow, husband, and produce the necessary and quality ingredients for ongoing experiments with food and wine. Restaurateurs and cooking schools have been attracted by the availability of honest local ingredients—organic produce, baked goods, cheeses, meat and poultry—as well as by the worldly destination designation.

The most important element may be the most intangible: the satisfaction and sense of being part of a place. Even the most developed areas, Napa and Sonoma, are still attuned to seasonal agricultural rhythms. Most people who live in wine country feel the benefit of independent grocers, cheese shops, butchers, farmers' markets, and fishmongers. They are part of the very pleasant, small-town friendly social life.

The prevailing flavor of the cuisine is western Mediterranean, as is natural in such a climate. Modern and historical Italian and French influences are strong, particularly Tuscan, Ligurian, and Provençal. Many Italian immigrants who settled here in the 19th century were from Tuscany and Liguria. The French came in the same post-Gold Rush waves from Bordeaux and Burgundy with their own vines and table traditions. Definite as these factors are, other people settled and are still settling in wine country and contributing to the cuisine. Asian, Southwestern, and Mexican are principal cultures and tastes influencing home cooks as well as professionals.

If the roots of evolving wine country cuisine are European, the flowers of food and wine pairings are American. Classic Old World matches such as Sauternes and foie gras or barolo and truffles have not been codified yet. The prevailing attitude of most winemakers and cooks is exploratory. Out of respect for the palate, most agree on a common-sense guide of simple wines with simple foods and more complex wines with more complex foods. Some will offer an opinion that this particular sauvignon blanc is perfect with that local fresh goat cheese, or that a fruity chardonnay is the best match with chile dishes. One cook may always choose pinot noir with her lamb, another cabernet sauvignon. Many more are open to the subtle surprises and new possibilities that such a young cuisine with so many flavors offers.

CUCUMBER SUNOMONO

Brix, Yountville

This simple, crisp, refreshing salad is ideal as an accompaniment for grilled seafood or served on top of chilled Asian noodles tossed in some of the marinade mixture. One delicious variation is to add some crabmeat, cooked shrimp, or smoked salmon to the salad just before serving.

The vegetables will become more vinegary as they sit in the dressing. If you want to store the salad without continuing the marinating, drain off the dressing after the ingredients have sat for 10 or 15 minutes. The salad is really best freshly made, though.

1 large English cucumber (about 1 pound), thinly sliced	*1½ cups seasoned rice vinegar*
½ large carrot, finely julienned (about 1 cup)	*1 tablespoon sugar*
½ sweet onion, finely julienned (about 1 cup)	*1 teaspoon salt*

IN A LARGE BOWL, combine the cucumber, carrot, and onion. Toss to mix well.

IN A MEDIUM BOWL, combine the vinegar, sugar, and salt. Let sit for a few minutes, then stir the dressing until the sugar and salt have dissolved. Pour the vinegar mixture over the vegetables, toss well, and set aside for 10 minutes before serving.

Makes 4 servings

GREEN PAPAYA SALAD

Lisa Hemenway's, Santa Rosa

Green papaya salad is a staple of Thai and other Southeast Asian cuisines, commonly served alone (sometimes with shrimp or other meats added) or alongside spicy curries or grilled meats. It has a spunky flavor all its own—from Thai fish sauce, fresh lime juice, and fresh hot chile—so pair it with flavorful foods that won't be overpowered by this crisp salad.

Asian shops where you'll find whole green papaya may also have shredded green papaya ready to go in plastic bags, if you're looking for a shortcut.

1 small green papaya (about 1½ to 2 pounds), peeled, seeded, and grated
2 plum (roma) tomatoes, halved and sliced
¼ cup Thai fish sauce (nam pla)
¼ cup freshly squeezed lime juice
1 small hot chile pepper, cored, seeded, and minced

1 tablespoon minced mint
1½ teaspoons minced garlic
1 teaspoon sugar
1 teaspoon minced cilantro

IN A LARGE BOWL, combine the papaya and tomatoes and toss to mix.

IN A SMALL BOWL, combine the remaining ingredients and whisk until the sugar is dissolved. Drizzle the dressing over the papaya and tomatoes, toss to mix well, and serve.

Makes 6 to 8 servings

BEEF TONGUE SALAD
with Leeks in Mustard Caper Vinaigrette

L'Amie Donia, Palo Alto

If fresh beef tongue is not available, most good delis and
charcuteries will have it precooked, notes chef/owner Donia Bijan. "The tongue
needs to be thinly sliced. Be sure to slice home-cooked tongue just before
serving or it will discolor to a dull gray."

You'll have extra meat if you cook the beef tongue yourself
(it's tough to buy half a tongue), but you can refrigerate the extra chunk, submerged
in its cooking liquids, for up to a week.

1 beef tongue (about 3 pounds)	*1 medium onion, coarsely chopped*
2 large carrots, coarsely chopped	*Bouquet garni of 1 bay leaf, a few sprigs of*
2 leeks, halved, rinsed, and coarsely chopped	*parsley, and thyme, tied in kitchen string*
3 stalks celery, coarsely chopped	

LEEK SALAD

5 large leeks, white and pale green parts only	*½ cup extra virgin olive oil*
2 tablespoons tarragon or white wine vinegar	*1½ teaspoons capers*
1 small shallot, minced	*1 teaspoon chopped tarragon*
1½ teaspoons whole-grain mustard	*Whole tarragon leaves, for garnish*
Salt and freshly ground black pepper	

THE TONGUE can be cooked a few days in advance. Rinse the beef tongue well under
cold running water. Put the tongue in a large pot with the carrots, leeks, celery, onion, and
bouquet garni. Add enough cold water to generously cover. Bring just to a boil, then
lower the heat and simmer until the tongue is very tender and the skin easily pulls away,
about 4 hours, adding more hot water as needed to keep the tongue covered. Take the
pan from the heat and let the tongue cool in the cooking broth, then refrigerate.

FOR THE LEEK SALAD, bring a large pot of lightly salted water to a boil and prepare a
large bowl of ice water. While the water is heating, tie the trimmed leeks together in a
neat bundle with kitchen string. When the water boils, add the leeks and cook until just

tender but still bright green, about 4 minutes. Drain well, then plunge the leeks into the ice water to stop the cooking and set their bright color. When cooled, untie the leeks, drain them well, and pat dry on paper towels.

IN A SMALL BOWL, whisk together the vinegar, shallot, and mustard, with salt and pepper to taste. Whisk in the olive oil in a thin stream to emulsify the dressing, then stir in the capers and chopped tarragon.

TEAR THE LEEKS into loose ribbons and put them in a large bowl. Drizzle about half of the vinaigrette over and toss to evenly coat. Pile the leeks high in the center of a large serving platter or on 4 to 6 individual plates.

TAKE THE TONGUE from the cooking liquids. Peel away and discard the skin. Thinly slice about half of the tongue and drape the slices around the bottom half of the leeks. Drizzle the remaining vinaigrette over the tongue, sprinkle tarragon leaves over, and season with a few extra grindings of pepper. Serve right away.

Makes 4 to 6 servings

CREAMED CORN AND MARINATED TOMATOES

with Assorted Basils

Sent Soví, Saratoga

"One of my favorite aspects of this dish is the temperature contrast of the cool, raw tomatoes and the hot creamed corn," says chef David Kinch. "It was created to take advantage of the different sizes, shapes, colors, and flavors of the heirloom tomatoes that we see in the markets at the end of the summer. The variety of tomatoes and the different shapes and sizes that you cut the tomatoes only add to the striking visual appeal of the dish."

At Sent Soví, the chefs benefit from a kitchen garden chock-full of many varieties of basil, and they generally use a bit of each in this recipe: lemon basil, sweet basil, opal basil, cinnamon basil, Thai (anise) basil, and chocolate mint (a basil cousin).

1½ cups whipping cream
3 pounds assorted heirloom tomatoes or other vine-ripened tomatoes
Salt and freshly ground black pepper
2 small bunches basil, preferably assorted types

2 shallots, finely minced
3–4 tablespoons top-quality olive oil
2 tablespoons red wine vinegar, or to taste
Kernels cut from 4–5 ears fresh sweet corn

PUT THE CREAM in a heavy saucepan over high heat, bring to a boil, then reduce the heat to medium, and simmer until the cream is reduced by about half.

WHILE THE CREAM IS REDUCING, core the tomatoes and cut them into varied, interestingly shaped pieces. Arrange the tomatoes in a single layer on a large platter and season to taste with salt and pepper.

PICK THE ATTRACTIVE TOPS from the basil bunches to use for garnish. Cut the remaining leaves into fine shreds. Sprinkle the shallots over the tomatoes, followed by the shredded basil. Drizzle the olive oil and vinegar over.

WHEN THE CREAM IS REDUCED, add the corn kernels and return to a boil. Season to taste with salt and pepper, and take the pan from the heat.

ARRANGE THE TOMATOES on 6 to 8 individual plates, with varied shapes and colors for each serving. Spoon the creamed corn over the tomatoes and garnish with the reserved basil sprigs. Serve right away.

Makes 6 to 8 servings

HEIRLOOM PRODUCE

The region's ingredient-driven cuisine thrives on very flavorful cultivars of fruits and vegetables. Every restaurant worth its salt has something heirloom on its menu. Produce offered as heirloom is usually tastier than the 10,000-acre monocrop kind, though older cultivars are not always more flavorful than modern hybrids. The term *heirloom* is used rather loosely, many times denoting cultivars that are simply unusual and not very old or out of commerce for any length of time. Some people include open pollination as a requirement for the heirloom designation.

From modest beginnings in backyards and very small truck farms, growing heirloom produce has become a fairly sizable, and certainly influential, enterprise. Larger-scale cultivation of such produce began during the back-to-the-land movement of the 1960s and '70s. Individuals had been saving seeds and cultivating these vegetables and fruits for many decades before this, of course. Some restaurants, notably Chez Panisse in Berkeley, used "special" backyard produce before the heirloom boom began to be seen in many restaurants and at farmers' markets about a decade ago.

The tomato has the largest number of heirlooms, though there are many others in the vegetable department: corn, cucumbers, greens, herbs, potatoes, shell beans, and zucchini, to name a few. Among common fruits are heirloom apples (see page 259), cherries, figs, grapes, melons, peaches, and plums.

Tastings (held at fairs, farmers' and other markets, and restaurants) prove that the flavors are distinctive. Some restaurants offer theme dinners of heirloom vegetables. One based on the tomato harvest might feature such cultivars as Brandywine, Marvel Striped, Cherokee Purple, Stupice, Green Zebra, Red Currant, and Lemon Boy.

It is increasingly common to see vegetables and fruits listed by cultivar names on menus and at markets. This partial list shows the mouthwatering, somewhat romantic appeal. Peppers include Chiltepin, Corno di Toro, Habanero, Mirasol, and Rocoto. Lettuces are Black-Seeded Simpson, Bronze Arrow, Four Seasons, and Red Deer Tongue. Melons include Blenheim Orange and Charentais Muskmelons, and Moon and Stars Watermelon. Grapes are Christmas Rose, Muscat, and Ribier. Among heirloom plums are Coe's Golden Drop, Italian Prune, Kirke's Blue, and Mirabelle.

INSALATA DI MELANZANE
(Eggplant Salad)

Café Maddalena, Dunsmuir

This simple, chunky salad can be served as is for a first course,
or it would be ideal served alongside grilled lamb or roasted chicken. You can make
the recipe up to a day in advance, but for more pronounced flavor, allow the
salad come to room temperature before serving.

2 large eggplants
2 tablespoons minced garlic
½ cup extra virgin olive oil
1 teaspoon dried oregano
Salt
3–4 tablespoons balsamic vinegar

10 ripe plum (roma) tomatoes or other ripe
tomatoes (about 2 pounds), cored and cut
in 1-inch cubes
10 mint leaves, torn into small pieces
½ teaspoon dried red pepper flakes

PREHEAT THE OVEN to 375°F.

CUT THE EGGPLANTS in half lengthwise and score the pulp at an angle at 1-inch
intervals, cutting through only the pulp and not the skin. Sprinkle the eggplant halves
with the garlic, pushing it into the cuts. Drizzle with half of the olive oil, the oregano, and
a pinch of salt. Put the eggplant halves cut side down on a rimmed baking sheet and bake
until just tender, 20 to 30 minutes (press lightly on the surface; it should feel soft but not
mushy). Take from the oven and let cool.

WHEN THE EGGPLANT is cool enough to handle, cut away and discard the stems.
Cut the eggplant in 1-inch cubes, using the slits already made as a guide. In a large bowl,
combine the eggplant with the tomatoes. Sprinkle the balsamic vinegar, remaining ¼ cup
olive oil, mint, and pepper flakes over, with salt to taste. Toss to evenly mix.

Makes 4 servings

MEDJOOL DATE AND CELERY SALAD

42 Degrees, San Francisco

"This is a remarkably simple composed salad. The key to its success
is in using the finest-quality ingredients: aged balsamic vinegar; good Italian cheese;
and sweet, plump fresh dates." This is good advice from chef James Moffat.
He wants diners to feel free to use their fingers for dishes such as this one, which
combines whole dates, big slivers of cheese, and whole parsley leaves.
But go ahead and use a fork if you prefer.

3 stalks celery
1 cup loosely packed flat-leaf (Italian)
parsley leaves
1–2 tablespoons aged balsamic vinegar (at
least 10 years old), or to taste
1–2 tablespoons extra virgin olive oil,
or to taste

Kosher salt and freshly ground black pepper
½ pound Medjool dates
About 2 ounces Parmigiano-Reggiano cheese,
in one piece

SET THE CELERY STALKS rounded side up on a cutting board and, working on a
long bias, cut the celery into very thin slices (as close to paper thin as possible). Combine
the celery and parsley leaves in a large bowl. Add about 1 tablespoon balsamic vinegar and
1 tablespoon olive oil, with salt and pepper to taste. Toss to evenly mix.

ARRANGE THE DATES in the center of 6 individual plates. Using a cheese shaver or
vegetable peeler, shave 6 to 8 large slivers of cheese over the dates. Spoon a small mound
of celery salad over the cheese. Drizzle a bit more balsamic vinegar and olive oil around
the salad on each plate, and serve.

Makes 6 servings

DUCK CONFIT
with a Frisée and Walnut Salad

Bistro Vida, Menlo Park

Note that you must start this delicious melt-in-your-mouth
duck confit at least 2 days before you plan to serve the salad. The method was
originally developed to preserve duck, so remember that you can make the confit as
far as a week in advance and store it, submerged in the duck fat, in the refrigerator.
It's a complete indulgence, but after using the confit, you could use the extra duck
fat to fry up some potatoes for a classic French complement to confit.

2 tablespoons unsalted butter	*1 tablespoon Dijon mustard*
1 cup walnuts, toasted	*¾ cup olive oil*
1 tablespoon Cajun spice mix	*Salt and freshly ground black pepper*
1 teaspoon ground cinnamon	*3 heads frisée, washed, tough outer leaves*
½ teaspoon salt	*trimmed, tender leaves separated*
½ teaspoon sugar	*3 tablespoons chopped flat-leaf*
¼ cup red wine vinegar	*(Italian) parsley*

DUCK CONFIT

6 duck legs	*2 bay leaves*
6 tablespoons coarse salt	*1 sprig rosemary*
10 juniper berries	*1 sprig thyme*
10 black peppercorns	*2½ pounds duck or goose fat*

FOR THE DUCK CONFIT, lay the duck legs in a dish just large enough to hold them.
Rub the salt over the legs, then scatter the juniper berries, peppercorns, bay leaves, rosemary, and thyme over the duck. Cover the dish with plastic wrap and refrigerate at least 8
hours or overnight.

THE NEXT DAY, preheat the oven to 250°F.

HEAT THE DUCK FAT in a medium saucepan over medium heat just until evenly
melted. Take the pan from the heat. Thoroughly wipe the salt from the duck and put the
legs in a heavy, deep pot, such as a Dutch oven. Add the herbs and other seasonings from

the dish, discarding the salt and collected juices. Pour the melted duck fat over the legs to fully cover them. Cover the pot and bake in the oven until the duck is very tender, 2½ to 3 hours. Take the pot from the oven and let cool, then refrigerate for at least 24 hours.

THE DAY YOU PLAN TO SERVE the salad, heat the butter in a small pan or skillet over medium heat until it is melted and turns a light nutty brown color. Take the pan from the heat, add the walnuts, and stir to evenly coat them in the butter. Add the Cajun spice, cinnamon, salt, and sugar, and toss to evenly mix. Return the skillet to medium heat and cook, stirring often, until the spices are aromatic and the nuts are well coated, 2 to 3 minutes. Set aside.

IN A SMALL BOWL, whisk together the vinegar and mustard, then slowly whisk in the olive oil. Season the dressing to taste with salt and pepper; set aside.

PREHEAT THE BROILER.

TAKE THE DUCK LEGS from the fat and lay them skin side up on a rimmed baking sheet. Broil the duck about 4 to 5 inches from the element until warmed through and crispy, 7 to 10 minutes. (Alternatively, you could pan-fry the duck legs in some of the duck fat until crispy and heated through, about 5 minutes.) While the duck is broiling, toss the frisée with the vinaigrette dressing. Add the spiced walnuts and toss to mix. Arrange the salad on 6 individual plates. Top each with a crispy duck leg, sprinkle with parsley, and serve.

Makes 6 servings

CHICKPEA SALAD
with Grilled Gypsy Peppers and Pickled Onions

Chez Panisse, Berkeley

This rustic salad is soul satisfying, with ingredients that each shine through individually. The gypsy peppers suggested here are a hybrid of the sweet bell pepper and are often yellow, though the peppers turn red when fully ripened. You can use small red or yellow bell peppers in place of the gypsies.

Note that the chickpeas need overnight soaking before they're cooked, so plan ahead. This recipe makes a crowd-serving quantity; you can halve it if you like.

3½ cups dried chickpeas (about 1½ pounds)	*Salt and freshly ground black pepper*
1 small carrot	*4 gypsy peppers, or small yellow or red*
1 small onion	*bell peppers*
½ stalk celery	*½ cup extra virgin olive oil, plus more for*
1 sprig thyme	*cooking peppers*
1 bay leaf	*2 tablespoons minced flat-leaf (Italian) parsley*
Pinch dried red pepper flakes	*1 teaspoon finely chopped marjoram*
1 large red onion, halved and thinly sliced	*2 cloves garlic, smashed to a paste or minced*
About 2 cups red wine vinegar	

PUT THE CHICKPEAS in a large bowl, add enough cold water to cover twice their volume, and let sit overnight.

THE NEXT DAY, drain the chickpeas and put them in a large saucepan with fresh cold water to generously cover. Add the whole carrot, whole onion, celery stalk, thyme sprig, bay leaf, and pepper flakes. Bring to a low simmer over medium heat and cook until the chickpeas are tender, 1½ to 2 hours, adding hot water if necessary so the chickpeas are always covered. Set them aside to cool in the cooking liquids.

PUT THE SLICED RED ONION in a medium bowl and add enough red wine vinegar to cover. Season with salt to taste and set aside to macerate for 15 to 30 minutes.

RUB THE PEPPERS with a little bit of olive oil and salt them lightly. Grill the peppers over a medium fire or under a broiler until tender, about 10 minutes, turning occasionally so they cook evenly. Set aside to cool. When cool enough to handle, stem and seed each pepper, slicing each in large strips.

WHEN THE CHICKPEAS ARE COOL, drain them, discarding the cooking liquids, vegetables, and herbs. Drain the red onions from the vinegar, reserving the vinegar. Combine the chickpeas and red onions in a large bowl. Add the peppers, olive oil, parsley, marjoram, and garlic with ¾ cup of the reserved vinegar. Taste the salad for seasoning, adding salt, black pepper, and/or more vinegar to taste. Serve at room temperature.

Makes 8 to 10 servings

THAI CHICKEN, RED GRAPE, AND MANGO SALAD

Bridges, Danville

The aroma of the stock used to poach the chicken for this salad is intoxicating and sets the stage for this flavorful and colorful salad. Asian pears have a very crunchy texture even when ripe, adding a welcome crispness, though a not-too-ripe regular pear could be used instead.

3 boneless, skinless chicken breasts (6 to 8 ounces each) | *4 ounces red seedless grapes, halved*
2 large shallots, thinly sliced | *½ Asian pear, peeled, cored, and diced*
Vegetable oil, for frying | *¼ cup finely chopped cilantro*
½ mango, peeled, pitted, and diced | *1 green onion, trimmed and finely chopped*

ASIAN STOCK

2 tablespoons salt | *1 slice ginger (about quarter size)*
2 cloves garlic, sliced | *¼ teaspoon fennel seeds*
2 cinnamon sticks | *¼ teaspoon coriander seeds*
2 star anise |

DRESSING

¼ cup vegetable oil | *1 teaspoon Thai fish sauce (nam pla)*
Juice of 1 lime | *or soy sauce*
1 tablespoon sugar | *Salt and freshly ground black pepper*

COMBINE THE ASIAN stock ingredients in a deep skillet or a saucepan large enough to hold the chicken breasts. Add 2 to 3 inches of cold water and bring to a boil. Reduce the heat to medium-low, add the chicken breasts, and simmer until the chicken is just cooked through, 15 to 20 minutes. Drain the chicken breasts and let cool.

IN A SMALL BOWL, stir together the dressing ingredients until the sugar has dissolved. Season the dressing to taste with salt and pepper and set aside.

SEPARATE THE SHALLOT SLICES into individual rings. Heat about 1 inch of oil in a small saucepan over medium-high heat. When hot, add the shallot rings in batches and fry just until lightly browned and crisp, about 2 minutes. Drain well on paper towels and set aside for garnishing the salad.

WHEN THE CHICKEN IS COOL, pull the breasts into rough shreds and put the chicken in a large bowl. Add the mango, grapes, pear, cilantro, and green onion. Drizzle the dressing over and toss to evenly mix. Arrange the salad on individual plates, scatter the fried shallot over, and serve.

Makes 4 servings

Main Dishes

JUMBO SEA SCALLOPS
with Kaffir Lime Beurre Blanc

Brix, Yountville

Kaffir lime leaves and lemongrass are both commonly used in Southeast Asian cuisines and should be available fresh in Asian markets or well-stocked grocery stores. If you're unable to find them, you can use a few strips of lime and lemon zest instead, though the flavor won't be as distinctive and aromatic.

24 jumbo sea scallops (about 1½ pounds)
2 stalks lemongrass, trimmed and
finely minced
1 cup dry white wine
2 tablespoons rice wine vinegar
1 tablespoon chopped ginger
1 tablespoon chopped shallot

6 kaffir lime leaves, finely chopped
¼ cup whipping cream
½ cup unsalted butter, cut in pieces
and chilled
Juice of 1 lime
Salt and freshly ground white or black pepper
1–2 tablespoons vegetable oil

LAY THE SCALLOPS on a plate and sprinkle them lightly with about half of the lemongrass. Set aside while preparing the sauce.

IN A SMALL, HEAVY SAUCEPAN, combine the wine, vinegar, ginger, shallot, kaffir lime leaves, and remaining lemongrass. Bring to a boil and reduce the liquids to a thick, syrupy consistency, about 20 minutes. Add the cream and simmer for 1 minute. Reduce the heat to very low and whisk in the butter one piece at a time, allowing each piece to melt creamily into the sauce before adding the next. Do not overheat the sauce at this point or it will become oily. After all the butter is added, stir in the lime juice with salt and pepper to taste. Strain the sauce (blending it first, if you like, to extract a bit more flavor), then return it to the pan. Keep warm over very low heat.

SEASON THE SCALLOPS with salt and pepper. Heat the oil in a large, heavy skillet over high heat. When the pan is very hot, add the scallops and cook until browned, 1 to 2 minutes. Turn and continue cooking until browned and medium-rare (still translucent in the center), 1 to 2 minutes longer. Arrange the scallops on 4 individual plates, spoon the kaffir lime beurre blanc around, and serve right away.

Makes 4 servings

HALIBUT ESCABÈCHE

42 Degrees, San Francisco

The cuisine of 42 Degrees is inspired by the honesty and simplicity of
peasant food, drawing upon Old World tradition and techniques. With its roots in
Iberia, escabèche is traditionally a way of preserving foods with vinegar. Chef/owner
James Moffet tempers the strength of the vinegar with wine and aromatic vegetables
and serves the escabèche as either an appetizer or a main course. The chef also
prepares this recipe with rockfish and cod, preferring fish that are on the flaky side
rather than those that are dense such as swordfish.

Because the fish is intended to cook from the heat of the hot vinegar,
it is important that the pieces be slender, about ½ inch thick. If you purchase one
fillet piece, cut it on the bias into individual ½-inch-thick pieces. (Be sure to remove
the pin bones first, to make cutting easier.) If the fish isn't fully cooked from the
vinegar, finish the cooking in the oven.

½ cup extra virgin olive oil
6 cloves garlic, slivered
1 small sweet onion, slivered
2 stalks celery, cut in 2-inch julienne strips
2 carrots, cut in 2-inch julienne strips
2 sprigs thyme
2 bay leaves
1½ teaspoons coarse salt
10 whole black peppercorns
¼ teaspoon cayenne pepper

1½ cups dry white wine
1½ cups sherry vinegar or other
  good-quality vinegar
2 pounds halibut fillet, cut in pieces
  about ½ inch thick
¼ head green cabbage, finely shredded
½ cup toasted whole almonds, roughly
  chopped after toasting
Juice of ½ lemon

IN A LARGE SKILLET, heat all but 2 tablespoons of the olive oil over medium-high
heat. Add the garlic and cook, stirring often, until lightly browned, about 2 minutes. Add
the onion, celery, carrots, thyme, bay leaves, salt, peppercorns, and cayenne. Sauté the vegetables, stirring occasionally, until tender, 8 to 10 minutes. Stir in the wine and vinegar,
bring just to a boil, then reduce the heat to medium and simmer for 5 minutes.

WHILE THE LIQUID IS SIMMERING, arrange the halibut pieces in a single layer in a
heatproof glass or ceramic baking dish. Pour the hot liquid and vegetables over the fish,

cover the heat-proof dish securely with foil, and let sit for about 15 to 20 minutes. The heat of the liquid should thoroughly cook the fish, but check the thickest part of 1 piece to make sure that it is opaque through. If not, put the pan in a 350°F oven for 3 to 5 minutes until the fish is cooked through, then take the pan from the oven and let sit for about 5 minutes before serving.

JUST BEFORE SERVING, combine the cabbage and almonds in a medium bowl. Drizzle the remaining 2 tablespoons olive oil and lemon juice over and toss to evenly mix.

TO SERVE, spoon the vegetables onto 6 individual plates and set the fish pieces on top. Drizzle about ¼ cup of the cooking juices over the fish. Garnish with the cabbage salad and serve right away.

Makes 6 servings

PAN-ROASTED SALMON

with Braised Napa Cabbage and
Beaujolais Nouveau Sauce

Left Bank, Larkspur & Menlo Park

Celebrated San Francisco chef Roland Passot (La Folie) uses his
Larkspur and Menlo Park restaurants as an outlet for really wonderful bistro-style
fare, more casual than what he serves in the big city. This earthy dish is a perfect
example. It was developed to help celebrate the arrival of Beaujolais Nouveau, an
annual event of national proportions in France (and beyond) each November.
The very young wine—fresh, fruity, and easy to drink—is available for only a few
weeks. In its place, you could choose another light, fruity red wine
such as Beaujolais Villages.

4 tablespoons olive oil	*½ cup dry white wine*
1 onion, cut in julienne strips	*4 salmon fillet pieces (about 6 ounces each),*
1 head napa cabbage (about 2 pounds), cored	*skin and pin bones removed*
and cut in julienne strips	*Thyme sprigs, for garnish*
2 tablespoons thyme leaves	

BEAUJOLAIS NOUVEAU SAUCE

2 tablespoons olive oil	*1 bay leaf*
6 small shallots, cut in julienne strips	*Salt and freshly ground black pepper*
1½ cups Beaujolais Nouveau	
2 cups veal or chicken stock, preferably	
homemade	

FOR THE SAUCE, heat the olive oil in a medium saucepan over medium heat. Add the
shallots and stir to evenly coat in oil. Lay a piece of foil loosely over the shallots and cook
until they are very tender and caramelized to a rich brown, about 15 minutes, stirring
occasionally. Add the Beaujolais Nouveau, bring to a boil, and boil until reduced by about
half, 8 to 10 minutes. Add the stock and bay leaf, return to a boil, and boil until reduced
by about half, 15 to 20 minutes. Discard the bay leaf, season the sauce to taste with salt
and pepper, and keep warm over low heat.

HEAT 2 TABLESPOONS OF THE OLIVE oil in a large skillet over high heat. When the skillet is very hot, add the onion and sauté, stirring often, until the onions are slightly browned and beginning to soften, about 5 minutes. Add the cabbage and continue sautéing until the cabbage and onions are tender, 5 to 10 minutes longer. Stir in the thyme, then add the wine. Continue cooking until the liquids have all evaporated, 10 to 15 minutes. Season to taste with salt and pepper and keep warm over low heat.

PREHEAT THE OVEN to 400°F.

HEAT THE REMAINING OLIVE OIL in a large, heavy ovenproof skillet over high heat. Season the salmon to taste with salt and pepper. When the oil just begins to smoke, carefully add the salmon pieces, fleshy side down, and sear for 1 minute. Transfer the skillet to the oven (do not turn the salmon pieces) and bake until the fish is nearly opaque through, 5 to 10 minutes, depending on the thickness of the fish. (The salmon will continue to cook a few minutes after coming from the oven.)

TO SERVE, spoon the braised cabbage into the centers of 4 individual plates. Carefully turn the salmon pieces in the skillet and set them on top of the cabbage. Drizzle the sauce around, garnish with thyme sprigs, and serve.

Makes 4 servings

LEMON BRAISED SEA BASS

with Star Anise and Baby Spinach

Pastis, San Francisco

Chef Gerald Hirigoyen made a splash in San Francisco when
he opened Fringale, a distinguished French bistro that is consistently a top favorite
among San Francisco diners. His more recent bistro, Pastis, continues the
tradition of classy but comfortable French fare.

Braising—whether the subject's meat or fish—is an ideal and easy way
to ensure moist and flavorful results from the oven. Here delicate sea bass is infused
with flavor from aromatic vegetables and a touch of spice from star anise.

4 sea bass fillet pieces (4 to 6 ounces each)	*1½ cups water*
Salt and freshly ground white pepper	*⅓ cup finely diced cucumber*
2 teaspoons olive oil	*⅓ cup finely diced tomato*
⅓ cup finely diced fennel bulb	*2 tablespoons finely diced apple*
¼ cup finely diced celery root	*4 cups lightly packed baby spinach leaves*
¼ cup finely diced carrot	*1 tablespoon extra virgin olive oil*
2 cloves garlic, minced	*Pinch mild cayenne pepper*
4 star anise	*2 tablespoons chopped parsley*
¼ cup freshly squeezed lemon juice	*2 tablespoons chopped chives*

PREHEAT THE OVEN to 475°F.

SEASON THE FISH FILLETS with salt and pepper and set aside. Heat the olive oil in a
large ovenproof skillet or sauté pan over medium-high heat. Add the fennel, celery root,
carrot, garlic, and star anise and cook, stirring, until the vegetables are tender and slightly
caramelized, 4 to 5 minutes. Add the lemon juice and cook for 1 minute, stirring to scrape
up flavorful bits stuck to the bottom of the skillet. Set the fish pieces on top of the vegetables, add the water, and cover the pan. Bake the fish until just cooked through, 6 to 9
minutes, depending on the thickness of the fish pieces. Take the pan from the oven and
use a slotted spatula to transfer the fish to a warm plate, covered with foil to keep warm.

ADD THE CUCUMBER, tomato, and apple to the skillet, bring to a boil, and boil until slightly thickened, about 2 minutes. Add the spinach, extra virgin olive oil, and cayenne, with salt and pepper to taste. Cook, stirring, just until the spinach wilts, about 1 minute.

SPOON THE VEGETABLES and braising liquids into 4 individual shallow soup bowls or rimmed plates and arrange the fish on top. Set a piece of star anise on top of each fish fillet, sprinkle the parsley and chives over all, and serve right away.

Makes 4 servings

FIRECRACKER SHRIMP

Cottonwood Restaurant, Truckee

You can take a hint from the name—this is one hot dish, thanks to the addition of an intense sweet and hot sauce. So, you're warned. But since you'll be the one cooking, add only as much sauce as you can tolerate. The rest will keep well, so you can work your way up the heat scale if you care to.

Salt	*1 green bell pepper, cored, seeded, and cut in*
2 tablespoons vegetable oil	*julienne strips*
1 tablespoon sesame oil	*2 cups finely shredded cabbage*
1½ pounds large shrimp, peeled, slit down the	*2 cups chicken stock, preferably homemade*
back, and deveined	*½ cup sweet and hot chile sauce (see below),*
2 tablespoons cornstarch	*or to taste*
2 carrots, cut in julienne strips	*¼ cup rice wine vinegar*
1 zucchini, cut in julienne strips	*½ teaspoon ground ginger*
1 stalk celery, cut in julienne strips	*1½ pounds dry soba noodles*
1 red bell pepper, cored, seeded, and cut in	*or angel hair pasta*
julienne strips	*2 tablespoons sesame seeds (black or white)*

PUT A LARGE POT of lightly salted water on to boil for cooking the pasta.

WHILE THE WATER IS HEATING, heat the oils in a very large skillet or a sauté pan over high heat. Toss the shrimp in the cornstarch to coat them evenly. When the oil is hot, add the shrimp and cook for about 30 seconds on each side (they will be only partially cooked at this point). Add the carrots, zucchini, celery, bell peppers, and cabbage, tossing a bit to mix.

IN A SMALL BOWL, stir together the chicken stock, about half of the sweet and hot chile sauce, the vinegar, and ginger. Add this to the pan, with salt to taste, and bring the liquid just to a simmer. Cook the sauce until it is slightly thickened and the vegetables are just becoming tender, 2 to 3 minutes. Taste the sauce for seasoning, adding more of the sweet and hot chile sauce to taste.

WHEN THE PASTA WATER IS BOILING, add the noodles and cook until just al dente, according to package directions. Drain the noodles well and arrange them in 6 to 8 large shallow soup bowls. Spoon the shrimp, vegetables, and sauce over, sprinkle with sesame seeds, and serve right away.

Makes 6 to 8 servings

SWEET AND HOT CHILE SAUCE

This sauce will keep for a long time, covered in the refrigerator.

¾ cup sugar	1-inch piece ginger, peeled and sliced
¾ cup white wine vinegar	3 cloves garlic, crushed
⅓ cup golden raisins	½ teaspoon salt
2 tablespoons cayenne pepper	½ teaspoon dried red pepper flakes

COMBINE ALL THE INGREDIENTS in a small saucepan and bring to a boil. Reduce the heat and simmer gently 20 minutes. Take the pan from the heat and let cool slightly, then purée the mixture in a food processor or blender.

Makes about 1½ cups

GRILLED PACIFIC SALMON

Sunsets on the Lake, Tahoe Vista

This recipe will be at its peak in late summer when the season's wild salmon
are still widely available and vine-ripe tomatoes are at their best. It is a gloriously
simple preparation that shows off the goodness of the ingredients. Chef Lewis Orlady
prefers mesquite for the charcoal fire, but you could also use other hardwood chips
such as alder, apple, or cherry. Chef Orlady also uses olive wood for grilling, another
hardwood available from olive orchards in the Napa/Sonoma region.

7 tablespoons extra virgin olive oil

3 tablespoons balsamic vinegar

2 large portobello mushrooms, stems removed,
caps wiped clean

4 vine-ripened yellow or red tomatoes, cored
and cut in slices about 1 inch thick

2 tablespoons minced basil

Salt and freshly ground (coarse) black pepper

4 salmon fillet pieces (about 6 ounces each),
skin and pin bones removed

4 cups washed and trimmed arugula
(about 6 ounces)

IN A SHALLOW DISH, stir together 4 tablespoons of the olive oil and 2 tablespoons of
the balsamic vinegar. Add the portobello mushroom caps, turning to coat them evenly.
Leave the mushrooms top down (dark gills up) in the marinade and set aside for 2 hours.

PREHEAT AN OUTDOOR GRILL, preferably with mesquite charcoal. If you like,
soak some mesquite (or other) wood chips in cold water while the grill heats. When the
grill is hot, drain the wood chips, if using, and scatter them over the coals. Grill the
tomato slices on only one side for 2 minutes. Turn them grilled side up onto a plate,
drizzle with 1 tablespoon of the olive oil and ½ tablespoon of the balsamic vinegar, and
sprinkle with basil and black pepper to taste. Set aside.

TAKE THE PORTOBELLO MUSHROOMS from the marinade, allowing any excess
to drip off, and grill them over the hot fire until just tender through, about 3 to 4 minutes
on each side. Set aside.

BRUSH THE SALMON FILLET pieces with 1 tablespoon olive oil and season with salt
and pepper. Grill the salmon over the hot fire until medium-rare, 1 to 3 minutes per side,
depending on the thickness of the fish. (Or you could cook the salmon to your taste,
adding 1 to 2 minutes per side if you prefer it medium to medium-well.)

WHILE THE SALMON IS COOKING, prepare the plates. In a large bowl, toss the arugula with the remaining 1 tablespoon olive oil and ½ tablespoon balsamic vinegar, with salt and pepper to taste. Arrange the arugula in the centers of 4 plates. Arrange the grilled tomato slices around the arugula. When the salmon is cooked to taste, set it on top of the arugula. Cut the portobello mushrooms in slices and set them on top of the salmon.

Makes 4 servings

A good number of cooks, in restaurants and at home, have fallen under the elemental spell of fire. About twenty years ago, the grill blazed through the scene, de rigueur for any cook with ambitions. The grill was, of course, the wood- or wood-charcoal-burning version, not the flattop grill of hash houses. Barely did this grill have a special menu section before the wood-burning oven and spit, or rotisserie, found homes in a number of restaurants wanting fire flavor of a different form. Some home cooks with the space and money also went for the wood, remodeling their kitchens to include wood ovens or buying imported Tuscan hearth grills. Others simply experimented with outdoor grills or put a grate on bricks in their fireplaces.

The differences in flavor these fiery methods yield are pronounced. The results depend chiefly on the kind of combustible material and the time elapsed for cooking. Charcoal grilling quickly cooks those foods able to withstand fairly intense heat. These are the classic grill foods: steaks, burgers, chicken pieces, fish fillets, and tender whole or sliced vegetables such as peppers and onions. These foods pick up simple smoky flavors, without the refinements of aroma and complex flavor that the wood oven and spit offer.

In Northern California, the choice of woods to burn is much greater than that of charcoals. Fruit orchards, nut plantations, olive groves, and vineyards are constantly being pruned, thinned, and replaced. Restaurants cultivate sources for cherry, almond, or apple woods, along with vine branches. Oak is a popular choice for its reliable hardwood qualities of high heat and clean burning. It is also in good supply. The home cook can count on finding retail sources of oak wood, and fruit woods and vines are becoming more available. Each of these woods has distinct aromatic properties, which can subtly alter the taste of foods.

Wood-fired ovens depend not on direct flames for cooking, but on the hot embers and reflected heat from the oven walls. The oven can be a more direct and energy-efficient use of wood than charcoal when the cook plans several dishes for one firing of the oven or when the oven is large enough to have different areas of heat intensity. Some dishes will be baked at a high temperature, some at a medium, and some when or where the temperature is low. The food may be courses of a meal and may also include dishes baked for later.

Restaurants try to maximize the use of their ovens for the variety of tastes they can offer customers, as well as for economy. The oven offers great depth of flavor for many foods, whether they are cooked quickly or slowly. For example, pizza and mussels are first courses that cook rapidly and take on very different taste dimensions when cooked in a hot wood oven. A wood-fire-burnished pizza crust—brushed with first-pressing olive oil and fresh herbs and topped with vegetables, cheese, or salami—is a pizza of a different order with the satisfying scent of slight smokiness. Put in front of anyone two pans of roasted mussels with the same shallots, herbs, and white wine—one opened in the wood oven, the other over a stovetop flame. Most people will choose the wood-oven dish, if not by aroma alone, then after a taste of the subtle alchemy of mussel juices, wine, and herbs wrought by smoke.

The same is true of dishes cooked at medium heat, from lasagna to breads to roast birds, lamb, and pork—in fact, any meat or fish suitable for roasting. Slow-cooked foods—such as cassoulet, vegetable gratins, stews, and the meats or poultry that call for the tenderizing effects of low temperatures—are likewise transformed from merely delicious to exceptional when baked in a wood oven.

Spit-roasting is a natural and relatively easy refinement of wood cookery. In restaurants, it's usually done in conjunction with a grill, sometimes with a wood-burning oven. The essentials are a holding/turning device—hand-turned, battery-operated, or official electric rotisserie—and a wood-burning source. This can be a fireplace or a sturdy backyard barbecue grill in which wood can be burned. Maintaining moderate direct flames, placing the meat a proper distance from the flames, and balancing the spit are the basic techniques. Spit-roasting is an excellent method for large roasts and whole birds, from chicken to quail. In effect, the rotation of the spit allows the meat to baste itself and cook evenly while absorbing the aroma of the wood. This results in a succulence that can't be matched by any other cooking method.

CRISPY HALIBUT

*with Braised Bok Choy, Japanese Eggplant
Chips, and Tapenade Butter*

Applewood Inn Restaurant, Pocket Canyon

A wonderful mix of flavors, colors, and textures, this dish blends a
Mediterranean-inspired tapenade with an Asian-influenced garnish of bok choy and
Japanese eggplant. It shows chef David Frakes's savvy and creativity in creating
the restaurant's distinctive prix fixe menus.

Vegetable oil, for deep-frying	*4 baby bok choy*
1 Japanese eggplant	*1 cup chicken stock, preferably homemade,*
Salt and freshly ground black pepper	* or water*
3 tablespoons extra virgin olive oil	*1 tablespoon unsalted butter*
2 tablespoons minced onion	*4 pieces halibut fillet (about 6 ounces each),*
½ teaspoon minced garlic	* skin and pin bones removed*
¼ cup dry white wine	

TAPENADE BUTTER

¼ cup unsalted butter, at room temperature	*½ teaspoon Dijon mustard*
2 tablespoons minced kalamata olives	*½ teaspoon minced anchovy (optional)*
1 tablespoon minced capers	*1 drop honey (optional)*

FOR THE TAPENADE BUTTER, combine the butter, olives, capers, and mustard in a
small bowl and mix with a fork until thoroughly blended. Mix in the anchovy and/or
honey, if desired. Set aside. (Refrigerate the butter if made more than 1 hour in advance
and let soften at room temperature before serving.)

HEAT ABOUT 2 INCHES OF OIL in a large saucepan to 375°F. Trim the eggplant and
cut it into ⅛-inch slices on the bias. (If you don't have a cooking thermometer, you can
test the heat of the oil by adding one of the eggplant slices; it should bubble vigorously
within a few seconds.) Add 6 to 8 of the eggplant slices to the hot oil one at a time (to
prevent them from sticking together), turn once, and fry until the slices are golden and
crisp, about 2 minutes. Scoop out the eggplant slices with a skimmer or slotted spoon and
drain on paper towels while frying the remaining eggplant. Season the slices to taste with

salt and pepper. (You could also add other favorite seasonings, such as red pepper flakes or thyme.) Keep the fried eggplant warm and crisp in a low oven.

HEAT 1 TABLESPOON OF THE OLIVE OIL in a large skillet over medium heat, add the onion and garlic, and cook, stirring, until fragrant and tender, 3 to 5 minutes. Add the wine, bring to a boil, and boil until the wine is fully evaporated, 2 to 3 minutes. Add the baby bok choy, chicken stock, and butter, with salt and pepper to taste. Cover the skillet and cook over medium heat until the base of the bok choy is just barely tender, 5 to 7 minutes (poke it with a fork to check). Take the skillet from the heat and set aside.

HEAT A LARGE, HEAVY SKILLET over high heat until very hot. While the skillet is heating, season the halibut pieces with salt and pepper to taste. Add the remaining 2 table-spoons of the olive oil to the hot skillet, swirl to evenly coat the pan, and quickly add the halibut pieces. Cook the halibut until nicely browned and crisp, about 3 minutes. Turn the fish pieces and continue cooking until the fish is just opaque through, 2 to 5 minutes longer (depending on the thickness of the fish).

TO SERVE, set a baby bok choy in the center of each of 4 plates and prop a piece of hal-ibut against the bok choy, poking some of the eggplant chips between and around the bok choy and halibut. Vigorously stir the tapenade butter to soften it, then drizzle the butter around the halibut. Serve right away.

Makes 4 servings

MEDALLIONS OF AHI TUNA
with Seared Foie Gras and Red Wine Sauce

Aqua, San Francisco

The veal demi-glace that serves as the base of this red wine sauce is a
prime example of why we pay a premium for meals out at restaurants such as Aqua.
It begins with a veal stock, cooked long and slow, often as many as 12 hours.
Then the strained stock is simmered until reduced to about one-quarter (or less)
of its original volume. The refined, deeply flavored sauce simply can't be achieved
any other way. At home, you could make a good beef or veal stock (without
necessarily cooking it 12 hours) and reduce it by at least half for a decent substitute.
Or look for demi-glace at gourmet food shops.

2 large portobello mushrooms	2 cups veal demi-glace
½ cup olive oil	2 large russet potatoes, scrubbed
3 tablespoons white wine vinegar	Salt and freshly ground black pepper
9 shallots: 3 minced, 4 sliced, 2 whole	2 tablespoons clarified butter or olive oil
2 cloves garlic, minced	1 pound spinach (about 1 bunch), washed
1 teaspoon thyme leaves, plus 1 sprig thyme	and dried, tough stem ends trimmed
1 cup cabernet sauvignon or other hardy	1½ pounds sashimi-grade ahi tuna, cut in
red wine	8 medallions
½ cup red wine vinegar	6 ounces fresh foie gras, cut in 4 equal pieces

TRIM THE STEMS from the portobello mushrooms and set the stems aside for adding
to the red wine sauce. Cut the mushroom caps into ½-inch slices. In a large bowl, combine ¼ cup of the olive oil, the white wine vinegar, half of the minced shallots, the garlic,
and thyme leaves and stir to mix. Add the mushroom slices, toss to evenly coat, and set
aside to marinate for at least 2 hours, tossing occasionally.

CHOP THE RESERVED MUSHROOM STEMS and put them in a medium saucepan
with the sliced shallots and 1 tablespoon of the remaining olive oil. Cook over medium
heat until tender, 2 to 3 minutes. Add the wine and red wine vinegar, bring to a boil, and
boil until reduced by about one-third, about 5 minutes. Add the demi-glace and the
thyme sprig, return to a boil, and reduce by about half, 8 to 10 minutes. Strain and set the
sauce aside in a warm place.

PREHEAT THE OVEN to 400°F.

WHILE THE SAUCE IS REDUCING, peel the potatoes and grate them. Grate the whole shallots as well. Combine the potatoes and shallots in a large bowl, season to taste with salt and pepper, and toss to mix well. Working one handful at a time, grab some of the potato mixture and squeeze it over the sink to extract as much liquid as possible. Heat 1 tablespoon of the clarified butter in a small skillet, preferably nonstick, over medium-high heat. Add half of the potato mixture, pressing it out into an even layer about 6 inches across, with tidy edges. Brown well, about 3 minutes on each side, then transfer the potato cake to a baking sheet. Repeat with the remaining clarified butter and potato mixture. Bake the potato cakes until cooked through and tender, 10 to 15 minutes. Cut each cake into 4 wedges and keep them warm in the oven (turned off).

HEAT ABOUT 1 CUP OF WATER in a large skillet over medium-high heat. When hot, add the spinach leaves, reduce the heat to medium, and cook until the spinach is tender, stirring occasionally, about 2 to 3 minutes. Drain the spinach and set aside to cool. When cool enough to handle, squeeze out all excess liquid. Heat 1 tablespoon of the remaining olive oil in the same skillet, add the spinach and remaining minced shallots, and warm over medium heat, stirring often. Season to taste with salt and pepper; set aside in the oven to keep warm.

PREHEAT A GRILL OR BROILER. Take the mushroom slices from the marinade and grill or broil them until just tender, 3 to 4 minutes per side. When cool enough to handle, cut the slices into ½ inch dice. Add the diced mushrooms to the red wine sauce and gently reheat.

RUB THE TUNA PIECES with the remaining 2 tablespoons olive oil and season the pieces with salt and pepper. Grill or broil the pieces until browned on the outside but still rare, 1 to 2 minutes per side for a piece about 2 inches thick.

JUST AFTER PUTTING THE TUNA on the grill, preheat a heavy skillet over high heat. Add the foie gras pieces to the hot pan and sear until well browned, about 1 minute per side, then take the pan from the heat.

TO SERVE, arrange 2 potato wedges on each of 4 individual plates and top the wedges with the spinach. Set the grilled tuna on the spinach and lay the foie gras over the tuna. Add the foie gras fat from the skillet to the red wine sauce (optional, for extra richness) and add salt and pepper to taste. Spoon the warm sauce over all.

Makes 4 servings

HAND-CUT LEMON PASTA

with Cold-Smoked Salmon

Jammin' Salmon, Sacramento

At this popular riverside restaurant, cold-smoked salmon
(such as lox) is served very thinly sliced atop the lemon-flavored pasta. You could also
use pieces of hot smoked salmon or cooked regular salmon. Because the delicate rich
flavor and texture of cold-smoked salmon quickly changes when it's heated, the
salmon is set on top of the pasta just before serving.

4 tablespoons extra virgin olive oil	*1 teaspoon minced garlic*
1 small red onion, thinly sliced	*¼ cup dry white wine*
½ cup loosely packed slivered fresh spinach	*2 tablespoons finely slivered basil*
½ cup slivered asparagus	*Salt and freshly ground black pepper*
2 tablespoons capers	*4–8 ounces cold-smoked salmon, thinly sliced*

LEMON PASTA

Juice and grated zest of 1 large lemon	*1 teaspoon salt*
3 eggs	*1½ cups semolina flour*
1 teaspoon olive oil	*1½ cups all-purpose flour*

FOR THE PASTA, combine half of the lemon juice, the lemon zest, eggs, olive oil, and
salt in the bowl of a mixer fitted with the paddle attachment. Blend until well mixed, then
add the flours, a little at a time, mixing until evenly blended. Change to the dough hook
attachment and knead the dough until it is smooth and satiny, about 5 minutes. Cut the
dough into quarters, cover with a cloth, and let sit for 30 minutes to rest before rolling.

BRING A LARGE POT of salted water to a boil.

WHILE THE WATER IS HEATING, use a hand-cranked pasta machine to roll out each
quarter of the dough to a thickness of about ¹⁄₁₆ inch (to setting 5 or 6). Using a ridged
pasta cutter or a sharp knife, cut the dough into strips 1 to 1½ inches wide and about
12 inches long. When the water comes to a rolling boil, add the pasta and cook until just
al dente, 2 to 3 minutes. Drain well and set aside.

HEAT 2 TABLESPOONS OF THE OLIVE OIL in a large, heavy skillet. Add the onion, spinach, asparagus, capers, and garlic and sauté over medium heat, stirring often, until slightly tender, 2 to 3 minutes. Add the wine, remaining lemon juice, and basil. Season to taste with salt and pepper and stir in the remaining olive oil. Add the cooked, drained pasta and toss to mix. Arrange the pasta on 4 individual plates, top with the smoked salmon, and serve right away.

Makes 4 servings

SKILLET-ROASTED SCALLOPS
with Curried Leeks and Blood Orange Sauce

The Lark Creek Inn, Larkspur

Sous-chef Jeremy Sewall created this recipe for something special on the
day that he proposed to his girlfriend. It very much represents chef/owner Bradley
Ogden's style and motto: "Keep it light, keep it simple." Chef Sewall originally made
the recipe with Maine Diver scallops, a true seafood delicacy gathered by hand in
Maine's cold waters, but home cooks on the West Coast might have difficulty finding
those scallops. You could use any large sea scallops, or even smaller bay scallops,
but reduce the cooking time accordingly to about 1 minute per side.

2 large leeks	*1 tablespoon curry powder*
2½ cups freshly squeezed blood orange juice	*Kosher salt and freshly ground black pepper*
or regular orange juice	*2–3 tablespoons olive oil*
3 sprigs thyme	*10 ounces large sea scallops*
4 tablespoons unsalted butter,	
at room temperature	

TRIM THE ROOT END and dark green leaves from the leeks. Split the leeks in half
lengthwise and rinse under cold water to remove all the dirt. Pat dry with paper towels
and cut the leeks into ¼-inch slices. Set aside.

COMBINE THE ORANGE JUICE and thyme in a small, heavy saucepan and boil until
reduced to about ½ cup, 20 to 30 minutes. Strain the juice and return it to the saucepan.
Set aside.

HEAT 2 TABLESPOONS OF THE BUTTER over medium heat and add the sliced
leeks. Cook gently, stirring often, for 3 minutes. Add the curry powder with salt to taste
and continue cooking until the leeks are tender, about 5 minutes longer.

WHILE THE LEEKS ARE COOKING, heat the olive oil in a large, heavy skillet, preferably cast iron, over high heat. Season the scallops with salt and pepper. When the oil just
begins to smoke, carefully add the scallops and cook until well browned, 1 to 2 minutes
on each side. The center of the scallops should remain slightly translucent.

WHILE THE SCALLOPS ARE COOKING, return the reduced juice to a boil. Take the pan from the heat and whisk in the remaining 2 tablespoons of the butter. Season the sauce to taste with salt and pepper.

SPOON THE LEEKS into the center of 2 warmed plates and top with the scallops. Spoon the blood orange sauce around and serve right away.

Makes 2 servings

NOT ONLY NAVEL: SPECIALTY CITRUS

Blood oranges (*Citrus sinensis*) grow well in Northern California and have been well received by the public. Crops have increased markedly in size and quality from those of twenty years ago. The Moro, Tarocco, and Sanguinelli span the season from January through March. Many find the lightly colored Moro pleasant, if not distinguished. Tarocco has a sugar-acid ratio and sprightly flavor that serves well for juice and desserts, as well as for sauces for savory dishes. Sanguinelli has the deepest red flesh and rind, with a distinctive spicy aroma and mild flavor.

The *C. reticulata* family contains mandarins and tangerines. Mandarins are the early-appearing, zip-peel, virtually seedless fruit popular for out-of-hand eating, garnishes, and fruit salads. Satsumas are the best varieties here; they have excellent low-acid flavor and a short December and January season. Several citrus hybrids are marketed as tangerines, including the tangors, the tangelos, and some mandarins. The Fairchild, Dancy, and honey clementine are grown locally. The season runs from December through March.

You can buy ordinary citron (*C. media*) to candy your own peel and the large segmented variety, Buddha's hand or bushukan, to scent your dining room with a dramatic centerpiece. Pomelo and pummelo are the same fruit, *C. grandis*. Though the pomelo resembles the grapefruit, it is less acid and less juicy, with a less bitter rind. After the flesh is eaten fresh or made into jam, the rind can be candied like citron; or the whole fruit can be made into marmalade. Kumquats finish the winter season with a flourish. They are in the citrus family and somewhat related in flavor and appearance but of a different genus, *Fortunella*. The combination of sweet rind and tart flesh in the kumquat is a surprise to those who haven't eaten one before. Because kumquats fill the palate with lingering flavor, they are used as an accent garnish with both sweet and savory dishes.

PAN-SEARED BODEGA BAY SALMON
with Fennel Cream Sauce

Huckleberry Springs Country Inn, Monte Rio

This is a wonderfully simple recipe with delicious results. Rich, yes,
with a delicate creamy sauce served with salmon, but the anise flavor from the fresh
fennel and a splash of Pernod complement the rich flavors beautifully. During the
summer, the inn chefs garnish the dish with fronds from wild fennel
that grows abundantly nearby.

2 tablespoons unsalted butter
½ large or 1 small fennel bulb, trimmed,
cored, and thinly sliced, fronds
reserved for garnish
1 tablespoon minced shallot
1 cup chicken stock, preferably homemade
¼ cup plus 2 tablespoons dry white wine
¼ cup whipping cream

1 teaspoon Pernod or other anise liqueur
Dash hot pepper sauce
Salt and freshly ground black pepper
1 tablespoon olive oil
4 salmon fillet pieces (about 6 ounces each),
skin and pin bones removed
Lemon wedges, for serving

HEAT 1 TABLESPOON OF THE BUTTER in a medium saucepan over medium heat.
Add the fennel and shallot and sauté until tender, about 5 minutes. Add the chicken stock
and ¼ cup of the wine, bring to a boil, and simmer until the liquids are reduced by about
half, 6 to 8 minutes. Whisk in the remaining butter, followed by the cream. Return the
mixture to a boil and simmer until the sauce thickens slightly, whisking often, about 3
minutes. Take from the heat and whisk in the Pernod and hot sauce, with salt and pepper
to taste. Set aside over low heat to keep warm.

HEAT A LARGE, HEAVY SKILLET over medium-high heat, then add the olive oil and
heat until nearly smoking. Add the salmon fillets fleshy side down and sear until nicely
browned, about 3 minutes. Turn the fillets and continue cooking for 2 minutes. Add the
remaining 2 tablespoons of the wine to the pan, take from the heat, cover, and let sit for
3 minutes. (If your salmon fillets are quite thick, you may need to heat the pan a couple
of extra minutes to cook the salmon to your taste.)

TO SERVE, arrange the salmon on 4 individual plates and spoon the sauce partly over and around the fish. Garnish the plate with fennel fronds and serve with lemon wedges for squeezing.

Makes 4 servings

WATSONVILLE AVOCADOS

Southern California may bring in the bumper crops, but avocados from Watsonville, Santa Cruz County, are an aficionado's dream. They are unctuous and full flavored, owing not only to their cultivar parentage, but also to their long maturing period. At this cool latitude, the avocado fruits stay on the trees an average of 18 months, rather than the 12 of warmer climates, time that allows more complex flavors to develop.

Two cultivars are grown, the Hass and the Bacon. Both trees are quite cold-tolerant and the fruits of both are high in oil content and therefore in flavor. The Hass has received the best press, probably from large Southern California growers, and is preferred by many cooks. It has distinctive purple black, bumpy and thick, leathery skin when ripe. For flavor and keeping qualities, the Bacon is quite comparable. It has thin, smooth, green skin when ripe. The Hass matures in the summer months and the Bacon from November to March.

Since all avocado trees flower in spring and the fruits require about 18 months to mature in Watsonville, any given tree has avocados in various stages of maturity. Growers gauge when to pick by fruit size and weight, taste, and oil content. On the trees, the fruits stay hard; they must be harvested before they can be brought to soft-ripe maturity.

The flesh of these avocados does not blacken, because they are not held under refrigeration. Chefs buy much of the small Watsonville crop, though part finds its way into San Francisco Bay Area homes though local and farmers' markets.

CURRY AND COCONUT
POACHED MONKFISH
with Cilantro-Avocado Butter

Restaurant 301, Carter House Victorians, Eureka

The cilantro and avocado both serve to cool down the fiery taste
of the green curry in this dish. Monkfish, firm and slightly sweet, holds up well to
the pronounced flavors in this recipe, with the added plus of being free of bones.
Depending on the size of the monkfish tail, you may require two or three tail
portions to make the two pounds needed. You could also use halibut,
swordfish, or other firm fish in its place.

Prepared green curry pastes can vary widely in their heat level. Start with the
amount listed here and then add more to taste.

The cilantro-avocado butter makes more than is needed for this recipe, but the
flavorful and brilliant green butter will keep for at least a week and is delicious tossed
on steamed vegetables. Or spread it on toasted bread and top with tiny cooked
shrimp or crabmeat for a tasty appetizer.

2 pounds monkfish, skinned and gray	*1½ teaspoons Thai green curry paste,*
membrane cut away	*plus more to taste*
2 tablespoons finely minced shallot	*1 tablespoon freshly squeezed lime juice*
⅔ cup unsweetened coconut milk	*Cilantro sprigs, for garnish*
1 tablespoon mild curry powder	

CILANTRO-AVOCADO BUTTER

1 small, ripe avocado	*1 tablespoon freshly squeezed lime juice*
½ cup unsalted butter	*Salt and freshly ground black pepper*
3 tablespoons minced cilantro	

PREHEAT THE OVEN to 325°F. Lightly grease a shallow baking dish large enough to
hold the monkfish.

RINSE THE MONKFISH under cold water and pat dry with paper towels. Sprinkle the shallot in the baking dish and lay the monkfish tails over the shallot.

IN A SMALL SAUCEPAN, combine the coconut milk, curry powder, and curry paste. Heat the mixture over medium heat, stirring often, until just simmering, 2 to 3 minutes. Taste for seasoning, adding more curry paste to taste. Pour the mixture over the monkfish and sprinkle 1 tablespoon lime juice over. Cover the dish with a lightly buttered piece of foil and bake the fish until it is just opaque through, 20 to 30 minutes (depending on the size of the monkfish tails).

WHILE THE FISH COOKS, prepare the cilantro-avocado butter. Peel, pit, and dice the avocado. Combine the avocado, butter, cilantro, and lime juice in a food processor and process until smooth. Season to taste with salt and pepper.

USING TWO SLOTTED SPATULAS, transfer the cooked monkfish to a chopping board and cover with the foil to keep warm. Carefully strain the cooking liquids into a small saucepan, bring to a boil, and boil until reduced by about half.

CUT THE MONKFISH into 1-inch slices and arrange them on 4 individual plates. Spoon a little of the reduced cooking liquids over and garnish with the avocado butter and sprigs of cilantro. Serve right away.

Makes 4 servings

SEARED SEA SCALLOPS
with Braised Oxtail

The Palace, Sunnyvale

Surf and turf does have a life beyond T-bone with lobster tail! In this easy preparation, oxtail portions are simmered in cabernet sauvignon to a rich, velvety tenderness. The oxtail meat is paired with the fresh crunch of sautéed mustard greens, topped with big, plump sea scallops.

At The Palace, chef Dennis Iczkowski uses jumbo dayboat scallops, the crème de la crème at generally over 1 ounce each, but choose the biggest and freshest you can find. Fresh scallops should smell sweet, with a subtle aroma of salty sea air. Scallops will continue to cook after they're taken from the pan, so be careful not to overcook them. The chef notes that there's nothing worse than an overcooked, rubbery scallop.

3 tablespoons unsalted butter	*½ teaspoon chopped thyme leaves*
2 pounds oxtail, cut in 1-inch pieces	*3–4 whole black peppercorns*
1 large onion, diced	*1 bottle (750 ml) cabernet sauvignon*
4 stalks celery, diced	*1 tablespoon olive oil*
1 medium carrot, diced	*Salt and freshly ground black pepper*
3 bay leaves	*4–6 large sea scallops (about 6 ounces total)*
3–4 sprigs thyme	

POTATO RÖSTI

1 russet potato (about 8 ounces)	*3 tablespoons olive oil*

SAUTÉED MUSTARD GREENS

1 tablespoon unsalted butter	*1 bunch mustard greens, rinsed, trimmed,*
1 shallot, thinly sliced	*and cut in 1-inch strips*

HEAT THE BUTTER in a sauté pan or large skillet over medium-high heat, add the oxtail, and cook, stirring occasionally, until well browned, about 5 minutes. Add the onion, celery, carrot, bay leaves, thyme sprigs, and peppercorns. Continue cooking, stirring occasionally, until the vegetables are tender and beginning to brown, 3 to 5 minutes longer. Reserve ½ cup of the cabernet sauvignon. Add the rest with enough water to just cover the oxtail. Cover the skillet and simmer gently over medium-low heat until the meat is very tender and falling from the bone, about 3 hours.

WHILE THE OXTAIL IS BRAISING, begin the potato rösti. Put the potato in a pan of cold water and bring to a boil. Reduce the heat and simmer until the potato is very tender (the skin will begin to crack), about 35 minutes. Drain the potato and let cool slightly, then refrigerate until thoroughly chilled, about 2 hours.

WHEN THE OXTAIL IS TENDER, scoop it out with a slotted spoon and set aside to cool. Strain the braising liquids and let sit until the fat has risen to the surface. Spoon away and discard as much of the fat as possible. Put the braising liquids in a small pan and bring to a boil, then simmer until reduced by about two-thirds.

WHEN THE OXTAIL IS COOL enough to handle, pull the meat from the bone and set the meat aside, discarding the bone and as much fat as possible. When the braising liquids have reduced, add the oxtail meat with the thyme leaves and the reserved ½ cup of the cabernet sauvignon. Cook over medium heat until most of the liquid has evaporated and the mixture has a velvety texture, 15 to 20 minutes, stirring occasionally. Season to taste with salt and pepper.

WHILE THE OXTAIL IS HEATING, finish the potato rösti. When the potato is cold, peel away and discard the skin, then coarsely grate the potato onto a large plate or chopping board. Season the pile of grated potato to taste with salt and pepper, tossing gently with your fingers to mix. Form the potato into 2 cakes about ½ inch thick and 3 to 4 inches in diameter. Heat the olive oil in a medium skillet, preferably nonstick, over medium heat. Add the potato cakes and cook until well browned and crisp, 4 to 5 minutes on each side. Transfer the cakes to a plate lined with paper towels and keep warm in a low oven until ready to serve.

FOR THE MUSTARD GREENS, heat the butter in a large skillet over medium heat. Add the shallot and cook until lightly browned and nearly tender, 3 to 5 minutes. Add the mustard greens and continue cooking, stirring often, until the greens are just tender and bright green, 1 to 2 minutes. (You may need to add the greens in a couple of batches, allowing some of the greens to wilt and make room for the rest.) Season to taste with salt and pepper and keep warm over low heat.

HEAT A HEAVY SKILLET over high heat until very hot. Carefully swirl in 1 tablespoon olive oil. Season the scallops with salt and pepper, add them to the hot pan, and sear until well browned, about 1 minute per side, being careful not to overcook.

TO SERVE, put the potato rösti in the bottom of 2 large shallow bowls or rimmed plates. Set the sautéed mustard greens on top of the rösti and spoon the oxtail mixture around. Set the seared scallops on top of the greens and serve.

Makes 2 servings

LATIN AMERICAN INGREDIENTS

Shopping in the Mission District of San Francisco or in Mexican stores in San Jose, Santa Cruz, or Salinas is like being in a *mercado*, with every flavoring necessary to make delicious dishes from many regions of Mexico. Tamarind comes in fresh pods or in pulp (with or without seeds) to make tamarind juice for flavoring main dishes and for beverages. Jars of *cajeta*, caramel syrup from goat and cow milk, are ready to spread on bread or to flavor custards. *Piloncillo,* pressed unrefined brown sugar, stands piled in small truncated cones to sweeten beverages and desserts.

Chiles of all sizes, colors, and shapes can be found in the bulk dried section for moles and sauces, in the canned goods for relishes and winter salsas, and in the produce department for rellenos, salsas, and pico di gallos in season. Also in season are tomatillos, for lightly roasting and then making into mole verde or salsa; plantains, for frying and adding to stews and soups; and nopales (cactus pads), for grilling or blanching before making salad or scrambled eggs.

For tamales, the choice is between masa (prepared dough) or masa harina flour, dried corn husks or parchment. Corn and flour tortillas are mostly factory-made, but a few stores occasionally offer handmade tortillas. Many herbs are available, usually fresh for flavoring and dried for tisanes: cilantro for salsas and garnish; epazote for bean dishes; jamaica (hibiscus flower) for a vitamin C–rich tea; manzanilla (chamomile) for a calming tea.

Salvadorean, Guatemalan, and Cuban stores carry many of the same semitropical fruits and vegetables. Spice blends such as adobo, special varieties of dried beans, pickles, and sundry imported ingredients distinguish the cuisines. Among the produce available are yuca or cassava *(Manihot esculenta),* unhusked coconut, and plantains and bananas of different varieties. Most of the tropical tubers resemble potatoes somewhat; each has a distinctive subtle flavor and texture. True yams or ñamé *(Dioscorea alata),* batata dulce or camote *(Ipomoea batatas)* await stewing, baking, deep-frying, boiling, or sautéing, according to the cook's inclination.

SUN-DRIED TOMATO TAMALES
Stuffed with Chicken and Topped with Castroville Avocado Salsa

The Whole Enchilada, Moss Landing

Coarsely ground corn masa is traditionally embellished with lard in tamale recipes, but Chef Luis uses corn oil instead, for a more contemporary approach. Making tamales definitely takes time. Have some friends over and make a party of it, with these delicious tamales (and maybe a few bottles of really cold beer) as a reward.

1 package (8 ounces) dry corn husks	2 large tomatoes, diced
8 ounces sun-dried tomatoes (not oil-packed)	½ onion, diced
3 cups chicken stock, preferably homemade	1 clove garlic, crushed
3 cups water	Salt and freshly ground black pepper
2 pounds corn masa (about 6 cups)	2 pounds boneless, skinless chicken breasts
3 cups corn oil	2 tablespoons vegetable oil
1 tablespoon sugar	¼ cup chopped cilantro
1 tablespoon baking powder	

CASTROVILLE AVOCADO SALSA

2 ripe avocados	½ onion, finely diced
¼ cup olive oil	1 cup drained artichoke hearts in water, finely diced
¼ cup balsamic vinegar	
Pinch sugar	¼ cup chopped cilantro
1 medium tomato, finely diced	1 clove garlic, minced

FILL A LARGE POT with cold water, add the dried corn husks, and soak overnight. Put the sun-dried tomatoes in a large bowl, add the chicken stock and water, and soak overnight as well. (For a shortcut, you could pour hot water over the husks and let them sit for a couple of hours; heat the chicken stock and water to a boil, pour the liquids over the sun-dried tomatoes in a large bowl, and let sit for about 1½ hours to plump.)

RINSE THE HUSKS WELL and cut off the tip of each husk. Cut any oversized husks in half lengthwise. Dry well with paper towels and set aside. Drain the sun-dried tomatoes, reserving the liquids, and purée half of them in a food processor or blender with 2 cups of the soaking liquids. Finely chop the remaining sun-dried tomatoes.

PUT THE PURÉED AND CHOPPED sun-dried tomatoes in a very large bowl, and gradually stir in the masa and corn oil, adding the sugar and baking powder about halfway through. Stir to mix well. Set aside.

HALF-FILL A LARGE SAUTÉ PAN or saucepan with water, add the tomatoes, onion, and garlic, with salt and pepper to taste, and bring to a boil. Add the chicken breasts, lower the heat to medium, and simmer until the chicken is just cooked through, 15 to 20 minutes. Take out the chicken breasts and set aside to cool, reserving the cooking liquids. Scoop the tomato, onion, and garlic into a food processor or blender, add ½ cup of the cooking liquids, and purée.

WHEN THE CHICKEN IS COOL enough to handle, finely shred it. Heat the vegetable oil in a large skillet over medium heat. Add the chicken and tomato purée and cook, stirring, until the liquids are almost fully evaporated, 10 to 12 minutes. Set aside to cool, then stir in the cilantro.

CUT THIN STRIPS from a few of the corn husks to use as ties for the tamales. Spread 3 to 4 tablespoons of the prepared masa evenly across one of the corn husks, almost to the edge but with at least 1 inch of each end open. Spoon 2 to 3 tablespoons of the chicken stuffing down the center. Fold the sides of the husk over the filling, overlapping the edges. Tie the ends with husk strips. Repeat with the remaining masa and filling. (You should get about 36 tamales.)

BRING A FEW INCHES OF WATER to a boil in a large steamer pot. Cover the steamer rack with corn husks and arrange the tamales on top, preferably upright. Cover the tamales with more corn husks and a dish towel. Put the lid on the steamer and steam until the husk can easily be peeled from one of the tamales, about 1½ hours. Keep an eye on the water level in the pot, adding more hot water as needed.

WHILE THE TAMALES ARE STEAMING, prepare the salsa. Peel, pit, and coarsely chop the avocados and put them in a food processor with the olive oil, vinegar, and sugar, with salt and pepper to taste. Process until smooth, then transfer to a large bowl. Stir in the tomato, onion, artichoke hearts, cilantro, and garlic.

TO SERVE, arrange the tamales, husks partially opened, on 8 individual plates. Top with a spoonful of the salsa and pass extra salsa alongside.

Makes 8 servings

TEQUILA-MARINATED CORNISH HEN

Las Camelias Mexican Restaurant, San Rafael

For big appetites, you could increase the number of hens to four and
serve them whole.

*2 Cornish hens (about 1½ pounds each),
rinsed and dried*

MARINADE

½ cup tequila	*¼ cup chopped onion*
¼ cup chopped garlic	*1½ cups water*
¼ cup chopped ginger	*Kosher salt and freshly ground black pepper*

SAUCE

1 pound tomatoes	*¼ cup minced cilantro*
1 tablespoon unsalted butter	*1–2 pickled jalapeño chiles, thinly sliced*
4 ounces mushrooms, trimmed and	*and seeded*
thinly sliced	

FOR THE MARINADE, combine the tequila, garlic, ginger, and onion in a food
processor or blender and blend until smooth. Add the water and pulse just to mix. Arrange
the hens in a pot deep enough to hold them snugly. Pour the purée over the hens and
season them with ½ teaspoon salt and ⅛ teaspoon pepper. Cover and marinate in the
refrigerator for at least 8 hours or overnight.

AFTER THE HENS HAVE MARINATED, preheat the oven to 375°F.

TAKE THE HENS from the marinade, reserving the marinade. Arrange the hens on a
roasting pan and roast until no pink juices appear when the thighs are pierced with a
sharp knife, about 1 hour. (Or you could check by lifting a hen above the roasting pan
and tilting juices out of the cavity; they should be clear, not pink.)

WHILE THE HENS ARE COOKING, prepare the sauce. Bring a medium pan of water
to a boil and prepare a large bowl of ice water. With the tip of a sharp knife, score a small

"X" on the bottom of each tomato. Add the tomatoes to the boiling water and blanch until the skin begins to split, 20 to 30 seconds. Scoop the tomatoes out with a slotted spoon and put them in the ice water for quick cooling. When cool, drain the tomatoes, then peel away and discard the skin. Quarter the tomatoes lengthwise, and scoop out and discard the seeds. Put the tomato pieces in a large bowl and mash them with a potato masher or a large fork.

WHEN THE HENS ARE COOKED, drain any cavity juices into the pan and set the hens aside on a platter, covered with foil to keep warm, reserving the cooking juices.

HEAT THE BUTTER in a large skillet over medium heat. Add the mushrooms and cook, stirring, until tender, 3 to 4 minutes. Add the mashed tomatoes and cook for 6 to 8 minutes longer. Stir in the cilantro and jalapeños and cook for 1 to 2 minutes. Add the reserved marinade with the reserved pan juices from roasting the hens and bring to a boil. Boil the sauce until thickened, stirring occasionally, about 15 minutes. Taste the sauce for seasoning, adding salt and pepper if needed.

WHILE THE SAUCE IS FINISHING, halve the hens with a large chef's knife or heavy kitchen shears. For extra crispness, you could sauté the halves in butter or broil briefly before serving. Arrange the hen halves on 4 individual plates, spoon the sauce over, and serve.

Makes 4 servings

DUCK BREAST

with Mendocino Pinot Noir–Wild Berry Sauce and Wild Mushroom Hash

MacCallum House Restaurant, Mendocino

Almost everything about this recipe reflects the region. Family-owned Sonoma County Liberty Farms provides the duck to MacCallum House, as it does to many top San Francisco Bay Area restaurants. The berries used in the vinegar come from the productive huckleberry bushes and blackberry vines that grow wild in many parts of this coastal area. And the wild mushroom hash combines locally foraged chanterelles and porcinis, which come into season with the first rain each fall. MacCallum House gets most of its mushrooms from Point Arena Gourmet Mushrooms, a small, owner-operated business just down the coast from Mendocino.

Chef Alan Kantor likes to add a good turn of black pepper to the sauce just before serving. "There's a great affinity between black pepper, berries, and duck, which is perfectly complemented by the notes in pinot noir. Don't forget a bottle to serve with dinner!"

The wild mushroom hash can be made a day or two in advance, refrigerated, and reheated just before serving. If wild mushrooms aren't available, you could use regular button mushrooms, shiitake mushrooms, or other cultivated mushrooms in their place. For a lighter version, you could omit the bacon and cook the vegetables in vegetable oil. Just imagine how delicious this hash would be at breakfast, too, with poached or scrambled eggs. Heaven!

4 duck breasts (6 to 8 ounces each)	*½ teaspoon salt*
2 shallots, finely chopped	*½ teaspoon freshly ground black pepper*
1 tablespoon finely chopped sage	*Fresh berries, for garnish*
1 tablespoon vegetable oil	

WILD MUSHROOM HASH

4 ounces bacon, preferably applewood smoked, chopped

1¼ pounds red potatoes (about 3 medium), cut in ½-inch dice

1 medium onion, finely diced

½ pound fresh porcini mushrooms, brushed clean and sliced

½ pound fresh chanterelle mushrooms, brushed clean and sliced

Salt and freshly ground black pepper

PINOT NOIR-WILD BERRY SAUCE

½ cup pinot noir

1 cup duck or chicken stock, preferably homemade

½ cup wild berry vinegar (see next page)

TRIM excess fat and skin from the edges of the duck breasts, if necessary. In a shallow dish, stir together the shallots, sage, oil, salt, and pepper. Add the duck breasts skin side up, rubbing the marinade evenly over them. Cover with plastic wrap and refrigerate for at least a few hours or overnight, allowing the flavors to infuse the duck meat.

WHEN READY TO COOK the duck, heat a large, heavy skillet over high heat until very hot. Take the duck from the marinade, wipe well, and set the breasts skin side up in the pan. Cook, without trying to move the breasts, for 2 minutes. Turn the breasts, reduce the heat to medium and cook until the duck fat under the skin is rendered, the skin is crisp, and the duck is medium done, 20 to 25 minutes.

WHILE THE DUCK IS COOKING, prepare the mushroom hash. Heat a large skillet over high heat, add the bacon, and cook, stirring, until the bacon is browned and crisp, 3 to 5 minutes. Scoop out the bacon with a slotted spoon and set aside in a medium bowl. Spoon out all but about 2 tablespoons of the bacon fat from the skillet and reserve. Add the potatoes and cook over medium-high heat, stirring occasionally, until the potatoes are golden and tender, 10 to 12 minutes. Transfer the potatoes to the bowl with the bacon and set aside. Add 2 tablespoons of bacon fat to the skillet (or oil, if there's not enough bacon fat), add the onion, and cook until lightly browned and tender, 2 to 3 minutes. Add the mushrooms and continue cooking until they are tender, 3 to 5 minutes longer. Return the potatoes and bacon to the skillet and stir to mix well. Season to taste with salt and pepper; keep warm over low heat.

WHEN THE DUCK IS COOKED, transfer the breasts to a plate and cover to keep warm while finishing the sauce. Pour the fat from the skillet and return the skillet to high heat. For the sauce, add the wine to the skillet and bring to a boil, stirring to dissolve flavorful bits stuck to the pan. Add the stock and vinegar, return to a boil, and boil until the mixture is reduced to about ¾ cup. Keep warm over low heat.

SLICE EACH DUCK BREAST on the bias and fan the slices on individual plates. Spoon some of the mushroom hash alongside, drizzle the pinot noir–wild berry sauce over the duck, garnish with berries, and serve right away.

Makes 4 servings

WILD BERRY VINEGAR

This flavored vinegar is a staple for the pinot noir–wild berry sauce served on duck at MacCallum House. Go ahead and use cultivated berries if you can't get wild berries. Extra vinegar will keep for a few weeks, refrigerated in an airtight container. It makes a delicious alternative to other vinegars used for vinaigrette dressing. Have fun experimenting to find your favorite uses for this tasty concoction.

3 cups wild berries (huckleberries, blackberries, or a combination)
½ cup honey

½ cup champagne vinegar or white wine vinegar

COMBINE THE BERRIES AND HONEY in a medium saucepan and cook over medium heat, stirring occasionally, until the honey is melted and the berries are soft, about 5 minutes. Let the berry mixture cool for a few minutes. Transfer to a food processor or blender, add the vinegar, and blend until smooth. Strain the mixture through a very fine sieve to remove the berry seeds, if you like, making sure to press as much pulp through the sieve as possible.

Makes about 3 cups

HYBRID BERRIES, JEWELS IN SUMMER'S CROWN

Rudolf Boysen and J. H. Logan, of Napa and Santa Cruz, gave the world the blackberry-raspberry hybrids that carry their names and spell summer for those who have grown up here. The boysenberry shows its raspberry parentage in aroma and soft flesh and its blackberry in purple black color, tart-sweet balance, and 1¼-inch or longer berries. The loganberry is also large, with an unusual wine maroon color that seems to have a silvery sheen; its flavor is more raspberry than blackberry. The olallieberry is a cross of crosses, progeny of the Logan and another blackberry-raspberry hybrid. It is altogether more at the blackberry end of the spectrum for color and flavor, with an elusive raspberry aroma. Many consider these berries the absolute best for pies, jams, and preserves.

The hybrids are truly special creatures, with flavors and aromas melding in a way that can't be replicated by eating raspberries and blackberries at the same time. Ideally, any blackberry or raspberry should be picked when fully—but not overly—ripe. If anything, this is more true of the hybrids, which show their full natures then. Hybrids are also rather more perishable and rarely shipped. For these berries, like figs, cold storage means they will lose some, if not most, of their flavor and aroma. They are commonly available in June and July.

STUFFED FREE-RANGE CHICKEN
with Garlic Mashed Potatoes

Kirby's Creekside Restaurant, Nevada City

At Kirby's Creekside, the chefs begin with a whole chicken and cut away the breast-wing portions, trimming the small wing tip and leaving the larger wing joint attached to the boneless breast. You could ask the butcher to portion a whole chicken using this technique, or you could simply start with boneless breast portions as we suggest here, though the breasts need to have their skin on.

¼ cup ricotta cheese	4 boneless free-range chicken breasts
2 tablespoons chopped sun-dried tomatoes	(6 to 8 ounces each), skin on
(oil-packed or plumped dried)	4 tablespoons olive oil
1 tablespoon plus 1½ teaspoons minced garlic	2 cups chicken stock, preferably homemade
1 tablespoon minced flat-leaf (Italian) parsley	¼ cup unsalted butter, cut in chunks
1 tablespoon minced chives	(optional, for sauce)
1 tablespoon minced thyme	3 small or 2 medium zucchini, trimmed
Salt and freshly ground black pepper	and thinly sliced lengthwise

GARLIC MASHED POTATOES

2 pounds russet potatoes, peeled and	¼ cup unsalted butter
cut in large chunks	2 tablespoons minced garlic
½ cup milk	

PREHEAT THE OVEN to 375°F.

STIR TOGETHER the ricotta cheese, sun-dried tomatoes, 1½ teaspoons of the garlic, the parsley, chives, and thyme in a small bowl. Season to taste with salt and pepper. Using your fingers, slide this stuffing between the flesh and skin of each breast. Heat 2 tablespoons of the olive oil in a large ovenproof skillet over medium-high heat. Season the stuffed breasts lightly with salt and pepper and add them to the skillet, skin side down. Cook until the breasts are just browned, 1 to 2 minutes. Turn the pieces over and put the skillet in the oven. Bake until the chicken breasts are just cooked through, 20 to 25 minutes.

WHILE THE CHICKEN IS BAKING, make the mashed potatoes. Put the potato chunks in a large pan of lightly salted cold water and bring the water just to a boil. Reduce the heat and simmer until the potatoes are tender, 15 to 20 minutes. When the potatoes are tender, drain well and return them to the pan. Add the milk, butter, and garlic and mash the potatoes with a potato masher or a large, heavy whisk. Season to taste with salt and pepper, adding a bit more milk if the potatoes are too thick. Keep warm over low heat.

HEAT ANOTHER TABLESPOON OF THE OLIVE OIL in a small saucepan over medium heat, add the remaining tablespoon of the garlic, and sauté until light golden, 1 to 2 minutes. Add the chicken stock, bring to a boil, and boil until slightly reduced, 3 to 5 minutes. For a richer sauce, you could whisk in the butter a few pieces at a time over very low heat so it melts creamily into the sauce. Season to taste with salt and pepper.

HEAT THE REMAINING TABLESPOON of the olive oil in a large skillet over medium heat, add the zucchini slices, and sauté until just barely tender, 3 to 5 minutes. Season to taste with salt and pepper.

TO SERVE, place a mound of the mashed potatoes to one side of each of 4 plates and lay the sautéed zucchini slices in a fan pattern alongside. Set a roasted chicken breast over the zucchini, leaning partially against the potatoes, and drizzle the sauce around.

Makes 4 servings

BREAST OF GUINEA HEN

with Organic Greens and Cranberry Vinaigrette

The Covey Restaurant, Quail Lodge, Carmel Valley

Chef Bob Williamson uses Guinea hen grown on a local farm, as well as produce from nearby growers, for this recipe. You could use boneless chicken breasts in place of the Guinea hen breasts, preferably organic free-range.

At the resort, the breasts are seared on a grill and then finished in the oven. We've adapted to sear quickly on top of the stove, then finish cooking in the oven. You could simply grill or bake until just cooked through, rather than combining the two techniques.

*1 medium jewel yam or sweet potato, peeled
and cut in ¼-inch slices
4 boneless Guinea hen breasts
Thyme-infused oil or top-quality
extra virgin olive oil
2 tablespoons butter*

*Kernels cut from 2 ears corn (about 2 cups)
⅓ cup diced tomato
2 tablespoons chopped green onions
1 pound mixed baby organic greens,
rinsed and dried*

CRANBERRY VINAIGRETTE

*1 cup fresh cranberries
½ cup water
¼ cup sugar*

*½ cup vegetable oil
Salt and freshly ground black pepper*

FOR THE VINAIGRETTE, combine the cranberries, water, and sugar in a small saucepan and bring to a boil. Reduce the heat to medium and simmer the cranberries until they are very tender, about 10 minutes. Let cool, then put the cranberry mixture in a blender or food processor with the vegetable oil and blend until smooth. Season to taste with salt and pepper and set aside.

PREHEAT THE OVEN to 375°F.

ARRANGE THE SLICED YAMS on an oiled baking sheet and roast them in the oven until tender, 18 to 20 minutes, turning the slices halfway through. Brush the Guinea hen breasts with the oil and season lightly with salt and pepper. Heat a large, heavy ovenproof skillet over high heat until very hot. Quickly sear both sides of the breasts in the hot skillet, 30 to 60 seconds per side, then transfer the skillet to the oven and bake until the breasts are just cooked through, about 10 minutes longer.

WHILE THE BREASTS ARE COOKING, heat the butter in a medium skillet over medium-high heat. Add the corn kernels, tomato, and green onions and sauté just to warm through. Season to taste with salt and pepper.

IN A LARGE BOWL, toss the greens with some of the vinaigrette. Arrange the greens in the centers of 4 large dinner plates. Spoon the corn mixture over the greens and arrange the roasted yam slices around, drizzling more of the vinaigrette around the salad. Slice each hen breast at a slight angle and arrange it over the corn. Serve right away.

Makes 4 servings

ROASTED OSTRICH LOIN
with Sweet and Sour Sauce

One Market, San Francisco

"Ostrich is very low in fat and full of flavor," notes chef Rabah Abusbaitan from One Market. Despite that, and despite the number of ostrich farms around the country, it can be hard to find in retail markets. You might have to ask your butcher to special-order it for you. Or you could use beef tenderloin in its place.

At One Market, this dish is embellished with gnocchi and a few other additions to the sauce, though this pared-down version is quite good, too.

12 pearl onions, peeled	4 ounces chanterelle mushrooms, trimmed,
1 tablespoon granulated sugar	wiped clean, large mushrooms halved
1 tablespoon unsalted butter	Salt and freshly ground black pepper
1 red bell pepper	2 bunches spinach, cleaned, stems trimmed
3 tablespoons olive oil	4 ostrich loin steaks (6 to 8 ounces each)
8 green onions, white and pale green	
portion only, cut in 2-inch pieces	

SWEET AND SOUR SAUCE

2 tablespoons olive oil	2 cups sherry vinegar
2 shallots, thinly sliced	3 cups veal or beef stock, preferably homemade
½ cup packed brown sugar	2 tablespoons minced chives

FOR THE SAUCE, heat the olive oil in a medium saucepan over medium heat, add the shallots, and sauté until tender and beginning to brown, 4 to 5 minutes. Add the brown sugar, increase the heat to medium-high, and cook, stirring, until the sugar is melted and beginning to bubble, 1 to 2 minutes. Slowly pour in the vinegar, turning your head away slightly so the vapors don't sting your eyes. Bring to a boil and boil until reduced to about ½ cup, 20 to 25 minutes. Add the stock, return to a boil, and boil until reduced to about 1 cup, about 30 minutes. Set aside.

PUT THE PEARL ONIONS in a small saucepan with the granulated sugar, butter, and enough water to just barely cover the onions. Cook over medium heat, stirring occasionally, until the water has evaporated and the onions are tender and caramelized, about 25 minutes.

ROAST THE RED PEPPER over a gas flame or under the broiler until the skin blackens, turning occasionally to roast evenly, 5 to 10 minutes total. Put the pepper in a plastic bag, securely seal it, and set aside to cool. When cool enough to handle, peel away and discard the skin. Remove the core and seeds and cut the pepper into strips. Set aside.

HEAT 1 TABLESPOON OF THE OIL in a medium skillet over medium-high heat. Add the green onion pieces and cook until partly tender and beginning to brown, 2 to 3 minutes. Add the mushrooms and continue cooking until the onions and mushrooms are tender, 2 to 3 minutes longer. Add the roasted pepper strips and toss just to heat through. Season to taste with salt and pepper. Add the vegetables to the sweet and sour sauce, taste the sauce for seasoning, and keep warm over low heat.

HEAT ANOTHER TABLESPOON OF THE OIL in the same skillet (you don't need to clean it out) over medium heat, add the spinach, and sauté until tender but still bright green, stirring often, 1 to 2 minutes. (You may need to add the spinach in a couple of batches, allowing some of the leaves to wilt and make room for the rest.) Season lightly with salt and pepper. Set aside.

PREHEAT THE OVEN to 375°F.

HEAT A LARGE, HEAVY OVENPROOF SKILLET over high heat. When hot, add the remaining tablespoon of the olive oil and turn to evenly coat the bottom of the pan. Season the ostrich steaks with salt and pepper, add them to the hot pan, and sear for about 1 minute on each side. Transfer the skillet to the oven and bake until the ostrich is cooked to your taste, about 5 minutes for rare or 7 minutes for medium-rare to medium. Take the skillet from the oven and let sit for 5 minutes before serving. Gently reheat the caramelized pearl onions and the spinach. Stir the chives into the sauce.

TO SERVE, arrange a pile of sautéed spinach in the centers of 4 large shallow soup bowls or rimmed plates. Cut each ostrich steak on the bias into 4 slices and set the slices on the spinach. Spoon the vegetables and sauce around the spinach, scatter the pearl onions around, and serve right away.

Makes 4 servings

GRILLED RACK OF LAMB

with Roasted Garlic, Whole-Grain Mustard,
and Honey Glaze

Albion River Inn, Albion

Locally raised Anderson Valley gourmet lamb is a terrific choice for this recipe.
Instead of broiling the lamb, you could also grill it for a bit of added flavor.

2 heads garlic	¼ cup balsamic vinegar
1 tablespoon olive oil	2 tablespoons whole-grain mustard
2 tablespoons unsalted butter	1 tablespoon honey, more to taste
2 large shallots, minced	Salt and freshly ground black pepper
6 tablespoons Madeira or dry sherry	2 whole racks of lamb (about 1 pound each),
1 cup veal or beef stock, preferably homemade	trimmed and cut into double chops

PREHEAT THE OVEN to 350°F.

SET THE GARLIC HEADS on a large piece of foil, drizzle the olive oil over, and wrap
securely. Roast the garlic in the oven until soft, 35 to 45 minutes. Take from the oven,
remove the garlic from the foil, and let cool. Squeeze the garlic from the individual cloves
and set aside.

IN A MEDIUM SAUCEPAN, heat the butter over medium-high heat until melted and
just lightly browned. Add the shallots and roasted garlic, reduce the heat to medium, and
cook, stirring, until tender and aromatic, about 2 minutes. Add the Madeira, bring to a
boil, and reduce until the pan is nearly dry, 3 to 5 minutes. Add the stock, vinegar, and
mustard. Bring to a boil and reduce by about half, 5 to 7 minutes. Take the pan from the
heat and stir in the honey, with salt and pepper to taste, adding more honey if desired. Set
aside over very low heat to keep warm, or reheat the sauce just before serving.

PREHEAT THE BROILER.

SEASON THE LAMB CHOPS with salt and pepper and arrange them on a broiler
rack. Broil the lamb about 4 inches from the heat source until cooked to taste: about
3 minutes on each side for rare, 4 minutes for medium-rare, or 5 minutes for medium.

Arrange the lamb chops on 4 warmed individual plates, drizzle the warm sauce over, and serve right away.

Makes 4 servings

GARLIC: GILROY'S GLORY

The midsummer gathering in Gilroy for the Garlic Festival has the flavor of ancient harvest festivals. Those who attend make a kind of pilgrimage for the gathering and sharing of rites. They celebrate—with the farmers, harvesters, braiders, packers, and other townspeople—what the earth gives, and they share the bounty with those in need.

The festival is an exemplar not only to its local fans, but also to small towns with big crops nation- and worldwide. From its beginnings in 1979 as a fund-raiser for high school band uniforms, the festival has taken on almost mythic status, inspiring dozens of towns across the United States to make the most of their main crops, whether cherries or collards. For the first festival, local farmers donated enough garlic to feed a few thousand, volunteers prepared the food, local television spread the word, and Gilroy launched into glory.

What makes it all possible is garlic. The humble yet magical allium found great growing grounds in Gilroy and enough receptive palates and minds in Northern California to keep the first festival volunteers recycling 3,000 tickets for 20,000 people. Now more than 150,000 people each year pay tribute to Gilroy's garlic; they love the flavor of it, the idea of it, the smell of it, the romance of it.

What also makes it possible is the good folks of Gilroy. More than 4,000 of the town's 30,000 citizens volunteer to help with the festival. Thousands of child, woman, and man years are spent each year in preparation for the three-day party during the last weekend of July. The proceeds from ticket and food sales are divided among volunteer groups according to how much work they contribute.

Organization is so seamless and thorough that the festival conducts international seminars on how to structure volunteer agricultural festivals. Chair positions for committees are four-year commitments, so each chair has a mentor, then performs the same service for the upcoming chair. Gilroy has discovered how small-town community feeling and large-scale monocrop agriculture can come together to benefit both. And how many people love to savor the flavor!

DAUBE PROVENÇAL

Fandango, Pacific Grove

The menu at this popular restaurant on the central coast is richly steeped
with exuberant Mediterranean fare. This rustic beef stew with roots in the south of
France is a perfect example. It's nothing fancy—but perfectly delicious.

Orange adds a subtly sweet flavor and aroma to this rich stew. So the zest pieces
can be easily removed before serving, use a vegetable peeler to peel away broad
strips of zest from the orange.

3½ pounds braising beef, cut in 2-inch cubes	*5 cloves garlic, mashed*
¼ cup olive oil, more if needed	*Peeled zest of 1 orange*
4 slices thick bacon, chopped	*4 cups beef stock, preferably homemade,*
1 onion, quartered	*or water*

MARINADE

2 onions, quartered	*Bouquet garni made from 1 sprig thyme,*
2 carrots, sliced	*1 sprig flat-leaf (Italian) parsley, and*
4 cups dry red wine	*1 bay leaf tied with kitchen string*
½ cup red wine vinegar	*Salt and freshly ground black pepper*

FOR MARINATING THE BEEF, combine the onions, carrots, wine, vinegar, and
bouquet garni with a good pinch of salt and pepper in a large bowl. Add the beef cubes,
stirring gently to mix. Cover and refrigerate overnight.

THE NEXT DAY, scoop the beef cubes from the marinade with a slotted spoon,
reserving the marinade and vegetables. Pat the beef dry with paper towels.

HEAT THE OLIVE OIL in a Dutch oven or another large, heavy pot over medium heat.
Add the bacon and cook, stirring, until the bacon is softened, 3 to 4 minutes. Add the
onion and cook until lightly browned, stirring often, about 5 to 7 minutes. Scoop out the
onion and bacon and set aside. Increase the heat to medium-high and brown the beef
cubes in batches, adding a bit more oil as needed. Return all the beef cubes to the pot
with the sautéed onion and bacon, add the garlic and orange zest, and cook, stirring

occasionally, for 5 minutes. Carefully pour over the reserved marinade and vegetables, bring to a boil, and boil until the liquid is reduced by about half, about 30 minutes. Add the stock, reduce the heat to medium-low, and simmer, partly covered, until the beef is very tender and the juices are well flavored, 2 to 2½ hours.

Makes 4 to 6 servings

PORK FRICASSEE
with Biscuit Topping

Bubba's Diner, San Anselmo

This hearty diner dish is a tasty variation on the chicken pot pie, with a rich pork mixture crowned with crumbled, cooked biscuit for a crisp—rather than soft—biscuit topping. At Bubba's, the dish is served with a sweet, slightly tangy apple butter alongside, echoing that longtime favorite pair of pork chops and applesauce. The pork mixture can be made up to a day in advance and refrigerated, then reheated and topped with biscuit just before baking.

2½ pounds pork roast, cut in 1-inch cubes

Salt and freshly ground black pepper

¼ cup vegetable oil

1 large sweet potato (about 1¼ pounds), peeled and diced

1 large onion, cut in 1-inch dice

2 large carrots, chopped

4 stalks celery, chopped

8 ounces mushrooms, wiped clean and sliced

4 tablespoons unsalted butter

2 tablespoons minced garlic

½ cup all-purpose flour

4 cups chicken stock, preferably homemade

2 tablespoons minced sage

Pinch cayenne pepper

BISCUIT TOPPING

2 cups all-purpose flour

½ cup unsalted butter, cut in pieces and chilled

2 teaspoons baking powder

1½ teaspoons sugar

½ teaspoon baking soda

¼ teaspoon salt

¾ cup buttermilk

PREHEAT THE OVEN to 375°F. Lightly grease a heavy baking sheet.

FOR THE BISCUIT TOPPING, combine the flour, butter, baking powder, sugar, baking soda, and salt in a food processor and pulse just until the mixture has a crumbly texture. Transfer the mixture to a bowl and stir in the buttermilk just until evenly blended. Take care not to overmix, or the biscuits will be heavy and tough. Turn the dough onto a lightly floured work surface and very gently knead for a few turns to smooth the dough. Press the dough into a rectangle about 1 inch thick. Cut 6 biscuits, about 3 inches square.

ARRANGE THE BISCUITS on the baking sheet and bake until puffed and browned, about 20 minutes. Set aside to cool.

SEASON THE PORK CUBES generously with salt and pepper. Heat the oil in a large, heavy pot, such as a Dutch oven, over medium-high heat. Working in batches, add the pork and brown well on all sides, 3 to 5 minutes total. Return all the pork cubes to the pot and add the sweet potato, onion, carrots, celery, mushrooms, butter, and garlic. Cook, stirring, until the vegetables begin to soften, about 5 minutes. Stir in the flour until evenly blended. Then stir in the stock, scraping up flavorful bits stuck to the bottom of the pan. Bring just to a boil, stir in the sage, then reduce the heat, and simmer until the pork is cooked through and the mixture is thickened and well flavored, about 30 minutes. Season to taste with cayenne, salt, and pepper.

PREHEAT THE OVEN to 400°F.

SPOON THE PORK MIXTURE into 6 individual deep baking dishes or into 1 large baking dish. Crumble the cooked biscuits evenly over (if you're using 1 big dish, you may not need all 6 biscuits) and bake until the topping is crisp, 10 to 15 minutes. Transfer the individual baking dishes to plates for easy serving, or spoon the fricassee from the large dish onto individual plates, and serve right away.

Makes 6 servings

SLOW-BRAISED VEAL CHEEKS
with Horseradish Whipped Potatoes

Montrio, Monterey

Chefs prize veal cheeks because of their firm texture that cooks to a supple tenderness when slowly braised in flavorful liquids. Not all butchers carry these, so you may have to special-order them. In place of the veal cheeks, chef Tony Baker suggests using lamb sirloin, though the recipe would be delicious with other braising meats as well. Veal cheeks come in perfect portion sizes, but if you use another variety of meat, cut it in roughly 2-inch square pieces.

At Montrio, the cheeks are wood-grilled before braising.
You can certainly do that as well, but to make things a bit simpler, we've adapted the recipe to all be done at the stove.

3 tablespoons olive oil, more if needed	*2 medium onions, 1 coarsely chopped, 1 diced*
2½ pounds veal cheeks	*3 cloves garlic, crushed*
Salt and freshly ground black pepper	*1 bunch thyme*
3 large carrots, 2 coarsely chopped, 1 diced	*½ cup sherry vinegar*
4 large stalks celery, 2 coarsely chopped, 2 diced	*1 bottle (12 ounces) dark ale*
	4 cups veal or beef stock, preferably homemade

HORSERADISH WHIPPED POTATOES

1½ pounds russet potatoes, peeled and quartered	*¼ cup unsalted butter*
½ cup half-and-half or milk	*2 tablespoons prepared horseradish*

PREHEAT THE OVEN to 300°F.

HEAT 2 TABLESPOONS OF THE OLIVE OIL in a heavy roasting pan over medium-high heat. Season the veal cheeks with salt and pepper and brown them well, about 2 minutes on each side. Set them aside on a plate. Add the coarsely chopped carrots, celery, and onion and the garlic to the roasting pan. Cook, stirring, until the vegetables begin to soften and lightly color. Set aside a few thyme sprigs for garnish and add the rest to the pan. Deglaze the pan with the sherry vinegar, stirring to lift up cooked bits from the bottom of the pan. Add the ale and boil until reduced by about two-thirds, about 5 minutes, then add the veal stock. Return the veal cheeks to the pan, with any accumulated juices, and braise in the oven until very tender, 3 to 4 hours (depending on the meat used).

ABOUT 30 MINUTES before serving, prepare the whipped potatoes. Put the potatoes in a large pot of cold salted water and bring to a boil. Reduce the heat and simmer until the potatoes are tender, 15 to 20 minutes. Drain the potatoes well and whip them with the half-and-half, butter, and horseradish in a mixer or with a large whisk until fluffy. Season the potatoes to taste with salt and pepper; cover and keep warm.

TRANSFER THE VEAL CHEEKS to a plate, cover, and set aside. Carefully strain the cooking liquids from the roasting pan into a bowl, discarding the vegetables. In a medium saucepan, heat the remaining tablespoon of olive oil over medium heat and sauté the diced carrot, celery, and onion until tender, about 5 minutes. Add the strained cooking liquids, bring to a boil, and boil until slightly thickened, 5 to 10 minutes. Taste the sauce for seasoning, adding salt and pepper to taste.

TO SERVE, spoon a mound of the horseradish whipped potatoes into the centers of 4 individual plates and top with the veal cheeks. Pour the sauce over and around, and garnish with thyme sprigs.

Makes 4 servings

PAVÉ DE BOEUF GRATINÉ AU CHEVRE

(Top Sirloin with Goat Cheese and Ratatouille)

Le Bilig, Auburn

At Le Bilig, the ratatouille is served sandwiched between
triangles of crisp puff pastry, and you can serve it the same way at home if you like.
The ratatouille recipe makes a generous amount, and you may have some left over.
It would be great tossed in pasta the next day.

The beef of choice for chef Marc Deconinck is from Niman Ranch, north of San
Francisco, and the goat cheese is from Laura Chenel, a Sonoma goat cheese producer
who is nationally recognized as a top American cheesemaker.

¼ cup pine nuts	*2 tablespoons olive oil*
2 tablespoons chopped tarragon	*2 cups veal or beef stock, preferably homemade*
6–7 ounces fresh goat cheese	*2–4 tablespoons unsalted butter*
4 top sirloin steaks (6 to 8 ounces each)	*Herb sprigs, for garnish*

RATATOUILLE

1 red bell pepper	*2 medium zucchini, trimmed and diced*
2 tablespoons olive oil	*6 plum (roma) tomatoes, peeled and diced*
1 large onion, chopped	*¼ cup chopped mixed herbs (thyme, sage,*
½ medium fennel bulb, trimmed,	*basil, and/or tarragon)*
cored, and chopped	*6 cloves garlic, minced*
2 small shallots, chopped	*Salt and freshly ground black pepper*
1 medium eggplant, trimmed and diced	

FOR THE RATATOUILLE, roast the bell pepper over a gas flame or under the broiler
until the skin blackens, turning occasionally to roast evenly, 5 to 10 minutes total. Put the
pepper in a plastic bag, securely seal it, and set aside to cool. When cool enough to handle,
peel away and discard the skin. Remove the core and seeds and chop the pepper. Set aside.

HEAT THE OLIVE OIL in a large saucepan over medium heat. Add the onion, fennel
bulb, and shallots and sauté, stirring often, until tender and aromatic, about 10 minutes. Add
the eggplant and cook until beginning to soften and lightly browned, about 10 minutes.

Stir in the zucchini, tomatoes, roasted bell pepper, herbs, and garlic. Continue cooking, stirring occasionally, until the vegetables are tender, about 20 minutes. Season the ratatouille to taste with salt and pepper. Set aside.

COMBINE THE PINE NUTS and tarragon on the chopping board and finely chop them together until well blended. If the goat cheese you're using isn't already in a cylindrical shape, form the cheese into a cylinder about 2 inches in diameter in a piece of plastic wrap. With a sharp knife, slice the cheese into 4 rounds. Discard the wrapping, then press the cheese into the pine nut–tarragon mixture to coat both sides. Set aside.

PREHEAT THE OVEN to 350°F.

SEASON THE SIRLOIN STEAKS with salt and pepper. Heat a large, heavy ovenproof skillet over high heat until very hot, swirl in the olive oil, and add the steaks. Sear the meat until well browned, about 2 minutes on each side, then top each steak with a slice of the goat cheese. Transfer the skillet to the oven and bake until the steaks are cooked to taste, about 5 minutes for rare, 7 minutes for medium-rare, or 10 minutes for medium. (Note that exact cooking time will depend on the thickness of the steaks; be sure to check as they cook.)

WHILE THE MEAT IS COOKING, bring the stock to a boil in a small pan and boil until reduced by about half. Take the pan from the heat, add the butter to taste, and swirl the pan to gently melt the butter into the reduced stock. Season to taste with salt and pepper. Reheat the ratatouille.

ARRANGE THE STEAKS on 4 individual plates and drizzle with the reduced stock. Spoon the ratatouille alongside, garnish the plate with herb sprigs, and serve.

Makes 4 servings

FRUIT AND SPICE LAMB SHANKS

Dorrington Hotel & Restaurant, Dorrington

The sweet tang of dried fruit and the warmth of spices are a perfect match
for lamb, the flavors all marrying beautifully after a long simmer together. This dish
would be great with rice pilaf or couscous alongside.

4 lamb shanks (about 5 pounds total)	*3–4 tablespoons sugar (optional)*
Salt and freshly ground black pepper	*2 tablespoons vinegar*
3 tablespoons olive oil	*½ teaspoon ground allspice*
1½ cups water	*½ teaspoon ground cinnamon*
1 cup dried apricots	*¼ teaspoon ground cloves*
1 cup prunes	

SEASON THE LAMB SHANKS well with salt and pepper. Heat the oil in a large, heavy
pot, such as a Dutch oven, over medium-high heat. Add the shanks 2 at a time and brown
them well on all sides, about 5 minutes total. Set the shanks aside on a plate. Add the
remaining ingredients to the pot and bring just to a boil. Reduce the heat to medium-
low and return the shanks to the pot. Cover with a tight-fitting lid and simmer until the
lamb is very tender, about 2 hours.

TRANSFER THE LAMB SHANKS to 4 individual plates, spoon the fruit and some of
the cooking liquids over, and serve.

Makes 4 servings

CHERRIES, APRICOTS, AND PLUOTS
BLOSSOM IN THE VALLEYS

When stone fruit and nut orchards covered the Silicon Valley, it was called Blossom Valley. Now the orchards have moved east to still-rural valleys that send the luscious cherries and apricots back to specialty and farmers' markets of the peninsular valley.

Sweet cherries *(Prunus avium)* have an all-too-brief season, mainly in June. Growers have been extending fresh cherry availability by planting more varieties. Favored purples are Duke, Bing, Blackheart, Tartarian, and Lambert. Yellow cherry favorites are Rainier and Royal Ann. Local sour cherries are seldom seen, though some imported Montmorency and Morellos show up in August.

Apricots *(Armenaica vulgaris)* were one of the main Blossom Valley crops, destined principally for the canneries during the first half of the century when canned fruit was a delicacy and one of the few ways in which people could enjoy fruits that didn't grow in their area. Locals wax nostalgic over the scent of apricot blossoms and tree-ripe fruit; some swear that Blenheim (also called Royal) is the best—others, Moorpark. A fine-flavored Iranian introduction, Ram Roc, is beginning to appear. Local apricots are mainly available in June and July.

Luther Burbank did many things to benefit fruits, vegetables, and humankind in Santa Rosa in the early twentieth century; hybridization of the pluot was one. In his day, the fruit was known as the *plumcot* or *aprium,* but the favored general term has become *pluot.* These are apricot-plum crosses. Varieties usually fall into the flavor-and-appearance camp of one of their parents. The Apex, one of Burbank's, is occasionally available in June; it has an apricot perfume and texture. Many pluots ripen later, in July. These cultivars have yellow or purple skin or flesh or a combination, like plums. The best—such as Rutland, another one Burbank developed—have a rich blend of apricot and plum flavor.

GRILLED PEPPERED T-BONE STEAKS
with Cherry-Lavender Relish

Restaurant 301, Carter House Victorians, Eureka

When buying balsamic vinegar, look for aged vinegar from the Modena region of Italy, which is where true balsamic vinegar is produced. The real thing is worth the extra expense—true balsamic is aged for up to 20 years (and longer) and develops a beautiful, mellow balance of sweet-sour flavors and velvety richness.

Bringing the meat to room temperature shortly before grilling will help ensure that it grills evenly. If fresh lavender isn't available, use fresh marjoram or rosemary rather than dried lavender.

2 T-bone steaks (12 ounces each), about 1½ inches thick	Coarse sea or kosher salt
2–3 tablespoons black peppercorns, very coarsely ground	1 clove garlic, lightly crushed
	1 tablespoon extra virgin olive oil

CHERRY-LAVENDER RELISH

1½ cups fresh Bing or Royal Ann cherries, halved and pitted	1 teaspoon finely minced ginger
1 cup off-dry young red wine	1 teaspoon finely minced fresh lavender flowers
1 teaspoon extra virgin olive oil	1 teaspoon balsamic vinegar, plus more to taste
2 tablespoons finely minced shallot	
½ cup diced jicama	
1 tablespoon finely minced or grated orange zest	

FOR THE RELISH, put the cherries in a large bowl, drizzle the red wine over, and let sit at room temperature to macerate for 1 hour. Meanwhile, heat the olive oil in a small skillet over medium heat and sauté the shallot until aromatic and beginning to soften but not browned, 1 to 2 minutes. Set aside.

PREHEAT AN OUTDOOR GRILL.

ABOUT 20 MINUTES before grilling the steaks, strain the cherries through a fine sieve and reserve 3 tablespoons of the macerating liquid. Combine the cherries, shallot, jicama, orange zest, ginger, and the reserved macerating liquid. Toss to mix and set aside.

RUB BOTH SIDES OF THE STEAKS with the pepper. Grill the steaks to taste over the hot grill, about 6 minutes on 1 side and 4 minutes on the other for rare, another 1 to 2 minutes per side for medium-rare to medium. (Reduce the cooking time if your steaks are less than 1½ inches thick.) After cooking the steaks on the first side, turn and lightly sprinkle the grilled side with salt. Just before removing the steaks from the grill, rub the top with the crushed garlic clove and drizzle with a bit of olive oil. Transfer the steaks to a warmed serving platter and loosely tent with foil; let sit for about 5 minutes before serving.

JUST BEFORE SERVING, stir the lavender and balsamic vinegar into the cherry relish. Arrange the steaks on 2 individual plates, spoon the cherry relish over, and serve.

Makes 2 servings

SPICED PORK TENDERLOIN
with Fresh Fruit Chutney

Covey Restaurant, Quail Lodge, Carmel Valley

This fresh chutney, with its sweet tang, is a wonderful accompaniment
to the spice-crusted pork tenderloin. You could also prepare this with one larger
piece of pork loin, though the baking time would need to be roughly doubled.
If you happen to have any leftovers, a cold pork sandwich with a smear
of the chutney is delicious.

*2 pork tenderloin pieces (about
¾ pound each)*

3 tablespoons vegetable oil

FRESH FRUIT CHUTNEY

*1 cup vinegar (such as cider, or red
or white wine)*
*½–1 cup sugar (depending on sweetness
of fruit used and your taste)*
½ medium onion, chopped
3 tablespoons chopped candied ginger
1 tablespoon minced garlic

1 cinnamon stick
3 whole cloves
4 cardamom pods
*2½ cups diced red or black plums (or other
ripe, tender fruit such as peaches, pears,
or apricots)*

SPICE BLEND

2 tablespoons yellow mustard seeds
4 teaspoons cumin seeds
4 teaspoons fennel seeds

1 tablespoon caraway seeds
2 tablespoons black peppercorns
Salt

FOR THE CHUTNEY, combine the vinegar, sugar, onion, ginger, garlic, cinnamon
stick, cloves, and cardamom pods in a medium saucepan and bring to a boil, stirring often
to help the sugar dissolve. Boil until the mixture thickens to the consistency of heavy
syrup, 15 to 20 minutes. Stir in the plums and cook over medium heat, stirring often,
until the fruit is soft, about 10 minutes. If you prefer a more traditional, thicker chutney,
continue cooking until it has a jamlike texture, 10 to 15 minutes longer. Set aside.

FOR THE SPICE BLEND, combine the mustard, cumin, fennel, and caraway seeds in a small dry skillet and toast over medium heat until they begin to lightly brown and smell aromatic, 2 to 3 minutes. Take from the heat and let cool slightly. Grind the spices with the peppercorns in a spice mill or coffee grinder, pulsing so that the spices still have some texture and aren't too powdery.

PUT THE SPICE BLEND on a plate and stir in salt to taste (1 to 2 teaspoons). Trim any fat or sinew from the pork tenderloins, then roll them in the spice blend to evenly coat.

PREHEAT THE OVEN to 350°F.

HEAT THE OIL in a large, heavy ovenproof skillet over medium-high heat. Add the tenderloins and brown evenly on all sides, being careful not to burn the spices, about 2 minutes total. Transfer the skillet to the oven and continue cooking until the pork is just firm to the touch, about 10 minutes. Take from the oven, cover with foil, and let sit 5 to 10 minutes before cutting into thin slices. Arrange the slices on 4 individual plates and spoon the fresh fruit chutney alongside. Serve right away.

Makes 4 servings

LAPIN AUX HERBES DE PROVENCE

(Rabbit Braised in Herbs)

Le Bilig, Auburn

You can ask the butcher to portion the rabbits for this dish if they're sold whole. Le Bilig's rabbit comes from Cloverdale Farms. The chef suggests serving this with fresh pasta or a potato gratin.

2 rabbits (about 2½ pounds each), each cut in 6 portions	¼ cup unsalted butter
	2 tablespoons chopped tarragon
1 cup all-purpose flour, more if needed	2 tablespoons chopped sage
3–4 tablespoons olive oil	2 tablespoons chopped marjoram
6 cups veal or chicken stock, preferably homemade	1 teaspoon tomato paste
	Salt and freshly ground black pepper
4 shallots, chopped	Thyme sprigs, for garnish

MARINADE

8 cups milk	4 sprigs thyme, chopped
2 large carrots, chopped	2 bay leaves
1 medium onion, chopped	2 teaspoons coarse salt
2 cloves garlic, chopped	1 teaspoon cracked black pepper

COMBINE THE MARINADE ingredients in a large dish, add the rabbit pieces, cover, and refrigerate for 8 hours or overnight.

DRAIN AND DISCARD THE MILK from the rabbit. Reserve the carrot, onion, and garlic. Pat the rabbit pieces dry with paper towels and dust them lightly with the flour, patting to remove excess.

HEAT 2 TABLESPOONS OF THE OLIVE OIL in a large, heavy pot, such as a Dutch oven, over medium heat. Working in batches, brown the rabbit pieces well on all sides, adding more oil as needed; set aside. Discard excess fat from the pot, then add ½ cup of the veal stock. Bring to a boil, stirring to dissolve cooked bits from the bottom of the pot, and boil until reduced by about half. Stir in the carrot, onion, and garlic reserved from the marinade, with the shallots, butter, tarragon, sage, marjoram, and tomato paste. Arrange the rabbit pieces in the pot and pour the remaining veal stock over. (Add a bit of water if needed so that the rabbit is just covered with liquid.) Cover the pot and simmer over medium-low heat until the rabbit is very tender, 45 minutes to 1 hour. Transfer the rabbit pieces to a warmed serving platter and cover to keep warm. Using an immersion blender, purée the vegetables and cooking liquids until smooth. (Alternatively, purée the mixture in batches in a food processor or blender.) Season the sauce to taste with salt and pepper and pour it over the rabbit. Garnish the platter with thyme sprigs and serve right away.

Makes 6 servings

THE CALL OF THE COUNTRY

Some are born in the country, while others hear its call. People who make their livelihood from food have been particularly attuned to an arcadian call in recent years. The usual reasons for moving to the country all apply: to find a less hectic pace and possibly less stress, to raise children in an environment where nature is part of the balance, to avoid the expense of city living. In addition, food people have other motivations: to start a business at an affordable cost, to bring different services to rural areas, and, most important, to be close to the basic materials of their métier.

The Northern California region has several attributes that foster such moves. Many towns and localities attract tourists. Vintners are emphasizing the fundamental wine-food partnership, so wine country is evolving into wine-and-food country. Agriculture of all kinds and levels is widespread. Distribution of goods is easy and regular throughout. Certain places are developing into specialized food centers. Sonoma, Mendocino, and Amador Counties, as well as the world-famous Napa Valley, are destinations for those who know fine wines. Marin, Mendocino, and Sonoma are renowned for their cheeses, meats, and poultry. The Central Valley is known for its fruit orchards, nut plantations, and olive groves.

While the trickle has not become a torrent, it could be called a trend; more and more urban and suburban food professionals find a way to do what they love in the country. Some become providers of lamb, rabbits, ducks, herbs, vegetables, or tree fruits. Others raise wine grapes or produce foie gras. Still others make cheese. Some people use local ingredients to produce mustards, jams, jellies, and other preserves for retail sales. Many bakers have settled in small towns, sometimes refurbishing existing bakeries.

A natural phenomenon is that food couples and families head for the hills. Sometimes they establish restaurants, working as chefs or dividing food and front-of-the-house responsibilities. For some, the role of innkeeper or bed-and-breakfast host fulfills a rural vision. They come from the cities of the area and beyond; some are from other countries, especially from France and Italy, Thailand and Vietnam. Certain regions attract clusters of immigrants. Cheesemakers are drawn to the coastal counties, particularly Sonoma. Several French chefs have settled in Gold Country environs.

Chefs who open restaurants find ample appreciation of their work from local and regional people, as well as from tourists from far away. Almost every nook in Northern California has a natural and/or human-made attraction that makes it a destination for city folks. Most enjoy exploring their own backyard country, especially when they can count on good food and wine almost everywhere they go. The chefs, in turn, know that they can count on a network of agricultural providers with sophisticated tastes and methods, who raise everything from beef and dairy cattle to olives and oysters. They find it inspiring to be able to work with special local treats—ranging from fish to berries, wine to cheese—and appealing to offer their creations to others who know and care.

This cross-fertilization of people, values, ideas, and raw materials may turn the definition of hick on its head. Food people in the country here are at ease, with a sophisticated understanding of natural and cultural influences and a sense of convivial community.

ESTOFADO DE CATALAN
(Spanish-Style Short Ribs)

Insalata's, San Anselmo

"This has become a real favorite at Insalata's," says chef/owner Heidi Insalata about this richly flavored stewlike dish. She suggests serving it with your favorite potatoes. Chef Insalata also suggests garnishing the ribs with gremolata, a mixture of finely chopped garlic, lemon zest, and parsley (here, it could be orange zest instead).

Commonly, beef short ribs are chunky, squarish pieces, with meat clinging to a short piece of the rib. Be sure to choose these and not the Korean-style short ribs, a long slender slice along the rib cage.

Salt and freshly ground black pepper	1 cup dry red wine
5 pounds beef short ribs	1 can (14 ounces) chopped plum tomatoes,
2–3 tablespoons olive oil	with liquid
1 onion, coarsely chopped	¼ cup tomato paste
1 carrot, coarsely chopped	1 sprig thyme
2 stalks celery, coarsely chopped	6 cups beef stock, preferably homemade
2 cloves garlic, crushed	

SAUCE

1 cup dry sherry	1 tablespoon unsalted butter
Grated zest of 1 orange	1½ teaspoons thyme leaves
½ ounce unsweetened chocolate, chopped	½ teaspoon chopped marjoram

PREHEAT THE OVEN to 300°F.

GENEROUSLY SALT AND PEPPER the beef ribs. In a heavy roasting pan, heat the olive oil over medium-high heat. Add the ribs and brown well on all sides, about 5 minutes. Transfer to a plate and set aside. Add the onion, carrot, celery, and garlic to the roasting pan and sauté, stirring often, until the vegetables are tender and caramelized, about 5 minutes. Add the red wine, increase the heat to high, and boil until the liquid is reduced by about half. Stir in the tomatoes (with their liquid), tomato paste, and thyme and stir to evenly mix. Return the ribs (and any accumulated liquid) to the pan and pour the stock over. Bring just to a boil, then transfer the roasting pan to the oven and bake until the meat is very tender and pulls easily from the bone, about 3 hours. Take the ribs from the pan and set aside, reserving the liquids.

FOR THE SAUCE, carefully strain the cooking liquids into a large saucepan and add the sherry. Bring to a boil and boil until the liquids are reduced by about one-third, 7 to 10 minutes. Add the orange zest, chocolate, butter, thyme, and marjoram, with salt and pepper to taste. Simmer, stirring, until the chocolate is melted. Add the ribs to the sauce and simmer for a few minutes longer before serving.

Makes 4 to 6 servings

ROASTED VENISON

with Big Sur Chanterelles and Foie Gras

Pacific's Edge, Highlands Inn, Carmel

Chef Cal Stamenov uses venison loin for this recipe but says that venison tenderloin would be fine as well. If you have trouble getting venison, beef tenderloin would be a delicious substitute. One of the country's two foie gras producers, Sonoma Foie Gras, is based on a farm in Carneros and produces foie gras from muscovy duck.

The sauce Chef Stamenov makes at Pacific's Edge is a bit more elaborate than the one here, essentially made up of two different sauces—one meat based and the other berry based—combined later. This modified version is also delicious, though, and is easier to make.

3 sweet potatoes
7 tablespoons unsalted butter
½ teaspoon freshly grated or ground nutmeg
Salt and freshly ground black pepper
12 pearl onions, peeled
2 carrots, diced

1 pound chanterelle mushrooms, brushed clean, large mushrooms halved or quartered
8 ounces fresh foie gras, cut in 4 even slices
1–2 tablespoons olive oil
1 pound venison loin, cut into 4 portions

SAUCE

1 tablespoon olive oil
½ pound venison or beef trimmings, cut in 1-inch pieces
1 onion, thinly sliced
1 leek, trimmed, cleaned, and thinly sliced

1 carrot, thinly sliced
1 cup ripe, sweet blackberries
1 cup dry red wine
2 cups veal or beef stock, preferably homemade

FOR THE SAUCE, heat the oil in a medium-size, heavy saucepan over medium-high heat. Brown the meat trimmings well on all sides, then add the onion, leek, and carrot. Reduce the heat to medium and cook, stirring often, until the vegetables are tender and lightly browned, about 10 minutes. Add the blackberries and cook for 5 minutes. Add the red wine, bring to a boil, and cook until the liquid is reduced to about ¼ cup. Stir in the stock and simmer gently over low heat for 1 hour.

WHILE THE SAUCE IS SIMMERING, preheat the oven to 350°F.

ROAST THE SWEET POTATOES, in their skin, until tender, about 1 hour. When cool enough to handle, peel the potatoes and put them in a large bowl. Add 6 tablespoons of the butter and the nutmeg, with salt and pepper to taste. Using an electric mixer, whip the potatoes until smooth and fluffy; set aside in a warm place.

BRING A MEDIUM PAN OF WATER to a boil, add the pearl onions, and simmer until just tender, about 10 minutes. Scoop out the onions with a slotted spoon, drain well, and set aside. Return the water to a boil, add the diced carrots, and simmer just until tender, 3 to 5 minutes. Drain well and set aside. Heat the remaining tablespoon of butter in a large skillet over medium-high heat, add the mushrooms, and sauté until tender, about 5 minutes. Add the pearl onions and carrots to the skillet, season to taste with salt and pepper, and stir to mix. Set aside.

STRAIN THE SAUCE and return it to the saucepan. Season the sauce to taste with salt and pepper and keep warm over low heat.

HEAT A HEAVY SKILLET over high heat until very hot. Add the foie gras and cook until nicely browned, about 1 minute. Turn and continue cooking until browned and just cooked through, about 1 minute longer. Set aside on paper towels and keep warm in a low oven.

WIPE OUT THE SKILLET, add the olive oil, and reheat over medium-high heat. Season the venison with salt and pepper and cook it in the hot skillet until browned on both sides and medium-rare, 2 to 3 minutes per side for pieces about 1 inch thick, longer for larger pieces.

TO SERVE, spoon the mushroom mixture onto 4 individual plates and top with the whipped sweet potatoes. Set a piece of venison on the potatoes, top with a piece of foie gras, and drizzle the sauce over and around. Serve right away.

Makes 4 servings

CARNITAS

North Coast Brewing Company, Fort Bragg

You have to work a bit for your supper with this dish. At North Coast Brewing Company, the carnitas are served with warmed flour tortillas, guacamole, pico de gallo, sour cream, and cilantro. Then it's up to the diners to assemble and eat as they like. You can do the same at home, or serve the meat simply as is, with a crisp salad and crusty bread alongside.

4 pounds boneless pork (butt or shoulder), excess fat trimmed from edges
2 bottles (12 ounces each) pale ale
2½ cups water
7 cloves garlic, crushed
2 teaspoons coarse salt
1 teaspoon toasted coriander seed, lightly crushed

1 teaspoon dried red pepper flakes
½ teaspoon freshly cracked pepper
½ teaspoon toasted cumin seed, lightly crushed
1–2 tablespoons olive oil, if needed

CUT THE PORK in 1½-inch cubes. In a large, heavy pot, such as a Dutch oven, combine the beer and water and bring to a rolling boil. Add the meat one handful at a time, allowing the liquid to return to a full boil before adding the next handful. When all the meat has been added, reduce the heat to medium-low and skim off any foam that rises to the top.

ADD THE REMAINING INGREDIENTS, except for the olive oil. Cover the pot and simmer until the meat is tender, about 45 minutes. Remove the lid and increase the heat to bring the liquids to a slow boil. Continue cooking until the liquids have completely evaporated, about 1½ hours. As the liquid is cooked off, you will need to reduce the heat to avoid scorching. Add 1 to 2 tablespoons olive oil if necessary to keep the meat from sticking. Cook until the meat is browned and slightly crisp on the outside. Serve hot, with garnish of choice alongside.

Makes 6 to 8 servings

ITALIAN INGREDIENTS

The love affair between Americans and Italian food reaches a passion point in this region, home to many Italians, present and past. One can find Ital-Asian, Ital-Cal, and North Beach Italian cuisines, as well as many regional Italian chefs cooking as close to the *la cucina genuina* as they can do in this country.

Consequently, many necessities of the Italian kitchen are available, not only in import stores, but in good supermarkets. In the latter, one can find decent, if not rare, balsamic vinegar, Arborio rice, and extra virgin olive oil. More markets are also stocking Italian regional cheeses—tangy Taleggio and Stracchino; nutty, buttery fontina; mellow pecorino fresco—as well as Parmigiano-Reggiano and aged pecorino for grating.

Imported specialties await the discriminating lover of Italian food in such shops as Vivande's Porta Via of San Francisco: rare, traditional balsamic vinegars; extra virgin olive oils from many regions in Italy; the finest artisanal pastas; dried porcini mushrooms; and other packaged goods.

From the earliest, Italian immigrants have produced some essentials locally. Fresh pasta, breads and pastries, and cured meats have distinctive flavor and many fans. They are worth savoring for themselves and can substitute nicely for imported Italian ingredients.

There are venerable *pastificii* in San Francisco's North Beach, notably the Florence Ravioli Factory, but pasta rolls out of towns and cities all over the region. The best is made by small producers and is often sold only at local stores and farmers' markets. Italian bakeries come in all sizes, from small family establishments, some more than 100 years old, to chain bakeries of very high standards. Independents are located mostly in San Francisco's North Beach. The Liguria Bakery makes *focaccie* equal to that of any regional baker in Italy. Il Fornaio is an Italian chain transplanted to California; its creditable factory breads are widely available in fine food markets. Molinari produces tasty commercial salami; especially good are their *finocchiona* and *coppa*.

Italian delicatessens can be found in most towns that have a hint of Italian heritage. They supply regionally produced ingredients such as biscotti, cheeses, pasta, and polenta. They also furnish salt-pack anchovies, capers, prosciutto di Parma, *baccalà* (salt cod), *amarene* (wild cherries in syrup), and many tastes of the Italian kitchen that aren't in most supermarkets.

GRILLED EGGPLANT PARMIGIANA

Prima, Walnut Creek

This is a very light version of the Italian classic, with the eggplant slices grilled rather than pan-fried. The oven-roasted tomatoes—which replace the traditional tomato sauce—can be made one to two days in advance and refrigerated.

10 large plum (roma) tomatoes, cored and halved lengthwise

¾ cup olive oil

4 cloves garlic, coarsely chopped

16 large basil leaves, rinsed, dried, and roughly torn

3 pounds Japanese eggplant (about 10)

2 teaspoons salt

2 tablespoons balsamic vinegar

12 ounces mozzarella, preferably fresh, thinly sliced

¼ cup freshly grated Parmesan cheese

PREHEAT THE OVEN to 200°F.

ARRANGE THE TOMATOES, cut side down, on a rimmed baking sheet. Heat ½ cup of the olive oil in a small skillet over medium heat, add the garlic, and cook until aromatic and just turning golden, 2 to 3 minutes. Drizzle the garlic and oil over the tomatoes and scatter with half of the basil. Bake the tomatoes until tender and wrinkly looking, about 3 hours. Let cool in the pan. Peel off and discard the tomato skin, coarsely chop the tomatoes, and set them aside on a plate. Carefully pour the remaining oil and cooking liquids into a small dish for using later.

TRIM THE EGGPLANTS and cut them in ¼-inch thick lengthwise slices. Sprinkle the salt over the slices and let drain in a colander for 1 hour to draw off any bitter juices. Wipe off the salt and pat the slices dry.

PREHEAT AN OUTDOOR GRILL, if using. (The eggplant slices can also be grilled stovetop, or broiled.)

IN A SMALL BOWL, combine the remaining ¼ cup of the olive oil with the balsamic vinegar and blend with a fork to emulsify. Brush both sides of the eggplant slices with the vinegar mixture. Grill or broil the slices until just tender and lightly browned, about 2 minutes on each side. Set aside.

PREHEAT THE OVEN to 375°F.

BRUSH A 9- BY 13-INCH BAKING DISH with some of the reserved tomato oil and arrange one-third of the eggplant on the bottom. Top with one-third each of the roasted tomatoes, remaining basil leaves, and sliced mozzarella. Sprinkle with one-third of the Parmesan cheese. (Don't worry about each ingredient fully covering each layer; just scatter each evenly.) Repeat the layering twice more, using the remaining ingredients, ending with the cheeses on top. Drizzle 1 to 2 tablespoons of the tomato oil over and bake the eggplant parmigiana until lightly browned on top and bubbly around the edges, about 30 minutes. Let sit for 5 minutes before cutting into pieces for serving.

Makes 6 to 8 servings

WILD MUSHROOM RISOTTO

Montrio, Monterey

This vegetarian entrée is aromatic with Madeira-soaked wild mushrooms. The risotto's richness is contrasted in color and flavor with the peppery crunch of arugula, added just before serving. It is important to use a short-grained starchy rice such as Arborio in order to achieve the distinctive creaminess of good risotto.

1 cup Madeira

1 ounce mixed dried wild mushrooms (such as porcini and morel)

5–6 cups vegetable stock, preferably homemade

3 tablespoons olive oil

1 onion, finely chopped

1½ cups Arborio rice

1 bay leaf

3 cloves garlic, minced

1 small bunch arugula (about 3 ounces), rinsed, tough stem ends removed, leaves picked

¾ cup freshly grated Parmesan cheese

Salt and freshly ground black pepper

2 tablespoons minced flat-leaf (Italian) parsley

COMBINE THE MADEIRA and dried mushrooms in a small saucepan and warm over medium-low heat until the mushrooms are fully reconstituted and tender, 10 to 15 minutes. Set aside.

IN A MEDIUM SAUCEPAN, bring the vegetable stock just to a boil. Reduce the heat to keep the stock at a low simmer.

IN A LARGE, HEAVY SAUCEPAN, heat 2 tablespoons of the olive oil over medium heat. Add the onion and sauté until just tender, 5 to 7 minutes. Add the rice and continue to cook, stirring constantly, until the rice is just evenly coated in oil, 1 to 2 minutes. Stir in about ½ cup of the warm vegetable stock with the bay leaf and cook, stirring, until most of the liquid has been absorbed by the rice, 2 to 3 minutes. Add another ½ cup of stock and continue cooking until the liquid is absorbed. Continue with this process, adding ½ cup of stock at a time and stirring constantly, until the rice is tender to the bite and the risotto has a creamy texture. As more liquid is added, it will take a bit longer for each addition to be absorbed. The whole procedure will take about 40 minutes. (You may have some stock left over, depending on the specific rice used and its absorbency.) Take the risotto from the heat. Remove and discard the bay leaf.

SCOOP THE MUSHROOMS from the Madeira and gently squeeze excess liquid back into the bowl. Trim tough stems if necessary and coarsely chop the mushrooms, reserving the soaking liquids. In a medium skillet, heat the remaining tablespoon of olive oil over medium heat. Add the mushrooms and garlic and cook, stirring, until just heated through and aromatic, 2 to 3 minutes. Stir the mushrooms into the risotto, along with the arugula and ½ cup of the Parmesan cheese. Season the risotto to taste with salt and pepper, and then spoon it into 4 individual shallow bowls. Drizzle a tablespoon or two of the reserved Madeira over the risotto and sprinkle with the reserved Parmesan cheese and the parsley. Serve right away.

Makes 4 servings

GOAT CHEESES GATHER THE GOLD

In the early 1980s, Laura Chenel's goat cheeses proved enough Americans hunger for farmhouse chèvres to support a dairy dedicated to making them. The demand was so great that others with similar passion and talent established dairies in the congenial North Coast environment and began to join Chenel in winning local and national acclaim for their work.

Redwood Hill of Sebastopol makes several kinds of goat cheese in addition to chèvre: Teleme and cheddar, as well as an award-winning Camembert-style cheese named Camellia. Yerba Santa of Lakeport makes a very hard, dry-aged Alpine Shepherd's chèvre that wins awards and raves for its rich, lingering flavor. Yerba Santa makes a range of fresh chèvres, as well. In Santa Cruz County, Sea Stars makes goat ricotta, feta, and award-winning *fromage blanc*. Sea Stars also has many fans for its fresh herb- and flower-decorated disks of delicate chèvre. Cypress Grove Chèvre is at home in sea-breezy Humboldt county, where more award-winning, rewarding cheeses are produced. Cypress Grove makes a full line of chèvres and specializes in pyramids and disks aged just enough to develop complexity, yet retain freshness. Cypress Grove and Laura Chenel wrap their aged cheeses in paper, as is traditional in France.

BUTTERNUT SQUASH AND GOAT CHEESE RAVIOLI
with Sage and Brown Butter Sauce

Hidden City Café, Point Richmond

Butternut squash and sage are two ingredients that are deliciously aromatic
and satisfying when it's cold and dreary outside. Here, the roasted squash is paired
with goat cheese to fill big ravioli, tossed in a simple sauce of sage leaves sautéed
in nut-brown butter.

½ butternut squash (about 1 pound), seeds discarded

Salt, preferably kosher, and freshly ground black pepper

¼ teaspoon freshly grated or ground nutmeg

6 ounces fresh goat cheese

Dry Asiago or Parmesan cheese, shaved or grated, for serving

PASTA

2 cups all-purpose flour, rice flour or cornmeal, for sprinkling

2 eggs

2 teaspoons water, plus more if needed

SAGE AND BROWN BUTTER SAUCE

6 tablespoons unsalted butter | 16 sage leaves

PREHEAT THE OVEN to 350°F.

SET THE SQUASH HALF cut side down on a rimmed baking sheet or roasting pan and
roast until tender, about 1 hour. Set aside to cool.

WHILE THE SQUASH IS BAKING, prepare the pasta. Combine the flour, eggs, and
water in a food processor and pulse until evenly blended. If the mixture is still dry, add up
to 2 more teaspoons of water. The dough may not form a ball in the food processor.
Pinch some of the dough between your fingers; if it is supple and holds together without
feeling dry, it is well mixed. Turn the pasta dough out onto a work surface and knead for a
few minutes to make a smooth dough. Wrap the dough in plastic and set aside for 1 hour.

WHEN THE ROASTED SQUASH IS COOL enough to handle, scoop the tender flesh into a large bowl, discarding the skin. Add 1 teaspoon salt, ½ teaspoon pepper, and the nutmeg and stir to mix. Crumble the goat cheese in small pieces, add them to the squash, and gently stir to mix.

AFTER THE PASTA DOUGH HAS RESTED, cut it into 2 pieces. Roll each piece out with a hand-cranked pasta machine to a thickness of about ¹⁄₁₆ inch (setting 5 or 6), using a bit of flour as needed to prevent sticking. The pasta sheet should be about 5 inches wide and more than 2 feet long. Lay the pasta sheet on a lightly floured work surface. Set tablespoons of the squash filling on half of the dough, leaving at least a ½-inch border around each. Dip your fingers in cool water and lightly rub the water on the pasta around each spoonful of filling. Fold the other half of the pasta over, pressing firmly between the filling to seal the 2 halves of dough. Try to remove any air pockets from each ravioli as you seal.

USING A PASTRY CUTTER or sharp knife, cut the filled dough to form individual ravioli. Sprinkle lightly with rice flour or cornmeal to prevent sticking while you make the remaining ravioli.

BRING A LARGE POT OF WATER to a rolling boil. Add the ravioli and when they float to the top of the pot, count 3 to 4 minutes longer for them to be fully cooked.

FOR THE SAUCE, while the ravioli are cooking, heat the butter in a large skillet or sauté pan over medium heat. Add the sage leaves and cook, stirring occasionally, until the sage is lightly browned and crisp and the butter is light brown with a nutty aroma, 3 to 5 minutes. Take care not to increase the heat or cook the sage too long; the butter may burn and become too bitter to use.

DRAIN THE RAVIOLI WELL, add them to the sauce, and toss to coat. Season the ravioli to taste with salt and pepper and arrange on 6 to 8 individual plates. Top with shaved or grated cheese and serve right away.

Makes 6 to 8 servings

DESSERTS

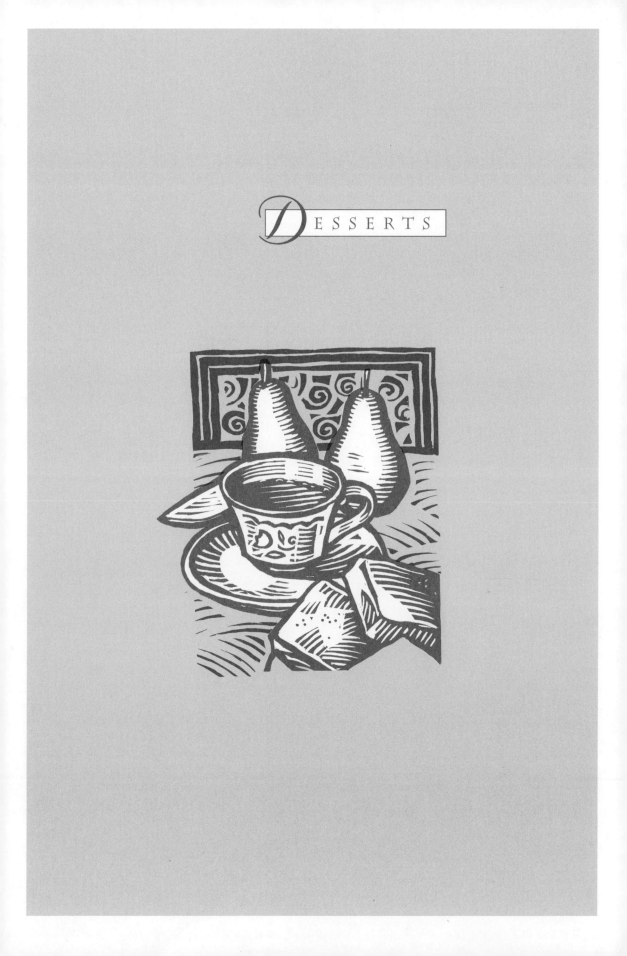

MENDOCINO MUD CAKE

North Coast Brewing Company, Fort Bragg

Mud never tasted so good. This rich, brownielike cake gets an intriguing hint of
hoppy bitterness from stout, a wonderful contrast to the chocolate. The North Coast
Brewing Company uses its Old No. 38 as the stout of choice, but any good stout will
do. The cake is often served there with a scoop of vanilla ice cream alongside.

1½ cups all-purpose flour	*2 cups milk*
1¼ cups granulated sugar	*3 tablespoons unsalted butter, melted*
¾ cup plus ⅓ cup cocoa powder	*and cooled*
¼ cup chopped walnuts	*1½ teaspoons vanilla extract*
1 tablespoon baking powder	*1¼ cups packed brown sugar*
¾ teaspoon salt	*½ cup stout*

PREHEAT THE OVEN to 350°F. Grease a 9- by 13-inch baking dish.

IN A LARGE BOWL, stir together the flour, granulated sugar, ¾ cup of the cocoa
powder, the walnuts, baking powder, and salt until well blended. Gently stir in the milk,
butter, and vanilla.

IN A MEDIUM BOWL, stir together the remaining ⅓ cup cocoa powder, the brown
sugar, and stout. Stir this into the batter until well blended, then pour the batter into the
prepared baking dish. Bake until a toothpick inserted in the center comes out clean, about
35 minutes. The cake will firm up a bit as it cools. Cut the mud cake into squares and
serve slightly warm or at room temperature.

Makes 12 to 15 servings

PEAR AND EGGNOG PARFAIT

One Market, San Francisco

This dessert makes a fun presentation at a dinner party, with the pear granité and eggnog ice cream layered in a tall slender champagne flute. You can also serve the parfait in other glasses, such as martini or large snifters. Have some fun with it. At One Market, the parfait might be served with pear chips (see below), but you could serve it with cookies, a couple of fresh berries, or edible flowers for garnish.

This ice cream recipe makes more than is needed for these parfaits, but it's hard to make in smaller batches (honest) and you'll be glad to have extra to enjoy later.

2 large pears, peeled, cored, and diced	1 teaspoon ground cinnamon
2 cups water	Mint sprigs, for garnish
½ cup sugar	6–8 pear chips (optional)
1 tablespoon freshly squeezed lemon juice	

EGGNOG ICE CREAM

3 cups milk	1 teaspoon freshly grated or ground nutmeg
2 cups whipping cream	¾ cup sugar
2 cinnamon sticks	6 egg yolks

FOR THE EGGNOG ICE CREAM, combine the milk, cream, cinnamon sticks, and nutmeg in a medium saucepan. Add half of the sugar and bring just to a boil, stirring occasionally to help the sugar dissolve. While the milk mixture is heating, combine the egg yolks and the remaining sugar in a medium bowl and whisk to thoroughly mix. When the milk comes to a boil, slowly pour about half of it into the egg yolks, whisking constantly. Pour this back into the saucepan and cook over medium heat, stirring constantly with a wooden spoon, until the mixture is thick enough to coat the back of the spoon, 3 to 5 minutes. Strain the ice cream base into a medium bowl, then set the bowl inside a larger bowl of ice water to quickly chill, stirring occasionally. When cool, pour the ice cream mixture into an ice cream maker and freeze according to the manufacturer's instructions. Transfer the ice cream to an airtight container and freeze until set, at least 2 hours.

COMBINE THE PEARS, water, sugar, lemon juice, and cinnamon in a medium saucepan and bring to a boil, stirring occasionally to help the sugar dissolve. Reduce the heat to medium and simmer until the pears are very soft, about 20 to 30 minutes (depending on the ripeness of the pears). Press the pear mixture through a fine sieve into a medium bowl, puréeing the pears and removing tough fibers. Set the bowl inside a larger bowl of ice water to quickly chill, stirring occasionally. When cool, pour the pear purée into a shallow baking dish and freeze, stirring every 20 to 30 minutes with a fork to break up the ice crystals. The granité should be fully set in about 2 hours.

TO SERVE, scoop some of the granité into the bottom of a champagne flute or another tall glass, follow with a scoop of the eggnog ice cream, and continue layering until the glass is full. Repeat with other glasses. Garnish with a mint sprig and pear chip in each glass, if using, and serve right away.

Makes 6 to 8 servings

PEAR CHIPS

These thin, crisp chips of pear are easy to make and are a great addition to the pear and eggnog parfait. The same could be done with apples as well. If you have a convection option on your oven, use it here. The circulating air is ideal for drying the pears. Otherwise, you might need to add an extra 30 minutes or so to the drying time.

Trim the stem end from 1 ripe but firm pear. Using a mandoline-type slicer if you have one, cut the pear in very thin (about ⅛-inch) slices, working from the stem end down through the core to the bud end. You don't have to cut out the core bits, just remove the seeds. Lay the slices on 2 very lightly oiled baking sheets and bake in a 200°F oven until dry looking and very lightly browned, about 1½ hours, turning the slices once halfway through. Transfer the slices to a cake rack to cool and crisp before serving.

RHUBARB CRUMBLE TART

L'Amie Donia, Palo Alto

Donia Bijan, chef/owner of L'Amie Donia, suggests serving this tart warm with a scoop of strawberry ice cream or lemon sorbet.

2 pounds rhubarb, trimmed and cut in roughly 1-inch pieces	*Grated zest and juice of 1 orange*
2 cups granulated sugar	*1 vanilla bean*

PASTRY DOUGH

1½ cups all-purpose flour	*2 egg yolks*
¼ cup granulated sugar	*2–3 tablespoons cold water*
¼ teaspoon salt	
5 tablespoons unsalted butter, cut in pieces and chilled	

CRUMBLE TOPPING

½ cup packed brown sugar	*¼ teaspoon salt*
½ cup all-purpose flour	*4 tablespoons unsalted butter, cut in pieces and chilled*
½ teaspoon ground cinnamon	
½ teaspoon freshly grated or ground nutmeg	

FOR THE PASTRY DOUGH, combine the flour, sugar, and salt in a food processor and pulse once to blend. Add the chilled butter pieces and pulse just until the mixture has a crumbly texture. Add the egg yolks and pulse a few times. Drizzle in just enough water to form a tender dough, pulsing a few more times. (Alternatively, you could mix the dough by hand: Stir together the flour, sugar, and salt and form a well in the center. Blend the egg yolks and butter in the well, then slowly incorporate the flour, adding water as needed.) Turn the dough out onto a lightly floured work surface and form it into a ball. Wrap the dough in plastic wrap and chill for at least 30 minutes.

IN A LARGE SAUCEPAN, combine the rhubarb, granulated sugar, and orange zest and juice. Split the vanilla bean lengthwise and run the tip of a knife blade down the bean to remove the vanilla seeds. Add the vanilla seeds with the split bean to the rhubarb mixture. Cook the rhubarb over medium heat until the rhubarb is tender but the fruit still holds its shape, 10 to 15 minutes, stirring occasionally. Take from the heat and let cool. Remove the vanilla bean before baking.

FOR THE CRUMBLE TOPPING, combine the brown sugar, flour, cinnamon, nutmeg, and salt in a food processor and pulse once to mix. Add the chilled butter and pulse just until the mixture has a coarse crumbly texture, not too fine. (Alternatively, combine all the ingredients in a bowl and use a pastry cutter or 2 table knives to cut the butter into the dry ingredients.)

PREHEAT THE OVEN to 350°F.

ROLL OUT THE CHILLED PASTRY dough on a lightly floured work surface to a circle large enough to line a 9-inch removable-base tart pan. Gently form the dough into the tart pan, pressing it well into the corners and trimming and fluting the edges.

USE A SLOTTED SPOON to scoop the cooled rhubarb into the tart shell, reserving the cooking juices. Sprinkle the crumble topping evenly over the rhubarb and set the tart on a baking sheet to catch drips. Bake the tart until the pastry is golden and the filling is bubbling around the edges, about 45 minutes. Boil the reserved cooking juices for a few minutes to thicken slightly. Let the tart cool slightly, then remove the rim and cut into pieces for serving. Drizzle a bit of the cooking juices over each piece if you like (or over the ice cream, if serving).

Makes 8 servings

CHOCOLATE WALNUT CRANBERRY
ESPRESSO BISCOTTI

Agate Cove Inn, Mendocino

These twice-baked cookies are chock-full of flavor—tart dried cranberries playing off the sweet chocolate, all wrapped in a subtle espresso dough.

2 cups all-purpose flour	*5 tablespoons espresso or strong*
1 cup sugar	*brewed coffee, cooled*
½ teaspoon baking powder	*4 teaspoons milk*
½ teaspoon baking soda	*1 teaspoon vanilla extract*
½ teaspoon salt	*1¼ cups semisweet chocolate chips*
½ teaspoon ground cinnamon	*¾ cup chopped walnuts*
¼ teaspoon ground cloves	*¾ cup dried cranberries or chopped*
1 egg	*dried cherries*

PREHEAT THE OVEN to 350°F. Lightly grease 1 or 2 heavy baking sheets.

IN A LARGE BOWL, combine the flour, sugar, baking powder, baking soda, salt, cinnamon, and cloves. Stir to mix well. In a small bowl, lightly beat the egg, then stir in the espresso, milk, and vanilla. Add the wet ingredients to the dry ingredients and stir gently until well blended. Stir in the chocolate chips, walnuts, and cranberries. Turn the dough out onto a well-floured work surface and divide the dough in half. Form the dough into 2 flat logs about ½ inch thick and 3½ inches wide and arrange them on the baking sheet. Bake until firm and cakelike, 20 to 25 minutes. Take from the oven and let cool on a cake rack. Reduce the oven temperature to 300°F.

WHEN THE LOGS ARE COOL, use a serrated knife to cut them in ½-inch pieces at a slight angle. Lay the slices cut side down on a baking sheet (or 2, if you need) and bake 6 to 8 minutes for medium-crunchy biscotti. For extra-crunchy biscotti, turn them and bake for another 6 to 8 minutes. Note that the biscotti will crisp up as they cool, so don't worry if they seem a bit soft when they come from the oven.

Makes about 3 dozen biscotti

THE MELLOW FRUITFULNESS OF PERSIMMONS

Persimmons are handsome trees throughout the year, with their large leaves, stately shape, and prolific fruit. In autumn, when the leaves have dropped, the ripening fruit still clings to the branches in a woodcut study of contrasting shapes and colors. The black branches and brilliant orange fruit against the deep blue October or November sky are as much a fall vignette for this region as the leaves of deciduous trees are for New England.

The cultivated persimmon *(Diospyros kaki)* comes from China through Japan with a venerable heritage. Ripening it requires a little knowledge and luck with the weather, as does the native wild persimmon *(D. virginiana)*, which does not grow well in California. Popular belief is that persimmons must be touched by frost to be free of astringency, but this is not completely true. Freezing temperatures, whether the fruit is on the tree or in a freezer, do hasten the softening part of the ripening process. If the fruit has not received enough warmth and light to completely develop its sugars, however, freezing will not bring it to ripeness. When picked at the proper stage, persimmons will soften at room temperature.

The most popular cultivars are the virtually seedless Hachiya and Fuyu, though others, such as Chocolate, are occasionally available. Hachiya is oblong-conical, deep orange when sugar-ripe, even though it may be very firm. It is often blushed purple black. It is an astringent type and must be completely soft-ripe, like jelly, before eating. The Fuyu is shaped like a flattened globe and is considered nonastringent. It may be eaten when firm-ripe, like an apple. If the sugar content of Fuyus is not high enough when they are picked, however, they will taste flat and dull. Even nonastringent persimmons taste best when they are somewhat soft-ripe.

BAKED PERSIMMON PUDDING
with Mandarin Orange Curd

Lark Creek Inn, Larkspur

In late fall and early winter throughout Northern California, fat, bright orange persimmons hang cheerily in their leafless trees. Local cooks have a heyday using the sweet, aromatic fruit in salads, breads, and pies. At chef Bradley Ogden's Lark Creek Inn, persimmons make their way into this easy spiced pudding, which is reminiscent of gingerbread.

If mandarin oranges aren't available, you could use the juice of sweet navel oranges for the curd.

⅓ cup sugar	¼ teaspoon salt
2 tablespoons unsalted butter, at room temperature	¼ teaspoon baking soda
	¼ cup milk
1 egg	¼ cup buttermilk
¼ teaspoon vanilla extract	½ cup persimmon purée (see below)
¼ teaspoon ground cinnamon	¾ teaspoon freshly squeezed lemon juice
½ cup sifted cake flour	¼ teaspoon grated lemon zest

MANDARIN ORANGE CURD

⅓ cup mandarin orange juice	1 teaspoon freshly squeezed lemon juice
3 egg yolks	2½ tablespoons unsalted butter, cut in chunks
1½ tablespoons sugar	

FOR THE MANDARIN ORANGE CURD, combine the mandarin juice, egg yolks, sugar, and lemon juice in a small, heavy, nonreactive saucepan and stir to mix. Add the butter and cook the mixture over medium-low heat, stirring often, until the curd has thickened and lightly coats the back of a spoon, 5 to 7 minutes. Pour the curd into a small bowl and set the bowl in a larger bowl filled with ice water to quickly cool and set. When fully cooled, refrigerate the curd until ready to serve.

PREHEAT THE OVEN to 350°F. Butter four ½-cup ramekins or other small baking dishes.

IN A MIXER, cream together the sugar and butter until light and fluffy. Add the egg, vanilla, and cinnamon and continue mixing until well blended, 1 to 2 minutes longer. In a medium bowl, stir together the flour, salt, and baking soda. Add the dry ingredients to the sugar mixture alternately with the milk and buttermilk. Stir together the persimmon purée, lemon juice, and lemon zest in a separate bowl. Fold this into the batter until evenly blended.

POUR THE BATTER into the prepared ramekins, set the ramekins on a baking sheet for easy handling, and bake until the tops spring back when lightly pressed, 40 to 45 minutes. Take from the oven and let cool slightly. Invert the persimmon puddings onto 4 individual plates, spoon some of the mandarin curd alongside, and serve.

Makes 4 servings

PERSIMMON PURÉE

If the persimmons you're using are very ripe and soft (which is best), you can simply press the pulp through a sieve to make the purée. You'll need 2 to 3 persimmons for the ½ cup purée needed for this recipe.

If your persimmons aren't quite as ripe, trim away the cores and coarsely chop the fruit. Put the persimmons in a small saucepan with ½ cup of water and cook over medium heat, stirring occasionally, until the fruit is quite tender and most of the water has evaporated, 20 to 30 minutes. Take from the heat and let cool slightly, then purée the persimmons in a food processor until smooth.

MERINGUE NESTS

Dorrington Hotel & Restaurant, Dorrington

Baked meringue is an old-time treat that, like a lot of good things,
never really goes out of style. Delicate and intriguing in their own right, these
meringues have the added benefit of being a blank canvas for the cook, essentially an
edible dish to be filled as you please. They could be filled with fresh fruit, ice
cream, sorbet, or lemon or orange curd. They could be drizzled with a fresh fruit
coulis, rich chocolate sauce, or light custard sauce. We offer just one possibility
here, something akin to peach Melba.

If you don't have a pastry bag and tip, you could make free-form nests,
spreading the meringue into a circle with the back of a spoon, pressing the
outer edges up as best you can.

1 cup powdered sugar	*1 teaspoon vanilla extract*
4 egg whites, at room temperature	*⅛ teaspoon cream of tartar*

FILLING

2 cups fresh or thawed frozen raspberries	*4 ripe peaches, halved, pitted, and peeled*
2 tablespoons powdered sugar	*8 good-size scoops vanilla ice cream*
1 tablespoon kirsch (optional)	

PREHEAT THE OVEN to 225°F. Draw eight 4-inch circles on a sheet of parchment
paper and set it on a heavy baking sheet.

SIFT THE POWDERED SUGAR onto a piece of waxed or parchment paper. Working
in a mixer or with electric beaters, whip the egg white until frothy, then whip in the
vanilla and cream of tartar. With the mixer running, begin adding the powdered sugar
about 1 tablespoon at a time, letting each addition be well incorporated before adding the
next. When all of the sugar has been added, the egg whites should be very stiff and hold a
firm peak.

SCOOP THE MERINGUE into a pastry bag fitted with a star or plain tip (about
½-inch size). Beginning at the outside of one circle on the parchment paper, pipe a solid
spiral of meringue, working toward the center of the circle. On top of that circle, pipe

1 single circle around the edge, followed by 1 more circle on top of that. Repeat for the remaining circles, piping 8 nests.

BAKE THE MERINGUES until fully set and crisp, about 1½ hours. When the meringues are done, turn off the oven and open the door, leaving the meringues in the oven to cool. (If the meringues are firm but not crisp after 1½ hours or so, they will generally crisp up while cooling.)

WHILE THE MERINGUES ARE COOLING, prepare the filling. Combine the raspberries, sugar, and kirsch (if using) in a food processor or blender and blend until smooth. Strain the sauce through a fine sieve to remove the seeds and set aside. Set each peach half on the cutting board and cut in slices, keeping the halves together.

TO SERVE, set the meringues on 8 individual plates and add a scoop of ice cream to each. Press gently on each peach half to partially fan the slices and set them on top of the ice cream. Drizzle the raspberry sauce over and serve.

Makes 8 servings

NECTARINE CRISP
with Cinnamon Buttermilk Sauce

Wente Vineyards Restaurant, Livermore

This simple, homey crisp has added aromatic flavor from fresh ginger, cinnamon, and freshly grated nutmeg. The sauce, infused with cinnamon stick, contributes a pleasant tangy complement thanks to the buttermilk.

6 ripe nectarines, peeled, pitted, and cut in ½-inch slices	*1 teaspoon vanilla extract*
	1 teaspoon grated ginger
¼ cup granulated sugar	*½ teaspoon freshly grated or ground nutmeg*
1½ teaspoons ground cinnamon	

CINNAMON BUTTERMILK SAUCE

1 cup milk	*6 tablespoons granulated sugar*
1 cinnamon stick	*½ cup buttermilk*
4 egg yolks	

TOPPING

½ cup all-purpose flour	*Pinch cinnamon*
½ cup packed brown sugar	*6 tablespoons unsalted butter, cut*
¼ cup granulated sugar	*in pieces and chilled*

FOR THE SAUCE, combine the milk and cinnamon stick in a small saucepan, bring to a boil, reduce the heat to low, and simmer gently for 15 minutes. In a medium bowl, whisk together the egg yolks and sugar until well blended. Scoop out and discard the cinnamon stick from the milk. Slowly add about half of the warm milk to the egg yolk mixture, whisking constantly, then add this back into the saucepan with the remaining milk. Cook the sauce over medium heat, stirring often with a wooden spoon, until it is thick enough to coat the back of the spoon, 3 to 5 minutes. Be sure not to let the sauce come to a boil or it will curdle. Set aside to cool completely. (For a very smooth sauce, you could strain it into a clean bowl.) When cool, stir in the buttermilk.

PREHEAT THE OVEN to 375°F. Grease a 9-inch square baking dish.

IN A LARGE BOWL, combine the nectarines, ¼ cup granulated sugar, 1½ teaspoons cinnamon, the vanilla, ginger, and nutmeg. Toss gently to evenly mix, then put the nectarine mixture in the baking dish.

FOR THE TOPPING, combine the flour, brown sugar, granulated sugar, and cinnamon in the bowl of a mixer. Using the paddle attachment, mix the dry ingredients just to blend. Add the butter and continue mixing until the topping has a crumbly texture. Sprinkle the topping evenly over the nectarines and bake until the fruit mixture bubbles around the edges and the topping is brown and crunchy, 30 to 40 minutes. Let cool slightly before scooping the crisp onto 6 individual plates. Spoon some of the cinnamon buttermilk sauce alongside, passing the rest separately.

Makes 6 servings

LE TARTE AU CITRON
(Lemon Tart)

Left Bank, Larkspur

This is a luxurious version of a lemon tart, the classic tart-sweet lemon curd filling made lighter by whipping the eggs before blending with the lemon and butter.

4 whole eggs	¾ cup freshly squeezed lemon juice
4 egg yolks	Grated zest of 4 medium lemons
1½ cups sugar	¾ cup unsalted butter

PASTRY DOUGH

1½ cups all-purpose flour	Pinch salt
½ cup unsalted butter, cut in pieces and chilled	3–4 tablespoons cold water, plus more if needed
1 tablespoon sugar	

FOR THE PASTRY DOUGH, combine the flour, butter, sugar, and salt in a food processor and pulse just until the butter has a crumbly texture. Gradually add the water, pulsing a few times just until the dough begins to form a ball. Turn the dough onto a lightly floured work surface and form it into a ball. Wrap the dough in plastic wrap and refrigerate for at least 2 hours (preferably overnight).

PREHEAT THE OVEN to 375°F.

ROLL OUT THE CHILLED PASTRY DOUGH on a lightly floured work surface to a circle large enough to line an 11-inch removable-base tart pan. Gently form the dough into the tart pan, pressing it well into the corners and trimming and fluting the edges. Refrigerate the crust for 30 minutes.

PRICK THE BOTTOM of the pastry a few times with a fork, then line the pastry with a double thickness of foil. (This is a technique for securing the pastry in the pan for blind baking; you could instead use pie weights on a single layer of foil.) Bake the pastry for 10 minutes. Take the pan from the oven, remove the foil, and continue baking until the pastry is set but not browned, 10 to 12 minutes longer. Set the pastry aside to cool.

FOR THE LEMON FILLING, beat the whole eggs, egg yolks, and sugar in a mixer until well blended and light, 2 to 3 minutes. Combine the lemon juice and zest in a medium saucepan and bring just to a boil. Stir in the egg-sugar mixture and the butter and cook over medium heat until the mixture thickens, 5 to 7 minutes, stirring constantly. Take from the heat and strain the filling into a medium bowl. Let cool, then refrigerate the filling for 1 hour.

REHEAT THE OVEN to 350°F.

POUR THE COOLED LEMON FILLING into the pastry crust and bake until the filling is set, 15 to 20 minutes. Let cool to room temperature before removing the rim and cutting the tart into pieces for serving.

Makes 8 to 10 servings

SWEET AND SOUR LEMONS

Chefs have taken to Meyer lemons like salmon to saltwater or bears to honey, using them in savory dishes as well as desserts (see pages 41 and 246). The juice retains good lemon flavor while having significantly less acid than common lemons, though Meyer is not classified as a "sweet" lemon. Many palates find this a pleasing balance. Others find the Meyer has less complex aromas.

The Meyer is problematic for growers because of its thin skin, reduced storage and shipping, and shorter season than the current commercial varieties. In addition, Meyers are often mistaken for oranges because of the color of their skin and flesh. But they are a premium fruit, selling for good prices during their winter season. Most Meyers retail at farmers' markets. If Meyers have not yet become a produce staple, it is probably a matter of time before demand puts them into that category.

Meyers are quite popular as fruiting landscape trees because they are only eight to ten feet tall and thornless. A single tree will provide a good harvest, but not enough to overwhelm the cook.

The main commercial lemons are the high-acid Eureka, Lisbon, and Sungold, a summer-bearing variety. Most are picked when green-ripe for storage. Any lemon will develop better flavor, aroma, and color if left to ripen naturally. Those who have a Lisbon in the garden can attest to a powerful, sweet perfume in the rind of the fruit, though the juice is quite acidic.

CHOCOLATE-COVERED SHORTBREAD IN CHERRY ICE CREAM

Applewood Inn & Restaurant, Pocket Canyon

This recipe is a change from the classic custard-based ice cream, in which
the egg, cream, milk, and sugar are cooked before freezing. Here the ingredients are
not cooked, so if you have concerns about eating uncooked eggs, you could use a
custard-style recipe for vanilla ice cream instead.

For a shortcut, you could purchase shortbread cookies and dip them
in the melted chocolate as described.

SHORTBREAD

6 tablespoons unsalted butter, at room temperature	1 egg yolk
⅓ cup sugar	¼ teaspoon vanilla extract
Pinch salt	1 cup cake flour
	2 ounces semisweet chocolate

CHERRY ICE CREAM

2 eggs	1 cup milk
¾ cup sugar	½ cup quartered, pitted fresh Bing cherries
2 cups whipping cream	

FOR THE SHORTBREAD, cream together the butter, sugar, and salt in a mixer or with
electric beaters. Mix in the egg yolk and vanilla until evenly blended. Working by hand,
stir in the flour to make a firm dough. Put the dough on a sheet of plastic wrap or waxed
paper and form it into a log about 2 inches in diameter. Wrap the log securely and chill
for at least 30 minutes.

PREHEAT THE OVEN to 350°F. Line a baking sheet with parchment paper or lightly
grease the baking sheet.

WHEN THE SHORTBREAD dough is chilled, remove the wrap and cut the dough
into ¼-inch slices. Bake the shortbread until firm and light golden, about 15 minutes.
Transfer the shortbread to a cake rack to cool.

WHEN THE COOKIES ARE COOL, melt the chocolate. Dip 8 of the cookies in the melted chocolate to coat and then let them cool on a piece of parchment or waxed paper. When the chocolate is set, break 4 of the coated cookies into small chunks (you should have about ½ cup). Save the rest of the undipped cookies to serve alongside the ice cream or for nibbling while it freezes.

FOR THE ICE CREAM, beat the eggs and sugar in a mixer or with electric beaters until very pale and fluffy, 5 to 10 minutes. Stir in the cream and milk and transfer the mixture to an ice cream freezer. Freeze the ice cream according to manufacturer's instructions, adding the cherries and chocolate-covered shortbread chunks shortly before the ice cream is set. (Alternatively, you could wait to stir in the cherries and shortbread until after removing the ice cream from the ice cream freezer.) Transfer the ice cream to an airtight container and freeze until set, at least 2 hours. When set, serve scoops of the ice cream with the reserved chocolate-covered and plain shortbread cookies, if you like.

Makes 1 quart

MANGO-COCONUT BARS

The Inn at Depot Hill, Capitola

If your afternoon needs a lift, these addictive tropical bars will do the trick.

1 large or 2 small mangoes, peeled, seeded, and chopped
⅔ cup sugar

1 egg white
Grated zest of 1 lemon or 1 orange

CRUST

¾ cup butter, room temperature
1 cup sugar
1 whole egg
1 egg yolk
1 teaspoon vanilla extract

2 cups all-purpose flour
1½ cups shredded unsweetened coconut
½ cup chopped almonds or macadamia nuts
¼ teaspoon baking powder

PREHEAT THE OVEN to 350°F. Lightly grease a 9- by 13-inch baking dish.

COMBINE THE MANGOES, ⅔ cup sugar, egg white, and citrus zest in a food processor and process until smooth. Set aside.

FOR THE CRUST, beat the butter with the sugar until fluffy. Beat in the whole egg and egg yolk with the vanilla. Stir in the flour, coconut, nuts, and baking powder to form a stiff dough. Press about ⅔ of the dough into the prepared baking dish. Spread the mango mixture over, then crumble the remaining dough evenly over the top. Bake until golden brown, 30 to 35 minutes. Let cool before cutting into bars.

Makes 12 to 15 bars

SPECIAL K COOKIES

Four Sisters Inns

These cookies are very easy to make and quite possibly the most
requested recipe at Four Sisters Inns, which include Maison Fleurie in Yountville and
Petite Auberge and White Swan Inn in San Francisco. The recipe is also good made
with raisin bran cereal and other similar flaky cereals.

The cookies are very delicate when they come right from the oven, so don't be in
too much of a hurry to move them to the cake rack to cool. If you're not careful, this
whole batch might be gobbled up in no time. Pace yourself.

1 cup unsalted butter	*1½ cups all-purpose flour*
1 cup sugar	*1½ teaspoons baking powder*
1 teaspoon vanilla extract	*2 cups Special K cereal*

PREHEAT THE OVEN to 350°F.

IN A MIXER or with electric beaters, cream the butter and sugar until fluffy. Beat in the
vanilla and set aside.

IN A SEPARATE BOWL, sift together the flour and baking powder. Stir the flour mixture into the butter mixture until thoroughly blended. Gently stir in the cereal. Drop the
dough by teaspoons onto a baking sheet, allowing a few inches between them. Bake until
lightly browned around the edges, 10 to 13 minutes. Let the cookies sit on the baking
sheet for a minute or two before transferring them to a cake rack to cool. Continue
baking the remaining dough in batches.

Makes about 4 dozen cookies

OLD-FASHIONED CREMA CATALANA
Perfumed with Fennel Seed

Sent Soví, Saratoga

This creamy dessert is a variation of a Catalan classic. Related to the French crème brûlée, this recipe has a subtle savory flavoring from fennel seed. Note the long cooking at a low oven temperature, which is key to the silky creaminess of the finished *crema*. Be patient, and you'll be rewarded.

2 cups whipping cream	1 tablespoon fennel seeds, lightly toasted
1¼ cups milk	9 egg yolks
Grated zest from ½ orange	½ cup sugar, plus more for caramelizing
Grated zest from ½ lemon	

PREHEAT THE OVEN to 215°F.

COMBINE THE CREAM, milk, and citrus zest in a medium saucepan and bring just to a boil, then take the pan from the heat. Add the fennel seeds, cover, and let steep for about 10 minutes.

MEANWHILE, whisk together the egg yolks and ½ cup of the sugar in a large bowl until they are well blended and the color begins to pale. Strain about ¼ of the cream mixture into the egg mixture, stirring constantly. Slowly strain in the remaining cream, stirring.

CAREFULLY LADLE the *crema* mixture into eight ½-cup ramekins or other small baking dishes. Arrange the dishes on a rimmed baking sheet for easy handling, then transfer them to the oven. Bake until the centers of the *crema* are firm when gently shaken, about 1¼ hours. Let cool completely at room temperature. Sprinkle a thin layer of sugar over each *crema* and carefully caramelize it with a small propane torch, or caramelize the tops under a broiler. Transfer to 8 small plates to make serving easier, and serve right away.

Makes 8 servings

FUSION FRUIT, FRUIT OF PASSION: POMEGRANATES

Punica granatum may not reach across as many cultures in late twentieth-century California as it did millennia ago, but it is beginning to appear on more menus here. Traditional dishes in Iranian, Italian, and Mexican cuisines use the tart-sweet, jewellike seeds or the juice. Chefs of all backgrounds find that the pomegranate's tangy, refreshing taste and beautiful appearance add excitement and balance to many dishes.

The fruit that spread over huge tracts of the ancient world—the Caucasus, Persia, Armenia, and then to the Mediterranean basin—has large colonies in the suburbs and orchards of Northern California, particularly in the area around the San Francisco Bay. The region's long warm season and mild winter serve pomegranates well. The Spanish missionaries first brought pomegranates to California, perhaps unaware of the fruit's long association with erotic love and fertility. The trees certainly look lush and fecund, especially in autumn when the abundant finger-shaped leaves provide a soft golden background for the carmine- or claret-colored fruit.

Several cultivars are grown commercially: Ruby Red, Spanish Sweet, Granada. Some producers sell frozen pomegranate juice at farmers' markets. It keeps well, even to the next season, and is a handy freezer ingredient, if you like dishes that use pomegranate juice. Juicing pomegranates is a messy business, and the juice does stain. At home, it is best done by rolling whole pomegranates on a table to soften them. Then cut them into quarters or sixths and squeeze the sections by hand into a deep bowl; strain the juice. An eight-ounce pomegranate yields about ¼ cup juice.

TARTE TATIN À L'ABRICOT ET GLACE À LA LAVANDE

(Apricot Tarte Tatin with Lavender Ice Cream)

Le Bilig, Auburn

The original *tarte Tatin* was created by the Tatin sisters in the early 1900s. After the famous Paris restaurant Maxim's began serving the richly caramelized apple tart, it quickly became a French national favorite. Apricots are a preferred variation of chef Marc Deconinck, but he notes that you could also use plums, peaches, or pears. And to simplify things a bit, you could instead make one large tart, using a deep pie pan about 12 inches across. For the individual tarts, choose pans that are at least 1½ inches deep to allow plenty of room for the caramel and apricots.

At Le Bilig, the lavender flowers are left in the ice cream, though you could strain them out before freezing if you prefer. You'll have more ice cream than needed to top the tarts, but that's not a problem, is it?

¾ cup unsalted butter	1 sheet frozen puff pastry, thawed
1½ cups packed brown sugar	in the refrigerator
18 medium apricots (about 2 pounds total),	Lavender sprigs, for garnish
halved and pitted	

LAVENDER ICE CREAM

2 cups milk, preferably whole	1 cup granulated sugar
1–2 vanilla beans, split lengthwise	1 tablespoon raw honey
1 tablespoon fresh or dried lavender flowers	2 cups whipping cream
10 egg yolks	

FOR THE ICE CREAM, combine the milk, vanilla bean(s), and lavender flowers in a heavy, medium saucepan. Bring the milk just to a boil, take it from the heat, cover, and set aside to infuse for 15 to 20 minutes.

MEANWHILE, combine the egg yolks, granulated sugar, and honey in a medium bowl and whisk until thoroughly blended and the mixture begins to lighten in color. Slowly pour the hot milk into the egg yolk mixture, whisking constantly, then pour this back into the saucepan. Discard the vanilla bean(s). (For added vanilla flavor in the ice cream, scrape some of the seeds from the beans into the milk mixture.) Cook the custard over medium heat, stirring constantly with a wooden spoon until the mixture has thickened enough to coat the back of the spoon, 5 to 7 minutes. Lift the spoon up and run your finger across the back; if the custard does not run into the path left by your finger, it is properly thickened. Take the pan from the heat, stir in the cream, let cool, then refrigerate until well chilled. When chilled, pour the mixture into an ice cream maker and freeze according to the manufacturer's instructions. Transfer to an airtight container and freeze until set, at least 2 hours.

PREHEAT THE OVEN to 375°F.

ARRANGE SIX 4-INCH PIE DISHES on a baking sheet and put 2 tablespoons butter and ¼ cup brown sugar in each. Put the baking sheet in the oven until the butter is melted, 5 to 7 minutes. Take the baking sheet from the oven and stir the butter and sugar in each pie dish. Continue baking until the mixtures are bubbly and the sugar is dissolved, 5 to 10 minutes longer. Take the baking sheet from the oven, leaving the temperature set at 375°F. Arrange the apricot halves cut side up in the caramel.

ROLL OUT THE PUFF PASTRY on a lightly floured work surface to about ⅛ inch. Cut the dough in circles large enough to cover the pie dishes and drape the pastry over the apricots. Bake the tarts until the pastry has puffed and nicely browned, about 20 minutes. Take the tarts from the oven and let sit a few minutes before serving.

USING PLATES at least a couple of inches larger than the tarts, invert the tarts onto the plates by first setting a plate on top of a pie dish, holding the two securely together, and inverting all at once. Lift off the pie dish, allowing the caramel to drizzle over the apricots. Place a scoop of lavender ice cream on top, garnish the plate with lavender, and serve right away.

Makes 6 servings

BITTERSWEET CHOCOLATE TART

with Hazelnut Cream and Pear Sauce

Domaine Chandon, Yountville

Everything about this recipe is rich and delicious, making it a spectacular way to end a special meal. It has several components and takes a bit of time to put together, but some parts can be prepared in advance. You can poach the pears and refrigerate them in their poaching liquids for a day or two. The pastry dough can be made a few days ahead and refrigerated. And the hazelnut cream recipe can be prepared and chilled up to a day in advance. As tasty as the hazelnut cream is, the tart would still be very good without it. Or, if you like, you could top the tart with lightly sweetened whipped cream with finely ground toasted hazelnuts folded in.

An easy way to make the chocolate shavings suggested for garnishing the tart is by scraping a vegetable peeler along the broad side of a piece of chocolate, letting the curls fall onto a piece of parchment or waxed paper.

¾ cup whipping cream	*1 egg, lightly beaten*
⅓ cup milk	*Chocolate shavings, for dusting*
3½ ounces semisweet chocolate, chopped	*Powdered sugar, for dusting*
3½ ounces bittersweet chocolate, chopped	

HAZELNUT CREAM

2 egg yolks	*1 cup milk*
¾ cup granulated sugar	*Powdered sugar, for dusting (optional)*
2 tablespoons all-purpose flour	*½ cup hazelnuts, roughly chopped*
1 vanilla bean, halved lengthwise,	*½ cup whipping cream*
or 1 teaspoon vanilla extract	

PASTRY DOUGH

¼ cup blanched almonds	1 egg
1 cup granulated sugar	1½ cups all-purpose flour
6 tablespoons unsalted butter, cut in pieces and chilled	Pinch salt

POACHED PEARS

5 cups water	½ cup freshly squeezed lemon juice
1½ cups granulated sugar	3 Bartlett pears, peeled, halved, and cored
½ cup dry white wine	

FOR THE HAZELNUT CREAM, combine the egg yolks with 2 tablespoons of the granulated sugar in a medium bowl. Whisk until well blended and beginning to lighten in color. Whisk in the flour until well blended. Combine the milk, 2 more tablespoons of the sugar, and half of the vanilla bean (or extract) in a small saucepan. (The remaining vanilla will be used for the poached pears.) Bring just to a boil. Slowly whisk about one-third of the milk mixture into the egg yolk mixture, then pour this back into the pan with the remaining milk. Cook the pastry cream over medium heat, whisking constantly, until it just comes to a boil. Continue cooking for 2 minutes, then pour the pastry cream into a medium bowl, discarding the vanilla bean (if using). Dust the surface lightly with powdered sugar to prevent a skin from forming, or lay a piece of plastic wrap directly on the surface of the cream. Set aside to cool completely.

COMBINE THE HAZELNUTS and remaining ½ cup of the sugar in a small, heavy saucepan and cook over medium-high heat until the sugar is caramelized and the nuts are toasty, about 5 minutes, stirring constantly once the sugar begins to melt. Immediately pour the mixture onto a lightly oiled baking sheet and let cool. When cool, break the praline into pieces and grind it to a fine powder in a food processor. Stir the ground hazelnut praline into the cooled pastry cream. Whip the cream until medium peaks form and gently fold it into the hazelnut cream. Refrigerate until well chilled, at least 2 hours.

FOR THE PASTRY DOUGH, finely grind the almonds in a food processor. In a mixer with the paddle attachment, cream the sugar and butter, then beat in the egg until evenly blended. Add the ground almonds, flour, and salt and continue mixing just until smooth and blended. Form the dough into a ball, wrap it in plastic, and refrigerate for at least 1 hour.

PREHEAT THE OVEN to 375°F.

ROLL OUT THE PASTRY DOUGH on a lightly floured work surface to a circle large enough to line a 9-inch removable-base tart pan. Gently form the dough into the tart pan, pressing it well into the corners and trimming and fluting the edges. Prick the base a few times with the tines of a fork to help prevent puffing. Bake the tart crust until just golden and set, about 15 minutes. Let cool.

FOR THE POACHED PEARS, combine the water, sugar, wine, lemon juice, and remaining ½ vanilla bean (or ½ teaspoon extract) in a large saucepan. Cook over medium heat, stirring, just until the sugar is dissolved. Add the pear halves and simmer until the pears are tender but still firm, 30 to 40 minutes (depending on the ripeness of the pears). Poke the tip of a knife into 1 pear half; it should go in with no resistance. Let the pears cool in the cooking liquid, then carefully scoop out the pears with a slotted spoon. Purée 3 pear halves with 1 cup of the poaching liquids in a blender or food processor. Finely dice the remaining pears and set aside.

REHEAT THE OVEN to 375°F.

FOR THE CHOCOLATE TART, combine the ¾ cup cream and ⅓ cup milk in a medium saucepan and bring just to a boil. Take the pan from the heat, add the chopped chocolate, and stir until melted. Set aside until almost cool, then add the egg and whisk until thoroughly blended. Pour the chocolate mixture into the tart crust and scatter the diced poached pears evenly over the chocolate. Bake the tart until the filling is mostly firm but still trembles a bit when gently nudged, about 30 minutes. Set aside on a rack to cool.

USING A PASTRY BAG fitted with a large star tip, pipe the hazelnut cream onto the cooled chocolate tart. (Alternatively, you could simply spread the cream on the tart with a spatula.) Scatter the chocolate shavings over the cream and dust lightly with powdered sugar. Cut the tart into wedges and serve a few spoonfuls of the pear sauce with each piece.

Makes 8 servings

BERRIES' BEST SEASONS

Berries are grown in Northern California during most months in most years; summer is, of course, the best season. In response to requests for more flavorful strawberries, growers are beginning to factor flavor into hybridization. Local and farmers' markets have reliable sources of flavorful berries from smaller growers throughout the season. Along the coast and in some forests grow several true natives for late-summer picking: thimbleberries, wild huckleberries, raspberries, and strawberries. Blackberries can also be found in the most remote places, but they are wildlings, escapees from cultivation that naturalize easily.

Strawberries come to market in March from the Central Valley and continue, from different areas, until September or October. A tasty early berry is Sequoia. Some of the best flavored, such as Quinault, are July-through September-bearing, though summer sun helps the flavor of most. Ogallala and Hecker are often the latest berries, available into October.

Blueberries from Sonoma County appear in July and August; most blueberries are imported from other states.

Red raspberries have a long season, from April to November in good years. Black raspberries have a short June and July season. Farmers' markets sometimes carry later-season cultivars into September. Golden raspberries are mid- to late-summer and early-fall berries. The hybrid boysenberry, loganberry, and olallieberry are June and July berries.

Fraises des bois are alpine berries that appear sporadically from March to November. They rarely appear in retail markets but are grown on a small scale for restaurants. Both red and white varieties are prized for their remarkable strawberry aroma. Many cultivars are easily garden grown, though the yields are quite low compared to large-fruited strawberries. Still, a few *fraises des bois* will help perfume and flavor ordinary strawberries, and they are a treat to savor singly or for breakfast.

STRAWBERRY SOUP
with Lemon Balm Granita

Lalime's, Berkeley

Pastry chef Judith Maguire shares the inspiration behind this refreshing dessert: "The recipe is the result of a bumpy bike ride I took home from the local farmers' market with two baskets of perfectly ripe organic strawberries. It is a wonderful way to use up berries that are bruised or just slightly overripe. Do not use moldy ones, though; even if you cut off the bad part, the flavor will be off. Use organic if you can, because they are well worth the extra expense."

You can make the granita with just about any herb. Mint is always available and works just fine, but more than half a bunch will be too strong. "This recipe has the added advantage of being fat- and dairy-free," notes chef Maguire. "We usually serve it with crispy meringue cookies to keep the course wheat-free as well."

2 pints ripe strawberries, preferably organic
½ cup freshly squeezed orange juice
¼ cup freshly squeezed lemon juice,
*   preferably Meyer lemon*

¼ cup honey
1 cup sparkling wine or seltzer

GRANITA

4 cups water
1 cup sugar
1 bunch fresh lemon balm or lemon verbena
(about 1 cup loosely packed)

¼ cup freshly squeezed lemon juice,
*   preferably Meyer lemon*

FOR THE GRANITA, combine the water, sugar, lemon balm sprigs, and lemon juice in a nonreactive medium saucepan. Bring to a boil, stirring occasionally to help the sugar dissolve. Take the pan from the heat and let the mixture cool slightly, then refrigerate until well chilled. Strain the mixture through a sieve lined with cheesecloth, wringing the cheesecloth well to extract as much flavor from the herbs as possible. Pour the mixture into a shallow baking dish and freeze until set, 2 to 3 hours, stirring every 30 minutes with a fork to make a crumbly texture. (Alternatively, you could freeze the granita in an ice cream freezer following the manufacturer's instructions.)

GENTLY RINSE THE STRAWBERRIES, leaving the hulls on, and set aside the 4 best for garnish. Purée the rest of the strawberries, hulls on, in a food processor. Strain the purée through a very fine mesh sieve. Scoop the seeds and hulls from the sieve into a small saucepan and add the orange juice, lemon juice, and honey. Bring the mixture to a boil, then cool to room temperature or cooler. (Setting the bottom of the saucepan in a large bowl of ice will speed the cooling.) Strain this mixture into the strawberry purée, discarding the seeds and hulls. Refrigerate until ready to serve.

JUST BEFORE SERVING, chop the reserved strawberries for garnish. Stir the sparkling wine or seltzer into the strawberry purée and ladle the soup into 4 individual bowls. Top with a scoop of the granita, scatter the chopped strawberries over the soup, and serve right away.

Makes 4 servings

UPSIDE-DOWN PECAN-APPLE PIE

The Village Pub, Woodside

Pastry chef Louise McLaughlin recommends serving this interesting upside-down pie with homemade vanilla or cinnamon ice cream.

6 tart apples, peeled, cored, and quartered	2 teaspoons ground cinnamon
¾ cup plus ⅓ cup packed brown sugar	3 tablespoons cornstarch
¾ cup water	2 tablespoons corn syrup
5 tablespoons unsalted butter	1 cup pecan halves

CRUST

2 cups all-purpose flour	½ teaspoon salt
¾ cup butter, cut in pieces and chilled	5 tablespoons buttermilk
1 tablespoon sugar	

FOR THE CRUST, combine the flour, butter, sugar, and salt in a food processor and pulse a few times until the mixture has a crumbly texture. Slowly add the buttermilk, pulsing a few times until the dough begins to pull together. (If the dough mixture remains crumbly looking, pinch some of it in your fingers to see if it forms a soft ball; if so, the dough's ready to be turned out.) Take care not to overmix the dough or it will become tough. Turn the dough out onto a lightly floured work surface and gently knead it a few times to smoothly blend the dough. Divide the dough in half, wrap each half in plastic, and refrigerate for 1 hour.

COMBINE THE APPLES, ¾ cup of the brown sugar, ½ cup of the water, the butter, and cinnamon in a large skillet or saucepan. Cook over medium-high heat, stirring often, until the butter melts and the sugar dissolves, 5 to 7 minutes. Stir together the cornstarch and 3 tablespoons of the water in a small bowl. Add some of the juices from the cooking apples to the cornstarch mixture and slowly pour the combination back into the apples, stirring constantly for a few minutes until the liquid thickens. Quickly pour the mixture onto a baking sheet to cool. The apples won't be cooked and tender at this point but will be nicely flavored with the sugar-cinnamon mixture.

PREHEAT THE OVEN to 350°F.

STIR THE REMAINING ⅓ cup of the brown sugar together with the corn syrup and the remaining tablespoon of water in a 9-inch deep pie pan. Spread the mixture to form a thin, even layer on the bottom of the pan. Add the pecan halves, rounded side down, in a spiral pattern, working from the outer edge toward the center.

ROLL OUT ONE OF THE DOUGH PORTIONS to a circle a little larger than the pie pan, using flour sparingly. Roll the dough round onto the rolling pin and unroll it over the pecan bed, laying excess over the edge of the pan. Arrange the apple pieces in snug circles over the dough and spoon the caramel mixture evenly over. Roll out the remaining dough portion to a circle large enough to generously cover the pie. Brush a little water on the edges of the first dough crust to moisten. Lay the second round of dough over the first and press the edges together to seal. Trim and flute to seal and form a decorative edge. Cut a vent hole in the center of the pie top. Put the pie pan on a baking sheet (to catch drippings) and bake until browned, about 50 minutes. Remove and let cool slightly.

CUT THE PIE into 8 wedges, leaving them in the pan. Lay a baking sheet over the pie pan and quickly but carefully invert both together. Set the baking sheet, with the inverted pie pan still on it, under the broiler to soften and help release the pecan topping. Take away the pie pan and transfer the pie pieces to individual plates. Add a scoop of ice cream, if you like, and serve warm.

Makes 8 servings

VANILLA-SCENTED YOGURT CREAM

Insalata's, San Anselmo

This dessert is so easy and delicious, you'll be amazed. "Goat yogurt makes this dessert divine," says chef/owner Heidi Insalata. She serves this with honeyed figs in the fall, blood oranges in the winter, and apricots in the summer. Chef Insalata prefers to use only the tiny, powerfully flavored vanilla seeds from inside the vanilla bean for flavoring the yogurt cream. You could save the bean to infuse flavor into milk for a custard sauce or ice cream, or into a light syrup for poaching fruit.

2 teaspoons (1 envelope) gelatin powder
¼ cup cold water
1 vanilla bean
1 cup whipping cream

½ cup sugar
2 cups plain yogurt, preferably made from goat's milk

LIGHTLY SPRAY six ½-cup ramekins or other small dishes with vegetable spray, or very lightly oil with a flavorless vegetable oil.

SPRINKLE THE GELATIN over the cold water in a small dish and set aside to soften for about 5 minutes.

SPLIT THE VANILLA BEAN lengthwise and run the tip of a knife down the bean to remove the vanilla seeds. Put the vanilla seeds in a small saucepan with ½ cup of the whipping cream and the sugar. Bring just to a boil, whisking to help the sugar dissolve. Take the pan from the heat and whisk in the softened gelatin, followed by the yogurt. Transfer the mixture to a medium bowl and set that bowl inside a larger bowl of ice water to quickly chill the mixture, whisking occasionally. While the yogurt mixture cools, whip the remaining ½ cup of the whipping cream to medium peaks. When the yogurt is cool, fold in the whipped cream.

SPOON THE YOGURT cream into the ramekins and refrigerate until set, 2 to 3 hours. The yogurt creams can be served right away with the fruit of your choice, or cover the ramekins with plastic wrap until ready to serve.

Makes 6 servings

FIGS OF MANY COLORS

The fig is another Mediterranean fruit for which the Northern California climate brings out the best. Figs flourish all over the state, but local growers find that microclimates with long, warm seasons moderated by coastal fogs and breezes produce the finest flavor in many varieties. Not coincidentally, these are the same conditions that favor wine grapes.

Most of the harvest is consumed locally, as figs must be picked tree-ripe and are quite perishable. Over the past few years, something of a boomlet has occurred in the varieties of fresh figs available at markets, farmers' markets, and restaurants. These are often identified by name, as is becoming common for many fruits and vegetables.

The Black Mission is still a popular variety, thought to be introduced by Spanish mission settlers in the 18th century. It has a black skin and amber flesh and is good fresh or preserved. Brown Turkey actually has a purple-red cast to its skin and a pinky amber flesh; it is best fresh. The Adriatic, when grown in a good climate, has a rich, figgy flavor; its flesh is a deep strawberry red color, a dramatic contrast to its grass green skin. Calimyrna's golden skin and amber flesh have a sweet, rich, nutty flavor; it is considered one of the best figs both fresh and dried.

Fresh figs are good in salads with radicchio and other chicories, with watercress and arugula, and with nuts. In compotes and chutneys, fresh or dried figs marry well with pears, apples, and lemons to accompany pork dishes. As part of a cheese course, figs provide delectable contrast with rich blues, such as Gorgonzola, and tangy, buttery, creamy types, such as St. André and Taleggio. Fig tarts, especially made from different-colored kinds together, are lovely to look at and to eat.

BERRY CRISP

Cottonwood Restaurant, Truckee

Use the best of whatever fruit the season has to offer for this crisp. Berries, apples, rhubarb, apricots, peaches, and pears would all be delicious. Keep in mind that you might need to alter the amount of sugar depending on the fruit's sweetness.

3 pounds fresh berries or berries and other
fresh fruit, chopped if necessary
⅓ cup sugar
2 tablespoons cornstarch

1 teaspoon freshly squeezed lemon juice
Vanilla ice cream or whipped cream,
for serving (optional)

TOPPING

1 cup all-purpose flour
1 cup sugar
½ cup butter, cut in pieces and chilled

¼ cup chopped toasted nuts (walnuts,
hazelnuts, or almonds)
¼ cup rolled oats (optional)

PREHEAT THE OVEN to 350°F.

PUT THE BERRIES (and other fruit, if using) in a large bowl. In a small bowl, stir together the sugar and cornstarch and sprinkle it over the berries, followed by the lemon juice. Very gently stir to evenly mix, then pour the fruit into an ungreased 9- by 13-inch baking dish.

FOR THE TOPPING, stir together the flour and sugar in a medium bowl. Using a pastry blender or 2 table knives, cut the chilled butter into the flour mixture until it has a crumbly consistency. (Alternatively, you could combine the flour, sugar, and butter in a food processor and pulse to mix.) Stir in the nuts and oats, if using. Sprinkle the topping over the fruit and bake in the preheated oven until bubbly and the topping is lightly browned, 50 to 60 minutes. Let cool slightly before spooning onto plates to serve, with a scoop of ice cream or whipped cream if you like.

Makes 10 to 12 servings

WARM CHOCOLATE SOUFFLÉ

The Dining Room at the Ritz-Carlton, San Francisco

Four simple ingredients put together in a deliciously tantalizing way make this a soufflé you could easily become addicted to. The texture is a bit denser and richer than those lighter-than-air soufflés, thanks to a generous addition of butter, with the result being a powerful chocolate flavor. At the Ritz-Carlton, this dessert is commonly served with bitter almond ice cream, though pastry chef Gregory Gourreau also suggests serving whipped cream with the warm soufflé.

⅔ cup (10 tablespoons) unsalted butter	*3 eggs, separated*
6 ounces extra bitter or bittersweet chocolate,	*½ cup sugar, plus more for coating ramekins*
finely chopped	

PREHEAT THE OVEN to 375°F. Generously butter six ½-cup ramekins. Coat the butter with sugar, tapping out the excess.

HEAT THE BUTTER in a small pan until fully melted and warm, then pour the melted butter over the chopped chocolate in a bowl. Stir until the chocolate is melted and the mixture is smooth; set aside.

IN A MIXER or with electric beaters, whip the egg yolks with all but 1 tablespoon of the sugar until light and pale yellow in color, about 5 minutes. Gently blend in the chocolate mixture.

WHIP THE EGG WHITES until peaks form. Add the remaining tablespoon of sugar and continue beating until glossy, 1 or 2 minutes longer. Fold about ¼ of the egg whites into the chocolate mixture to lighten it, then gently fold this back into the remaining egg whites until evenly blended. Spoon the soufflé mixture into the prepared dishes (about ¾ full), set them on a baking sheet for easy handling, and bake until well puffed but still a little soft in the center, about 15 to 17 minutes. At the Ritz-Carlton, the soufflés are unmolded onto individual plates before serving. You could do the same, or set each dish on a plate and serve as is from the oven.

Makes 6 servings

LEMON CURD CAKE
with Crème Fraîche and Mixed Berry Compote

Pastis, San Francisco

This pairing of lemon and berries is wonderfully light and full of flavor.

GENOISE

⅓ cup sugar | ½ cup all-purpose flour
2 eggs |

LEMON CURD

2 teaspoons (1 envelope) gelatin powder | 4 eggs
¼ cup cold water | 1 cup unsalted butter, cut in pieces and
1⅓ cups sugar | softened at room temperature
¾ cup freshly squeezed lemon juice |

BERRY SAUCE

2 tablespoons unsalted butter | 1 cup fresh raspberries
2 cups fresh blueberries | ½ cup sugar
2 cups hulled and quartered strawberries |

GARNISH

1 cup crème fraîche | 8 mint leaves

PREHEAT THE OVEN to 400°F. Butter and flour a 9-inch springform pan.

FOR THE GENOISE, combine the sugar and eggs in the bowl of a mixer or in the top of a double boiler and whisk to mix. Set the mixture over (not touching) gently simmering water. Continue whisking until the mixture feels lukewarm, about 2 minutes. Take the mixture from the pan of water and beat with the mixer or with handheld electric beaters until the mixture is very light and thick, 8 to 10 minutes. When you lift the beaters, a ribbon of the batter should fall gently onto the surface and hold its shape for a few seconds. Sift the flour over the batter and gently fold it in with a rubber spatula. Pour the genoise batter into the prepared pan, spread the top smoothly, and bake until the cake springs back when gently pressed in the center, about 15 minutes. Turn the cake onto a cake rack to cool completely. Thoroughly clean and dry the springform pan.

WHILE THE CAKE IS COOLING, prepare the lemon curd. Sprinkle the gelatin over the cold water in a small dish and set aside to soften. Combine the sugar, lemon juice, and eggs in a medium saucepan and whisk to blend. Cook the mixture over medium heat, whisking constantly, until it just comes to a boil, about 5 minutes. (The mixture should become very frothy and increase slightly in volume.) As soon as it begins to boil, reduce the heat and continue cooking, whisking briskly, for 2 minutes longer. Take the pan from the heat, add the softened gelatin, and whisk until well blended.

POUR THE CURD MIXTURE into the bowl of an electric mixer and whip on high speed until the mixture cools slightly, about 5 minutes. (Alternatively, beat the curd in a large bowl with handheld electric beaters.) Reduce the speed to medium and add the butter a few pieces at a time until all the butter is incorporated and the curd is very smooth, 2 to 3 minutes.

ASSEMBLE THE CAKE in the same springform pan the genoise was baked in. Using a large serrated knife, carefully cut the genoise into 2 even layers. Pour about one-third of the lemon curd into the bottom of the springform pan and top it with 1 cake layer. Repeat with half of the remaining curd and the second cake layer. Pour the remaining curd over the top, spreading it evenly. Cover with plastic wrap and refrigerate until set, 2 to 3 hours.

WHILE THE CAKE IS CHILLING, make the berry sauce. Melt the butter in a large skillet over medium heat. In a large bowl, combine the berries with the sugar and toss gently to evenly coat. Add the berry mixture to the skillet and cook, stirring occasionally, just until the berries begin to soften and the sugar is dissolved, 2 to 3 minutes. Take the skillet from the heat and set aside until ready to serve.

WHEN THE CAKE IS SET, run a knife around the edge and remove the springform sides. Cut the cake into 8 wedges and set them on individual plates. Garnish each slice with a dollop of crème fraîche, several spoonfuls of the berry sauce, and a leaf of mint.

Makes 8 servings

MOCHA FLAN

MacCallum House Restaurant, Mendocino

Note that the flans need to chill for a couple of hours before serving, so be sure to allow yourself enough time. They can be made up to a day in advance and refrigerated. At MacCallum House, the flans are often garnished with edible wildflowers or local huckleberries. Even the chocolate and coffee are regional notables: the coffee is MacCallum House's organic Thanksgiving blend from a local roaster, and the chocolate is from Scharffen Berger, a San Francisco Bay Area company founded by John Scharffenberger (of local wine fame) and Robert Steinberg.

Making caramel can be intimidating, especially when it comes to deciding when to take the cooked sugar from the heat. While it is important to avoid overcooking the caramel, which leaves it bitter tasting, it is also important to cook it beyond a simple "golden" color to a more flavorful bronzy brown.

1½ cups sugar
½ cup water
2 cups whipping cream
3½ ounces bittersweet chocolate,
finely chopped

¼ cup espresso
4 egg yolks

FOR THE CARAMEL to line the ramekins, combine 1 cup of the sugar and the water in a small, heavy saucepan. Cook the sugar and water over medium-low heat, stirring occasionally, until the sugar is dissolved, about 5 minutes. Increase the heat to high and continue cooking, without stirring, until the mixture reaches a deep caramel color, about 15 minutes longer.

CAREFULLY POUR THE CARAMEL into six ½-cup ramekins or custard cups, and quickly tilt and turn each so the caramel evenly coats the bottoms, and about two-thirds of the way up the sides of the dishes. Set the prepared ramekins aside in a baking dish.

PREHEAT THE OVEN to 350°F.

IN A MEDIUM SAUCEPAN, bring the cream just to a boil. Take the pan from the heat, add the chocolate and espresso, and stir until the chocolate is melted. In a small bowl, whisk together the egg yolks with the remaining ½ cup sugar. Slowly whisk in about ¼ of the cream mixture, then whisk this back into the remaining cream until thoroughly blended.

CAREFULLY POUR or ladle the custard into the ramekins. Add warm water to the baking dish so it comes about halfway up the sides of the ramekins. Bake the custards until set, about 1 hour. (Insert the tip of a knife in the center of one of the flans to check; it should come out clean.) Take the ramekins from the water bath, and let cool. Refrigerate for a couple of hours until well chilled.

TO SERVE, hold the bottom half of each ramekin in a pan of hot water for about 1 minute. Run a paring knife around the edge and wipe off the ramekin. Set a small serving plate over the top of the ramekin and quickly flip both together so the ramekin is upside down on the plate. Lift off the ramekin, allowing the caramel to drip down the sides of the flan. Scrape out any extra caramel with a spoon. Repeat with the remaining flans. Serve right away.

Makes 6 servings

GRAVENSTEIN APPLE BREAD PUDDING

Huckleberry Springs Country Inn, Monte Rio

This bread pudding is a few steps up from the ordinary, with apple cider in the custard and rich amaretto sauce spooned over for serving. The recipe won first place honors in the sweet category for professional chefs at the 1996 Gravenstein Apple Fair held in Sebastopol.

1 (10-ounce) loaf stale French or other country-style bread	1 cup granulated sugar
	1 cup chopped walnuts or pecans
4 Gravenstein apples, cored, peeled, and finely chopped	½ cup unsalted butter, melted and cooled
	3 eggs, lightly beaten
2½ cups milk	2 tablespoons vanilla extract
1½ cups apple cider	2 teaspoons ground cinnamon

AMARETTO SAUCE

1½ cups powdered sugar	2 egg yolks
½ cup unsalted butter, cut in chunks	¼ cup amaretto liqueur, plus more to taste

PREHEAT THE OVEN to 350°F. Grease a 9- by 13-inch baking dish.

TEAR THE BREAD INTO SMALL PIECES and put them in a large bowl. Add the apples, milk, cider, sugar, nuts, butter, eggs, vanilla, and cinnamon and stir to evenly mix. Put about ⅓ of the mixture in a food processor and pulse a few times to finely chop, then return it to the bowl. Stir to mix, then pour the bread mixture into the prepared baking dish. Bake until the top is brown and the pudding is set, about 1¼ to 1½ hours.

WHILE THE BREAD PUDDING IS BAKING, prepare the amaretto sauce. In a small saucepan, combine the powdered sugar and butter and cook over medium heat, stirring, just until the butter is evenly incorporated into the sugar. Take from the heat and stir in the egg yolks, followed by the amaretto. Stir well to mix, then set aside to cool, stirring often. The sauce will thicken as it cools.

WHEN THE BREAD PUDDING IS COOKED, let it cool slightly. Cut the warm bread pudding into pieces, spoon the amaretto sauce over, and serve.

Makes 8 to 10 servings

APPLE HIGHWAYS AND BYWAYS

The Gravenstein Highway wends through western Sonoma County near the town of Sebastopol, perfumed spring and late summer with blossoms and fruit of the eponymous apple. The Gravenstein flourishes in these parts, and also grows in other Northern California locales. It's a handsome green yellow apple, blushed with shades of red, prized for cooking and out-of-hand eating.

The gently rolling hill country around Watsonville in Santa Cruz County is also filled with apple orchards, many of these off small roads. So are the more dramatic Sierra foothills, the gold country stretching east and south from Yuba County to Nevada and Placer Counties. Some of the orchards were planted midcentury and offer apples of those times: Red and Golden Delicious, McIntosh, Newton Pippin, Granny Smith. Lately, something of a Johnny Appleseed movement has touched all these regions.

Inherited orchards are sometimes being replanted by the next generation. Other times enthusiastic newcomers—often engineers or doctors, as in vineyard country—are starting with a new passion. In either case, heirloom apples and new hybrids are coming to market now and will usher in the next millennium. A few of the dozens and dozens available locally include Banana, Black Twig, Braeburn, Cox's Orange Pippin, Mutsu, Pink Lady, Prairie Spy, Sierra Beauty, and Winesap. Last but not least is Winter White Pearmain, traceable to 13th-century England.

Since these apples are largely harvested tree-ripe and often are sold locally, they offer a full range of perfume and flavor. A Newton Pippin is a marvel of clove and basil scents, tart and sweet to the taste. A Winesap reveals how aptly it's named; nostrils quiver and taste buds tingle with it just as they do with a glass of fine wine.

APPENDIX:
RESTAURANTS & INNS

42 DEGREES
235 16th Street
San Francisco, CA 94110
(415) 777-5559

ABIGAIL'S
2120 G Street
Sacramento, CA 95816
(916) 441-5007

AGATE COVE INN
11201 N Lansing Street
Mendocino, CA 95460
(707) 937-0551

ALBION RIVER INN
3790 Highway 1
Albion, CA 95410
(707) 937-1919

APPLEWOOD INN & RESTAURANT
13555 Highway 16
Pocket Canyon, CA 95446
(707) 869-9093

AQUA
252 California Street
San Francisco, CA 94111
(415) 956-9662

BELLE DE JOUR INN
16276 Healdsburg Avenue
Healdsburg, CA 95448
(707) 431-9777

BISTRO VIDA
641 Santa Cruz Avenue
Menlo Park, CA 94205
(650) 462-1686

BRIDGES
44 Church Street
Danville, CA 94526
(925) 820-7200

BRIX
7377 St. Helena Highway
Yountville, CA 94558
(707) 944-2749

BUBBA'S DINER
566 San Anslemo Avenue
San Anselmo, CA 94960
(415) 459-6862

BUZ'S CRAB
2159 East Street
Redding, CA 96001
(530) 243-2120

CAFÉ MADDALENA
5801 Sacramento Avenue
Dunsmuir, CA 96025
(530) 235-2028

CARTER HOUSE VICTORIANS/
RESTAURANT 301
301 L Street
Eureka, CA 95501
(707) 444-8062

CHEZ PANISSE
1517 Shattuck Avenue
Berkeley, CA 94709
(510) 548-5049

CITY HOTEL
P.O. Box 1870
Columbia, CA 95310
(209) 532-1470

COTTONWOOD RESTAURANT
10142 Rue Hilltop
Truckee, CA 96160
(530) 587-5711

DOMAINE CHANDON
1 California Drive
Yountville, CA 94559
(707) 944-2892

THE DINING ROOM AT THE
RITZ-CARLTON
600 Stockton Street
San Francisco, CA 94108
(415) 296-7465

THE DORRINGTON HOTEL AND
RESTAURANT
3431 Highway 4
Dorrington, CA 95223
(209) 795-5800

DUNBAR HOUSE, 1880
271 Jones Street
Murphys, CA 95247
(209) 728-2897

FANDANGO
223 17th Street
Pacific Grove, CA 93950
(831) 372-3456

FARALLON
450 Post Street
San Francisco, CA 94102
(415) 956-6969

FLUME'S END BED & BREAKFAST
317 S Pine Street
Nevada City, CA 95959
(530) 265-2245

THE GABLES INN
4257 Petaluma Hill Road
Santa Rosa, CA 95404
(707) 585-7777

GLENELLY INN
5131 Warm Springs Road
Glen Ellen, CA 95442
(707) 996-6720

GREY WHALE INN
615 N Main Street
Fort Bragg, CA 95437
(707) 964-0640

THE GROVELAND HOTEL
18767 Main Street
Groveland, CA 95321
(209) 962-4000

HALF DAY CAFÉ
848 College Avenue
Kentfield, CA 94904
(415) 459-0291

HIDDEN CITY CAFÉ
109 Park Place
Point Richmond, CA 94801
(510) 232-9738

HIGHLANDS INN/PACIFIC'S EDGE
P.O. Box 1700
Carmel, CA 93921
(831) 624-3801

HUCKLEBERRY SPRINGS COUNTRY INN
8105 Old Beedle Road
Monte Rio, CA 95462
(707) 865-2683

INDIAN CREEK BED & BREAKFAST
21950 Highway 49
Plymouth, CA 95669
(209) 245-4648

THE INN AT DEPOT HILL
250 Monterey Avenue
Capitola, CA 95010
(831) 462-3376

INSALATA'S
120 Sir Francis Drake Boulevard
San Anselmo, CA 94960
(415) 457-7700

JAMMIN' SALMON
1801 Garden Highway
Sacramento, CA 95833
(916) 929-6232

JOHNSON'S COUNTRY INN
3935 Morehead Avenue
Chico, CA 95928
(530) 345-7829

KIRBY'S CREEKSIDE RESTAURANT
101 Broad Street
Nevada City, CA 95959
(530) 265-3445

L'AMIE DONIA
530 Bryant Street
Palo Alto, CA 94301
(650) 323-7614

LALIME'S
1329 Gilman Street
Berkeley, CA 94706
(510) 527-9838

LARK CREEK INN
234 Magnolia Avenue
Larkspur, CA 94939
(415) 924-7766

LAS CAMELIAS MEXICAN RESTAURANT
912 Lincoln Avenue
San Rafael, CA 94901
(415) 453-5850

LE BILIG
11750 Atwood Road
Auburn, CA 95603
(530) 888-1491

LEFT BANK, LARKSPUR
507 Magnolia Avenue
Larkspur, CA 94939
(415) 927-3331

LEFT BANK, MENLO PARK
635 Santa Cruz Avenue
Menlo Park, CA 94025
(650) 473-6543

LISA HEMENWAY'S
714 Village Court
Santa Rosa, CA 95405
(707) 526-5111

LOST WHALE BED &BREAKFAST
3452 Patrick's Point Drive
Trinidad, CA 95570
(707) 677-3425

MACCALLUM HOUSE RESTAURANT
45020 Albion Street
Mendocino, CA 95460
(707) 937-5763

MAISON FLEURIE
6529 Yount Street
Yountville, CA 94599
(707) 944-2056

MENDOCINO HOTEL
45080 Main Street
Mendocino, CA 95460
(707) 937-0511

MONTRIO
414 Calle Principal
Monterey, CA 93940
(831) 648-8880

NORTH COAST BREWING CO.
444 N Main Street
Fort Bragg, CA 95437
(707) 964-3400

OLIVETO RESTAURANT
5655 College Avenue
Oakland, CA 94618
(510) 547-5356

ONE MARKET
1 Market Street
San Francisco, CA 94105
(415) 777-5577

THE PALACE
146 S. Murphy Avenue
Sunnyvale, CA 94086
(408) 739-5179

PASTIS
1015 Battery St.
San Francisco, CA 94111
(415) 391-2555

PETITE AUBERGE
863 Bush Street
San Francisco, CA 94108
(415) 928-6000

PRIMA
1522 N Main Street
Walnut Creek, CA 94596
(925) 935-7780

QUAIL LODGE/COVEY RESTAURANT
8000 Valley Greens Drive
Carmel, CA 93923
(831) 624-1581

QUAIL MOUNTAIN BED & BREAKFAST
4455 St. Helena Highway
Calistoga, CA 94515
(707) 942-0316

ROSE PISTOLA
532 Columbus Avenue
San Francisco, CA 94133
(415) 399-0499

SCHAT'S COURTHOUSE BAKERY
AND CAFE
113 S. Perkins Street
Ukiah, CA 95482
(707) 462-1670

SEAL COVE INN
221 Cypress Avenue
Moss Beach, CA 94038
(650) 728-7325

SENT SOVÍ
14583 Big Basin Way
Saratoga, CA 95070
(408) 867-3110

SUNSETS ON THE LAKE
7320 N. Lake Boulevard
Tahoe Vista, CA 96148
(530) 546-3640

SUTTER CREEK INN
75 Main Street
Sutter Creek, CA 95685
(209) 267-9155

THE VILLAGE PUB
2967 Woodside Road
Woodside, CA 94062
(650) 851-1294

WENTE VINEYARDS RESTAURANT
5050 Arroyo Road
Livermore, CA 94550
(925) 456-2450

WHITE SWAN INN
845 Bush Street
San Francisco, CA 94108
(415) 775-1755

THE WHOLE ENCHILADA
7902 Highway 1
Moss Landing, CA 95039
(831) 633-3038

WINE SPECTATOR RESTAURANT
AT GREYSTONE
2555 Main Street
St. Helena, CA 94574
(707) 967-1010

WOODROSE CAFÉ
911 Redwood Drive
Garberville, CA 95542
(707) 923-3191

INDEX

S

ABOUT THE AUTHORS

Cynthia C. Nims, food editor of *Seattle* magazine, attended La Varenne cooking school in Paris. The coauthor of *The Northwest Best Places Cookbook,* she is based in Seattle.

Carolyn Dille, author and coauthor of numerous cookbooks, was the first chef at the famed Chez Panisse Cafe in Berkeley and served as recipe editor of the *Chez Panisse Menu Cookbook.* She lives in San Jose.